ON THIS GROUND

ON THIS GROUND

Hardship and Hope at the
Toughest Prep School in America

Anthony DePalma

WILLIAM MORROW
An Imprint of HarperCollins*Publishers*

HarperCollins books may be purchased for educational, business, or sales promotional use. For information, please email the Special Markets Department at SPsales@harpercollins.com.

hc.com

FIRST EDITION

Designed by Michele Cameron

Library of Congress Cataloging-in-Publication Data has been applied for.

ISBN 978-0-06-346439-1

25 26 27 28 29 LBC 5 4 3 2 1

For Brother David Van Hollebeke, FSC:
a giant in a black robe and white collar whose
belief in me has made all the difference

And for Bob, Carmine, Dave, George, Mike, Pat, Sil, and Steve:
my own brotherhood of tough Jersey guys who've been with me the
whole way

The ground is holy and the need
has never been greater.

—*Father Edwin Leahy, O.S.B., Headmaster,
St. Benedict's Preparatory School*

Wherever American cities are going,
Newark will get there first.

—*inscribed on the granite base of a bronze statue
of Kenneth A. Gibson, Newark's first Black mayor,
that stands in front of Newark City Hall*

Stability in this community, pursuit of perfect
charity through a monastic way of life.

—*lifelong vow of Newark Abbey's Benedictine monks,
handwritten on parchment and preserved in the office of the abbot*

CONTENTS

I WAS GIVEN extraordinary access to what everyone at St. Benedict's calls "the property"—the urban medley of old and new that is Newark Abbey, St. Mary's Church, and the remarkable prep school run by an inimitable gang of downtown monks. Once I cleared a formal background check, they issued me a photo ID and a password for the security gate so I could enter the grounds unannounced whenever I wanted. I roamed freely, sitting in on classes, observing group-counseling sessions, and interviewing students and staff wherever I found them.

The freedom I was permitted during the more than two years I spent at the school raised delicate issues of privacy. I have used the real names of all the adults mentioned in these pages. However, I have changed the names of some students so their high school indiscretions don't someday hamper their ambitions. Other students were so outstanding that I felt it would be an injustice not to use their given names.

Most of the contemporary events I describe took place during St. Benedict's 50th anniversary school year, which began on July 31, 2023, and ended with the boys division graduation on June 2, 2024.

The story of what happens every day in this old, deeply scarred, often overlooked city illuminates the astonishing ability of faith to alter destiny, be it of a school, a society, or several generations of kids who otherwise might have been lost. The struggles of the monks, the heartaches of their students, and the gritty perseverance of their city demonstrate how trying, and ultimately triumphant, life can be when tough men keep their promises, tough kids are given enough love, and a tough city fights back. It is my unreserved hope that the enduring lessons of courage, brotherhood, and resilience outlined here resonate powerfully in other schools in other American cities, fulfilling the wistful prediction that wherever American cities are heading, Newark has gotten there first.

CHAPTER I

Of One Accord

ON A RESILIENTLY crisp 75-degree Monday morning in late July 2023, Anthony Badger parked his twenty-one-year-old beige Acura TL in the lot behind the Radel Library, an ennobling edifice that did not exist when he was a student at St. Benedict's Prep. He walked up the stairs to the Henry and Agnes Brennan Center—with its swimming pool and basketball court to die for—that was dedicated in 1988, long after he'd graduated. Dressed in shorts, sneakers, and a black and white T-shirt, he felt at home in the gym where, in a few weeks, he'd start another season as coach of the St. Benedict's freshman basketball team, the team he hoped to join when he showed up at the school one morning exactly fifty years before.

This place and all it represents still leaves him awestruck. High on the wall above one end of the court is a poster-sized photo of St. Benedict's legendary coach Joseph "Joe K" Kasberger, who, in the thirty-seven years he led the school's football and baseball teams, suffered fewer than a handful of losing seasons. Next to him is Ernest "Prof" Blood, St. Benedict's basketball coach from 1925 to 1950, whose name is inscribed in the national Basketball Hall of Fame. Banners laud St. Benedict's long list of national championship teams and salute individual standouts like Claudio Reyna, the soccer star who played on several U.S. Olympic teams, and Ed Cheserek, the best high school cross-country runner the United States had in 2012.

The gathering that was about to begin was roughly the ten thousandth since the first one in 1973, when Badger was one of the eighty-nine students enrolled in the experimental school that was reopening in the heart of Newark almost exactly one year after the century-old traditional St. Benedict's Prep had closed. The old school had been mostly white. The new one was almost entirely Black, like him.

These mandatory morning get-togethers—they're called "convocations" to stress their importance—are far more involved than the assemblies held at other schools. Think of them as a mash-up of spiritual revival and military muster fortified with the energy of a pep rally and the sanctity of a Catholic novena. They can be as complex and, at times, as rowdy as a circus big top, the students cheering wildly as one act follows another. And yet there are moments when this gym teeming with more than 750 teenagers falls as respectfully silent as if it were a chapel, a temple, or a mosque.

Regardless of the weather, or Newark's brutal rush hour traffic, every student is expected to be here before eight a.m. every day to take part in this ritual. For the Rev. Edwin D. Leahy, O.S.B. (Order of St. Benedict), the crankily charismatic headmaster who's ruled the school for half a century—and who just about everyone calls Father Ed—"convo" is one of the most important things St. Benedict's does. It is a recurring reminder that the students—who run each convo, along with a lot else in the school—belong to a compassionate community where they watch out for each other, just as the monks in the monastery have one another's back. It's tempting to think of it as one big family, but do so and Father Ed will quickly correct you. You don't have to do anything to be born into a family, he says. But it's a privilege to belong to a community like this, a privilege that has to be earned, and one that can be lost.

Badger grabbed a seat in the center section of the bleachers, a couple of rows up from the floor. When he was a student, St. Benedict's was small and struggling to survive. Now it sprawls over both sides of Dr. Martin Luther King Jr. Boulevard in downtown Newark. To the west stand the library, gym, and dormitory that are the stirring signs of the resurrected school's success. They are linked via pedestrian skybridge to a block of antique buildings straight out of the old school's nineteenth-century beginnings.

Since St. Benedict's 1973 reboot, the school has evolved into a powerhouse of urban education that sprawls over several acres in the heart of Newark's concrete and asphalt downtown. Father Ed and the other monks bristle when they hear it called a campus, which implies that the monastery and church were plunked down next to the school. St. Benedict's is situated on the sacred grounds of Newark Abbey, and the walls and fences surrounding the abbey distinguish everything that goes on inside from the rest of the city. Father Ed is often heard proclaiming, "The ground is holy and the need has never been greater," which neatly sums up the monks' reason for being, and for being in Newark.

The prep school now enrolls about 650 students who share the abbey grounds, a.k.a. "the property," with another 120 youths in grades seven and eight. Another 200 youngsters in grades K-6 have their own building a few blocks away. After nearly 150 years as an all-boys school, St. Benedict's Prep is now officially co-institutional; girls have their own classes in a separate building on the property. Around 85 percent of St. Benedict's students are Black or Latino; many but not all come from homes mired in poverty in and around Newark. But poverty alone doesn't begin to cover the range of liabilities some of them confront when they are not in school. Addiction, abandonment, crime, and domestic violence are constants that scar many. They are left to cope with layers of depression, resentment, anger, and fear that, without counseling, would short-circuit their chance at learning and eventually compromise their futures. St. Benedict's has found a way to overcome those liabilities by paying strict attention to the students' heart as well as to their mind, and in the process toughening their character to prepare them for whatever the future brings.

The freshmen sitting on the gym floor, awkward and uncomfortable in the shirt and tie they were forced to wear on this first day of the school year, hadn't yet earned the right to wear the St. Benedict's uniform of black pants, a black polo in warmer months, and a coveted black hoodie the rest of the year. Nor had they fully adapted to the MO concerning "the hand." Few of them noticed when one student—a trim young man with dark hair, brown skin, and broad shoulders—approached the podium in the center of the gym. But then he raised his right hand high into the air, and something extraordinary happened.

Without him saying a word, most everyone in the bleachers raised their hands too. The beginners sitting on the floor shyly followed along and, like water circling a drain, the uproar gradually dissipated. Over the course of the eleven-month school year, the raised hand would trigger an almost immediate reaction, the goal being not only silence but an anticipated respect for whoever was about to speak. On this first day, the response was sloppy, but the student at the podium let it slide because he was focused on getting through his initial appearance as senior group leader, the most powerful person under twenty-one in the school. He liked the sound of that—Reynaldo, the eldest son of Ruth and Thomas, a street kid known to everyone as Rey, just a few years out of an ordinary public elementary school in North Newark's *nada del otro mundo* Latino neighborhood, taking charge at St. Benedict's Prep like he'd been born to it. Who could have imagined?

Rey remained silent, having already learned that once you raise your voice to quiet the room, the hand is no longer effective. He took a moment to scan the bleachers, organized according to the school's leadership structure of large sections comprising smaller groups that mix students from all four years so that no one gets forgotten. On Rey's far left, hugging the wall, was the Gray section, long known as the rowdiest bunch in the school, guys who know how to get under Father Ed's skin.

They are the ones the headmaster constantly reminds to stop yapping, sit up, and stay awake. One of Rey's closest friends was in Gray, and Father Ed loved to single him out whenever he wanted to get a laugh by picking on the section's fabricated deficiencies, like their inability to remember whether to spell the gray in Gray Bees, the school's mascots, with an A or an E, even though it's written out in gigantic letters on the gym wall facing them. To Rey's far right was the Maroon section, and in between White, led by his buddy Noah, and Blue, where another one of his pals was in charge. The two new girls sections, Black and Garnet, were just to the right of Maroon. Freshman girls nestled onto the side bleachers, and the freshman boys sat on the same floor where they'd just spent the first night of their week-long boot camp, with the middle-division minions sitting cross-legged along the back wall.

"Hands down," Rey snapped. Every hand dropped. Every pair of lips closed.

Student broadcasters are in charge of streaming convo on their own YouTube channel every day. On this morning, nearly one hundred alumni signed on to watch from Arizona, England, Korea, and wherever else they happened to be. While student leaders took attendance, the alumni caught up. "Happy 50th Anniversary convo," one wrote in the comments section, and another responded, "Yes, fifty years, thankful to the Brothers who walked before me." When one alumnus, Minga Batsukh, '06, wished everyone a good morning, several others reacted with surprise and wanted to know where he was. Minga responded that he was at home, in Mongolia.

The live stream goes blank during attendance, but calling it attendance is misleading. More accurately, it is an inventory of all that is most dear at the school. The students themselves are in charge of accounting for everyone—all their peers who are present in the stands as well as anyone who, for whatever reason, is not at convo that morning, and why. Each missing student is named individually, and their reason for not being there is shouted out for everyone to hear: Home, sick. At the dentist's. College visit. In counseling. The message is unmistakable—this is your place, you belong here, and even when you're not here, you're with us.

After all are accounted for, the live stream resumes. Soon after, on this first morning, Rey left the podium, and Jonathan, a lanky third-year student who usually was accompanied by a golden retriever puppy he was training for the Seeing Eye organization, stepped up. "Good morning," Jonathan read. "Welcome to convocation for July 31st. Let's begin with prayer." What followed was a twenty-first-century version of the Benedictine practice of *morning prayer*, a meditative reading of scriptures that monks everywhere have practiced for 1,500 years. This day began with a reading from *The Rule of St. Benedict*, the revered sixth-century guide to monastic life. "Listen carefully, my son," Jonathan recited, "to the master's instructions, and tend to them with the ear of your heart."[1]

The seventy-three chapters of *The Rule*, and the Benedictine values of obedience and brotherhood that they outline, guide life in Newark Abbey as well as in St. Benedict's Prep, their lessons repeated endlessly and applied to the daily trials that students encounter both within and beyond the Abbey's walls.[2] It is a surprisingly effective transfer of age-old lessons to the contemporary life of these kids. The basic concepts of love and selflessness are conveyed in ways that do not always seem Catholic, and sometimes are not even distinctly Christian, but are always bountifully humanistic. After the readings, students shout out prayers for sick grandparents, world peace, and victories for their teams. Then they sing simple verses written especially for them by the late Rev. Peter Winstead, a Black preacher from one of Newark's storefront churches who for years played the piano at convo. Winstead died a decade ago, but his songs continue to rock the gym.

"When I woke up this morning, I knew I had a miracle," they sang on this first morning after prayers, their voices filling the gym with so much energy that even half-awake upperclassmen came alive. The songs are easygoing earworms that returning students knew well, each an invitation to drape their arms over each other's shoulders and sway to the rhythm. At other inner-city schools, that would be unthinkable. But here, even the toughest guys and baddest girls join in without lashing out. One song leads to the next expression of optimism—a remedy for first-day-of-school-in-the-middle-of-the-summer blues. "You can't take my miracle away; You can't make me sad today." As the energy builds inside the gym, it's possible to feel their spirit growing larger as their outside lives, with all their troubles and issues, recede. "God gave me life and that's good," they belt out. "When I woke up this morning I really understood; Today—woooh!—I'm living in a miracle."

As a graduate of an all-boys Catholic prep school, I recognized the gawky companionship that was so unashamedly on display in the bleachers, guys sporting wispy facial hair to hide a sea of pimples, who shared similar dreams and fears, all reaching for that sweet spot between "dude" and "dork," searching for someone to admire, and for others to admire them. It was familiar in other ways too. Like the monks, the men who lectured me and my classmates also wore black, also projected strength and discipline, and also demanded more of us than we thought we had to give.

Rey raised his hand again, and once the gym quieted down, one of the girls division leaders read out the names of alumni, including a few who'd come back to give opening-day pep talks. "Where's the boss?" Father Ed looked around, then handed the microphone to Maurice Boyd, class of 1995, public safety director of the nearby city of East Orange.

"Like a lot of you," said Boyd, a burly Black man with braids down to his shoulders, "I grew up in the city of Newark, and saw a lot of crime. A lot of drugs. Saw people die. But one thing I can tell you is the decision my mother made to send me to St. Benedict's was the best decision of my life." Father Ed then called up Mark Comesañas, '98, an educator and community activist in Newark who is the father of two Benedict's

men. He shaves his head, wears a full dark beard, and speaks with the
cadence of the city so heavy in his voice that when he utters the word
"Newark," it comes out as *Nork*, just the way it does for most of the kids.
This son of a preacher started with a New Testament reference from
Acts, Chapter Two. "It begins by saying that on the day of Pentecost,
they were all in one accord and in one place," he explained. That shared
vision, the mutual commitment to the same goal, he said, is the source
of St. Benedict's strength. He flipped the story around so the students
could understand how it applied to them. "Reynaldo, this is for you.
And whoever the young lady is, senior group leader of the girls division,
this is for you also. The reason that everybody's hands should go up, the
reason why everyone should be in uniform, is not because we are forcing
you to do something. It should be because you have a desire to be of one
accord. The reason you start with gray before you get to black is because
it's measuring your commitment to being of one accord. Because not just
everybody can be down with all this from the beginning."

He said that other educators ask him how they can replicate what
St. Benedict's does. It's not easy to get them to understand what happens here, he said, because their prejudice gets in the way. They could
look at all of you in your uniforms, he told the students, keeping quiet
when the senior group leader raises his hand, and think it's all about
control. A kind of penitentiary discipline, the way to keep minority kids
in line. They may see freshmen being yelled at by older kids, and think
it's about keeping all of you scared.

"But they've got it all wrong." He raced around the podium, mic
in hand. "It's not about controlling young men and women." What St.
Benedict's does, he pronounced, is guide each student to make the same
commitment to each other, to be of one mind about what it means to
live with others, whether in a monastery on a mountaintop or on the
rough streets of a Northeastern city that's seen better days, and to give
up what they want for the sake of what they all collectively need—a

message of altruism and toughness that has become synonymous with
St. Benedict's.

"And if that happens," he told the students, "then this place will
continue to always be a place of power. A light on a hill. And everywhere I go, people will always say, 'Hey, you ever heard of that spot, St.
Benedict's?' And then when I say, 'Yeah, actually I went there, and my
son went there, and my other son goes there now.' And then their eyes
light up and ask, 'Is it everything that they say?'"

The answer, he tells the students, will always be yes, it's everything
they say, and more.

The alumni tales, the bespoke gospel songs, and the ancient urgings
to listen with the ear of your heart—these are the essential elements
that make St. Benedict's far more than a prep school. It's apparent—
from the perpetual presence of the headmaster and his brother monks,
the prolonged commitment of alumni who return year after year, the
lay staff who are on the job in July while most other schools are closed
for the summer, along with Rey's tentative insistence as he tried to project his authority and silence the gym by simply raising his hand—that
something happens here that doesn't happen in other schools in other
cities. St. Benedict's Prep is recognized as one of the most successful
inner-city educational initiatives in the country, with an almost perfect
graduation rate and a record of sending nearly all its students on to
college regardless of their origin. Neither a charter school nor one that
relies on vouchers, it is a multiracial, multi-ethnic, multicultural college
prep without selective admissions standards.

St. Benedict's achievements are many. Some are easy to identify,
like the group system that makes accountability a requisite, and en-
sures that everyone belongs. But there are also intangible elements, like
the way that the spirit of community inside the Benedictine monastery
infiltrates the school. The two institutions are physically joined at the
main lobby, where one door leads to classrooms and another door opens

onto the monks' residence. The tide between the two constantly ebbs and flows, the dedication and stability of the monks enriching the students, just as the courage and determination of the students constantly enhances the monks' life of prayer and service.

Urban teenagers like those in the bleachers this morning represent some of the thorniest challenges in education today. The academic underachievement associated with this group of adolescents has little to do with cognitive shortcomings and everything to do with the limited resources and abundant emotional turbulence they live with, which their better-off suburban peers don't often face. At St. Benedict's, that inner turmoil has a name. It is "the ugly," and it is what adolescents bring with them to school as surely as they bear the books in their backpacks. The national statistics about young Black and Latino men in particular should alarm even the most disinterested. Minority males are severely underrepresented in honors courses, while they are vastly overrepresented in dropout rates, disciplinary problems, and every other index of failure. In his book *The Trouble with Black Boys*, sociologist and dean of the University of Southern California's school of education, Dr. Pedro A. Noguera, theorized that young Black males have been taught to see themselves as incapable, even inferior. Because most urban schools do not champion these young men the way they need in order to learn, the only way to break that cycle of failure, Noguera argues, is if they are given some degree of control over issues that affect their lives.[3]

That is the brand of empowerment young people get at St. Benedict's, where student leaders make sure everyone shows up for school on time, eleven months of the year. They have the authority to alter the daily schedule, and interview faculty candidates. Students here push each other to take advanced classes, including chemistry, calculus, and Latin, and attend college courses for credit. They hold competitions that keep daily attendance from falling below 95 percent, with all but a handful showing up every day in uniform and on time. And they apply to and are accepted by colleges and universities that prove the "prep" part of the school's name is not just for show.

No other prep school in the country demands as much from its students. Beyond their academic and disciplinary challenges, students here are forced to face the limits of their physical stamina and personal courage, which provides a wellspring of grit they can tap as they face the many rigors ahead. These are kids who already are proficient at the art of survival. St. Benedict's aims to help them thrive in an unfair, unjust, and unforgiving world. Before the year is over, boys and girls who've never left the city will have to tough it out for a week on a winding trail through the mountains. Black kids who are five times more likely than white kids to drown will learn how to be safe in water. To prove it after they've been trained, they must step, fully clothed and blindfolded, off a high platform into the deep end of a pool. And city kids who can't tell a maple tree from a spruce will learn how to survive off the grid by relying only on their wits, stamina, and teamwork.

St. Benedict's is a contradiction in terms. It teaches like Outward Bound, but it is not a wilderness academy. It bears the prep school name, but it possesses none of the traditional prep school's entitlement, pretense, or privilege. The way it physically tests its students is like a military academy, but it tends to their hearts like a support group. And although it is a Catholic school with a proud tradition of producing priests and brothers, most of its students today are not Catholic.

All this takes place in one of America's oldest cities, and one of its unluckiest, condemned to forever be overshadowed by the urban behemoth that is New York, one train stop away. Newark's decline has been catastrophic, and for years it was a place where just about anybody who had the chance to leave, did. But its stubborn refusal to give up makes it a metaphor for the sustained viability of urban centers everywhere. For decades it has been said that wherever American cities are going, Newark will get there first. The city is now in a place where the worst is behind it, and more opportunities than disappointments lie ahead.

* * *

Someone more concerned with anniversaries than Father Ed might have made a bigger deal about celebrating the fiftieth year of something as unlikely to have lasted as the remade St. Benedict's. He kept the morning low key for more than an hour before he finally called everyone's attention to what made the day special.

"Where's Ant? Is Badge still here?" Father Ed's voice is still as raspy and impossible to ignore as it was decades ago when one graduate described it as sounding like his own conscience. His inescapable puns are still as welcomed as brain freezes, his dedication to his students just as ferocious as it was on that first day that St. Benedict's transitioned from an almost all-white prep to an almost all-Black prep. There's a bit of Theodore Hesburgh of Notre Dame in him, and a touch of Boys Town's Father Flanagan too. He is unapologetically still a schoolboy, and even looks it, despite closing in on eighty. His hair is still light brown, and he combs it with the same conservative side part he had in the 1950s. Unlike other monks who've grown beards, some down to their chest, he's always clean-shaven, and prone to wearing a zip-up hoodie over his long black robe. He makes wisecracks just as he did when he wrestled for St. Benedict's, and revels in pranks and ball-busting as much as any of his students. He's usually voluble and outspoken, but he rarely boasts of his own achievements. He has been honored countless times as an educational leader, and has served on innumerable boards, including the Foundation for Newark's Future. But at the recent ceremony where he was inducted into the New Jersey Hall of Fame with journalist Gay Talese, actress Meryl Streep, and the *Brilliant Mind* Nobel Prize–winner, Dr. John Forbes Nash Jr., he recounted how, when he applied to St. Benedict's Prep when he was thirteen, he was initially rejected. His father had to plead with the monks to give him a second chance, which they did.

Second chances remain a hallmark of St. Benedict's, and a way out of the traps a city like Newark can set for someone like Anthony Badger, who Father Ed called down from the bleachers. "So, sitting in the room . . ." The headmaster waited as Badger crossed the gym floor, moving not as nimbly as he had as a star player on the Gray Bees' varsity basketball team, but spritely enough for a trim, high-energy, sixty-four-year-old retiree. "Fifty years ago, not exactly today but this convocation, the first one happened fifty years ago." It wasn't stirring rhetoric, but that's part of what makes him so relatable to the teenagers who are young enough to be his grandkids, or even great grandchildren. His black robe might awe them, and the title "Headmaster" throw fear into their hearts. But when he speaks and sounds like them, they listen.

"He was in the room as a kid, a ninth grader. A lot of you guys know him because he coached you in basketball when you were freshmen, but I wanted to give him a chance because he was in the room. Just a ragtag group of 89 guys we kind of pulled together to start this, with no idea folks, no idea, that those 89 would turn into 980 this year," referring to the entire K-12 enrollment.

Badger hadn't prepared anything special to say, but the gym floor is his second home, and coaching has taught him how to get through to kids. He started with a three-minute résumé: He played basketball and ran cross country at St. Benedict's. Father Ed drove him to his first day of college in Pennsylvania. With his degree in hand, he returned to St. Benedict's as college admissions counselor and freshman basketball coach and stayed for nearly a decade. Went on to a lengthy career in youth sports and social services. Retired three years ago with a big part of his retirement plan being to come back and coach. He left out the time that the city overwhelmed him, the way it does so many. Captive to heroin, he spent several years harassed by cops, swindled by other addicts, and isolated from family and friends. All he said about that dark chapter of his life was that it was the lessons that Father Ed and the other monks taught him that gave him the strength to recover from his mistakes. "The foundations of my life that I got while I was here," he declared in front of the entire school and everyone watching online, "are the reason why I'm standing here today."

The odds against Badger succeeding in life were as great as those the monks faced when they opened their new school to him fifty years ago. Those same hard-luck odds also applied to the city of Newark, which many people had given up for dead back then. Like one of the parables Father Ed often preaches, all of them—Badger, St. Benedict's, and the city of Newark—had to symbolically die before they could be reborn and eventually become what they are today. None of it was easy. It has taken the legendary efforts of a tough bunch of downtown monks, men whose unyielding moral brawn is often hidden beneath the glossier version of their history, who refused to abandon a roughed-up city that also was too proud to give up, who stuck around when others fled, to create, and then run for half a century, a school for ill-starred kids who learn that failure is not the only option for underdogs like them. Over the decades, these selfless individuals have sown courage, confidence, and compassion on this hilltop of asphalt and concrete, and harvested plentiful yields of what can best be summarized as hope. In the end, the proof of their success can be found in the lives of those kids who reflect the city of Newark in their attitudes, their accents, and their actions, who have proven time and time again that they should not be counted out simply because of their histories.

This is their story.

CHAPTER 2

A Showcase for Others

IN THE SUMMER of 1967, when Anthony Badger was eight years old, his curiosity got the better of him. He was at home in one of Newark's threadbare neighborhoods just off the busy commercial drag of Springfield Avenue, and when no one was looking, he crept to the front window of his third-floor apartment, drawn by the sirens and the shouting and his mother's stern warning to keep away. He pulled back the curtain far enough to see army jeeps roaring down his street carrying uniformed white soldiers wearing helmets and holding rifles like they were heading to war. He was too dumbstruck to hear his mother coming up fast behind him to swat the back of his head and yell at him to get his butt away from the window, or else. Like a startled cat he jumped back, but not before he'd glimpsed what looked like a tank rumbling down the same street he crossed every day to play basketball in the asphalt "parking lot" that was his second home.

Anthony lived at the tail end of what the *Newark Evening News* called "a mile and a half battleground"[1] that ran from where St. Benedict's Preparatory School sat on what then was High Street in downtown Newark, up the commercial spine of Springfield Avenue, to South 10th Street, just past his home. The avenue was where his mother shopped at Foodtown and Marty's Meats, and where she sifted through bins at

John's Bargain Stores looking for inexpensive clothes for him and his two brothers. Once in a while, if she had a little extra money, she'd take them all to the avenue for hot dogs, or ice cream. But Springfield Avenue and all the familiar places he knew so well were strictly off-limits now that his neighborhood had been turned into a combat zone.

This was not at all what the Badgers had expected to find when they had set out for Newark three years earlier. Coming as they did from an impoverished corner of the backcountry South, the city promised opportunity, bountiful and blessed. And for a while it seemed to deliver on those promises, at least for them. Anthony's father, Willie, found work as a barber. Mildred, his mother, rented this nice, seventy-dollar-a-month apartment on Brenner Street just by asking a woman she ran into on the sidewalk if it was available. The Waverly Avenue School that Anthony attended two blocks away was a real school, not like the rundown and poorly equipped excuses that passed for schools where they'd come from.

On any other day he'd be in "the parking lot" playing basketball, or exploring the wild places in the cemetery across Brenner Street from his home. There, surrounded by Newark's jammed-up Central Ward, was an unkempt forest of thirty-five acres of twisty lanes and small hills that were perfect for the bikes Anthony and his friends rode. The elegant brownstone entrance to Woodland Cemetery was just a few yards from his front door, and most days it was unlocked and unguarded. In summer, the Brenner Street boys raced down the cemetery's hills. Wintertime meant sledding down the same hills, whizzing by tombstones engraved with peculiar names like Schoenamsgruber, Brunngraber, Hellriegel, and Schweikert. The grave markers seemed impossibly ancient to them, bearing dates from the mid-1800s, and they wondered what it all meant. But their wonder evaporated as soon as their bikes or sleds picked up speed. It wasn't until years later that Anthony understood that the tombstones signified that there was more to Newark than just him and his friends. Those names looked nothing like the names of anyone he knew in Newark, where nearly everyone on Brenner Street and at Waverly School was Black. Where had those people with the strange names come from, and where had they all gone?

Newark's past remained a mystery, but wandering through the cemetery gave Anthony a hint that, despite their concrete, brick, and steel, cities can change just as people can. Newark wasn't always what it was in 1967. When Woodland Cemetery was started in 1855, German immigrants were pouring into Newark. Fed up with the chaos in Europe and hungry to start anew, they settled on the city's outskirts, which then was a modest slope traversed by an unpaved thoroughfare called High Street. Many of them were Catholic, which meant they were not welcomed by the mostly Anglo-Saxon Protestants whose ancestors had founded Newark two centuries before.

That dispiriting pattern of settlement followed by resentment was repeated when vast numbers of Black Americans started showing up in Newark after the First World War. Many came, as Anthony's family would, from the southern United States in what is now known as the Great Migration. The Badgers were on the tail end of that migration, traveling the 775 miles up Highway 1 from Scotia, South Carolina, in 1964. Scotia was a tiny, mostly rural, mostly Black enclave in South Carolina's Hampton County. "Just a little place you go through, like a little town with four stores," Mildred Badger recalled. "Before you start goin' through it, you're out." Black families left Scotia because they "got tired of living there," she said. "Nothin' to do." They came north looking for work, settling in Chicago, New York, and, to a lesser extent, smaller cities where they already had family, like Philadelphia and Newark. Anthony's family was among the last to leave Scotia. By the time they packed up and headed north, Scotia's population had dropped from an all-time high of 324 in 1930 to fewer than 100.

Despite the influx of so many newcomers, Newark also was shrinking. White flight and suburbanization sucked out more people than the Great Migration brought in. By 1960, Newark's population had dropped to 405,000, a steady decline from its all-time high of 442,000 in 1930.[2] As the overall population shrank, and more Black families arrived, the city underwent the most dramatic racial transformation of any major U.S. city at that time, going from 10.6 percent Black in 1940 to a majority of 54 percent Black by 1970. By some accounts, Newark had become America's first Black city.[3]

White families continued to flee the city as key parts of the massive interstate highway system made commuting to downtown Newark from wealthy suburbs easier. Blockbusting scared homeowners into selling before prices dropped even lower, leaving rows of aging houses that were sold to absentee landlords. At the same time, the *Newark News* carried pages of advertisements for suburban developments boasting modern design and bigness: big rooms, big kitchens, and big yards. The Garden State Parkway opened to traffic in 1954, triggering a massive surge of suburban development and accelerated white flight.

"Quick pleasant commuting three ways," promised a 1956 ad in the *Newark News* for a Parkway-inspired development called Fleetwood Park near Middletown, New Jersey, thirty-five miles south of Newark, where a four bedroom, one-and-a-half bath Georgetown Colonial with a separate dining room and a paneled basement rec room could be purchased with a thirty-year mortgage for as little as eighty-six dollars a month. The underlying message was well understood: leave the overcrowded, increasingly violent, increasingly Black city behind.

Cities all over America hemorrhaged residents and businesses in the '60s but few declined as drastically as Newark. Conditions in the city were so grim by 1967 that Newark willingly labeled itself one of the worst cities in America, hoping that by doing so it could snare federal funds through the new Model Cities Program. Because presenting the worst case made the best case for being picked to receive the money that the Johnson administration was promising, Newark's application showcased the city's failings rather than trying to hide them. City Hall unashamedly boasted that the FBI had listed Newark as the number one city in the country in overall crimes reported four years in a row. In almost every negative category, Newark was at or near the worst— seventh in negligent manslaughter, ninth in forcible rapes, tenth in burglaries, eleventh in robberies, fourteenth in auto thefts, and fifteenth in murders. As the population shrank, the city's negatives intensified. With fewer businesses to help carry the burden, property taxes—the principal source of income to pay for municipal services, including Newark's troubled schools—soared, creating by 1967 the highest per capita property tax burden in the country.[4]

At one point, the Model Cities submission turned prophetic. "Newark remains an uncommon challenge," the three-inch-thick proposal concluded, "big enough to count and small enough to manage. It is as close to a perfect testing ground for the techniques of tomorrow as America is likely to see."

As those who could pack up and get out of Newark took off, the city's limited physical size and its energetic embrace of high-rise, low-income, public housing—Newark built more per capita than any other city—meant that the pockets of Black poverty grew denser, with the highest concentrations occurring in what had once been the German section of the Central Ward.

The German immigrants had moved up and out by then, but the monastery and prep school that Benedictine priests from Germany had established there in the mid-nineteenth century remained a stabilizing presence on High Street. St. Benedict's had been educating boys there since 1868, first Germans, then Irish, then Italian, but very few Blacks. As the prep approached its centennial, the monks hired professional planners to study the school's prospects for continued success in the city. The consultants came back with an upbeat set of recommendations that ignored the portrait of Newark presented in the city's Model Cities application. They found that although the school was no longer a primarily Newark-centered institution, the city's substantial transportation network continued to draw students from all over northern and central New Jersey. With legions of baby boomers ready to enroll, the consultants predicted that a regional high school like St. Benedict's was sure to gain.[5]

They also acknowledged that St. Benedict's deteriorating neighborhood would probably hurt the number and quality of applicants, but they were confident that the city's urban renewal program would revitalize the blocks around the school. The consultants recommended upgrading older buildings, improving the prep school curriculum, recruiting more high-achieving students, and increasing scholarships.

By the 1960s, the prep had already educated thousands of young men, nearly all of them white. Some went on to hold powerful positions in the church, the state, and especially in Newark, government. Hugh A. Addonizio, a six-term congressman who had starred as quarterback for St. Benedict's in the 1930s, had recently won a second term as mayor. Alumni held important positions throughout the city, including in the police and fire departments, which were overwhelmingly white. During Addonizio's tenure, officials had become cozy with organized crime, which operated openly. Mobster Ruggiero "Tony Boy" Boiardo had his fingerprints on many city contracts. Illegal gambling was commonplace, and it was no secret that if you wanted something done in Newark, you'd better include an envelope stuffed with cash.

Every member of the city council but one was white, as were most department heads. The Addonizio administration antagonized the city's Black residents when it skipped over a qualified Black man for a position as secretary to the Board of Education in favor of a white man with political ties to City Hall. Addonizio then triggered a full-blown community crisis when he tried to convince state leaders that Newark, and not suburban Madison, was the best place to build New Jersey's first publicly funded medical school. In order for the school's planners to even consider Newark, they had first demanded 150 acres of cleared land for the construction of a new hospital and adjacent buildings. The response from City Hall was an enthusiastic "no problem."

The administration decided that the perfect place for the school was the city's Central Ward, the most predominantly Black neighborhood in Newark.

Addonizio ran Newark as if no one were watching. But many people were. At the same time the city was submitting its Model Cities application, Dr. Martin Luther King Jr. was boldly predicting that Newark and ten cities from coast to coast would "explode in racial violence" that summer.[6]

Newark officials took great offense at King's ominous prediction. Police director Dominick A. Spina deplored King's prophecy of violence and boldly claimed that Newark was a striking example of "racial tranquility." Even the city's first Black council member, Irvine Turner, pushed back at King's warning: "Rather than being a potential powder keg as Mr. [sic] King claims, Newark can continue as a showcase for others," read his statement to the papers.[7]

Three months later, Turner's showcase exploded.

CHAPTER 3

Open Rebellion

WHEN A CITY'S best hope is to be recognized as the worst city in America, there's little chance of anything good coming to pass. By the summer of 1967, the neighborhood around St. Benedict's had turned into one of the roughest sections of a city filled with block after block of no-go zones. And then one Wednesday night in the middle of July, the uprising that Dr. King had forecast ignited a conflagration that would one day be recognized as the moment when one Newark ceased to exist and another, short on luck and love, took its place.

At the center of it all was John Smith, a stocky Black man with a goatee and a name so common it could have belonged to anyone, or to no one at all. Smith drove for the Safety Cab Company, hustling throughout the Central Ward to cover the $16.50 a day it cost him to rent the car with a little left over to save for new front teeth. He'd lost his own in an accident while playing the trumpet back home in Salisbury, North Carolina, and had come north hoping to find work, a new smile, and a chance to get paid for his music.[1]

On that hot and humid Wednesday night, Smith cruised the Central Ward hoping for a good fare. Finally, as it was growing dark, a middle-aged woman flagged him down near City Hospital on Bergen Street and 12th Avenue. Less than five minutes and a few blocks later,

Smith slowed almost to a stop behind a Newark police cruiser that was double-parked with two officers sitting inside. He blinked his high beams and pulled around the cruiser, as he'd done many times before when he needed to pass a car. He didn't think much of it until he heard the police tap their siren and signal for him to pull over. "They said I had popped the intersection, that I had run through without having the right of way," Smith recalled years later.

To this day there are two versions of what happened next.[2] Smith claimed the two white officers insulted the woman who was in his cab before ordering her to get out. Then they forced him into the back seat of their cruiser and beat him. The police officers would testify that when they demanded Smith's license and registration, he became abusive. When they ordered him out of the car, he opened the door so forcefully that it struck one of the officers hard enough to injure him. Smith claimed the cops beat him for no reason. The police alleged that Smith attacked them and had to be subdued. Whether he was hurt, or being uncooperative, when they got him to their station house—what was then known as the Fourth Precinct on 17th Avenue, directly across the street from the massive Hayes Homes housing project—the officers grabbed Smith by the arms and legs and carried him inside. By the time Smith was booked and charged with assaulting a police officer, resisting arrest, and using offensive language, it was 9:30 p.m.

The surrounding streets were filling with people escaping the stifling heat of the projects. The sight of the white police officers dragging Smith into the precinct house immediately set off rumors. Had the police beaten another Black man to death? In the absence of answers about Smith, the angry crowd supplied its own. "He's gone, brother. They killed him,"[3] shouted the line of taxi drivers that drove up, inciting the crowd. Most Newarkers had no trouble believing that the police had it in for Smith. For years there had been repeated calls in Newark for a civilian review board to investigate charges of police brutality. What happened to Smith that night simply released the pent-up anger and frustration that had been building for decades. "We don't want to talk about Smith," one woman was reported to have told the police inspector after he brought a few protesters inside the precinct house to see for themselves that Smith was alive. "We want to talk about what we see here happening every day, time and time again."[4]

Smith was eventually taken to the hospital cut, bruised, and nursing a fractured rib. The next morning, the police piled traffic citations on top of the assault charges, then released him on bail. But by then, the knowledge that he was alive mattered little. That night, anger, frustration, and rage poured into the streets. Rioters pelted the police precinct with bottles, rocks, even firebombs. They trashed several police cruisers and torched an abandoned car.

The police forced the people on the street to disperse, but many didn't go home. Packs of angry men took out their frustration on local stores. When somebody smashed the front window of Harry's Liquors on Belmont Avenue, people helped themselves to all the beer and whisky they could grab. On Springfield Avenue, where the mile and a half heading west from High Street was jammed with stores, many owned and operated by Jews who, until the 1950s, had represented a sizable percentage of Newark's inhabitants, were systematically looted. In his autobiography, poet Amiri Baraka—who was known as LeRoi Jones until he switched to the African name—described what he and a few friends saw on a long slow drive up Springfield Avenue. It was an eruption of long stifled violence that shattered not only windows and storefronts but the city's sense of its own destiny. He witnessed crowds casing Springfield Avenue's stores as if they were on a mission, strategically heading for the places that would satisfy their unrequited desire for the things they saw advertised on television but could not afford. As restraint faded, he saw whole families working together to grab sofas and television sets too big for one person to carry.[5]

Before Baraka and his friends had finished cruising the avenue, Newark police stopped them, searched their car, and found two .32

caliber handguns. They roughed up Baraka and arrested him. He spent the rest of that night in jail, twenty stitches in his head. He understood that the city where he had been born would never be the same.

One of the policemen on patrol that night was Officer Richard Nazareta, a Newark native who had graduated from St. Benedict's in 1958. He and his partner were patrolling Springfield Avenue when they spotted looters breaking into a jewelry store. As Nazareta pulled the patrol car to the curb, somebody hurled a whisky bottle his way, shattering the driver's-side window. "I was grabbing my eyes," Nazareta said, "and the other guys in the car came to my aid, and they called it in that I was hurt. They pulled me out of the car onto the pavement on Springfield Avenue. And then you could hear people yelling 'shoot the cop!'" When another patrol car showed up, Nazareta was rushed to the hospital where doctors removed the glass from his eyes.

Despite the attack on the station house, and the wanton destruction of Springfield Avenue that night, the following day's *Newark News* ran an article on page one (below a large photograph of the crowning of Miss Tall Universe) that reflected more hope than reality. The article described the unrest as an "isolated incident," and quoted Mayor Addonizio declaring, "We're concerned, but not unduly concerned."

* * *

While his sons had strict orders to stay inside, Anthony Badger's dad, Willie, left the Brenner Street apartment to get to his barber shop in the South Ward, on the other side of town. At least, that's what he told his family. But when he came home after the eleven p.m. curfew with his hand and arm bleeding, his wife was furious. He told her it was just an accident, but she doubted he was telling the truth. Willie eventually confessed that he and a few friends had followed the crowds into an appliance store and he had cut himself on broken glass before hightailing it back to Brenner Street and stashing the loot two houses down with

Mr. Joe, the neighborhood bookie who ran numbers, sold beer on Sundays, and knew how to unload things that fell off of trucks.

As the number of people hurt, killed, or arrested in Newark multiplied, the flustered mayor admitted that, contrary to his dismissive earlier statement, there was much to be concerned about. At around two a.m. Friday morning, he called Governor Richard J. Hughes to ask for help. Hughes responded quickly, ordering in several hundred state police troopers, who started arriving before daybreak. Then, as the sun rose, the first of several thousand National Guardsmen took up positions on and near Springfield Avenue. Eventually more than five thousand troops, along with their jeeps and armored personnel carriers, would be deployed, some coming from armories as far away as Salem County, at the southern tip of the state, where Newark was nothing but a bad image best avoided.

As the guardsmen and troopers joined the city's thirteen hundred police officers, the violence escalated. Most of the soldiers were young, white, and scared to have been thrown into a running battle in the state's largest and now most unruly city. Local residents felt besieged. Kevin Washington, who would in a few years be Anthony Badger's classmate, lived at the foot of Springfield Avenue, where he had a clear view of both St. Benedict's and the growing confrontation between rioters and police. He recalled the same unreal images as Anthony—National Guard trucks and tanks roaring up the streets where he usually played ball. "There was a sniper in the apartment building across the street from where I lived, and I could hear the gunfire of the cops shooting up from my building to that building," he told me. "We had to duck down in the house."

The first night of the riot passed relatively unnoticed inside the Benedictine abbey on High Street. St. Benedict's Prep was closed for the summer and most of the monks were visiting family or traveling. As the disturbances escalated throughout the city, the young monks who were stuck at the abbey couldn't ignore what was happening. At night, a few of them climbed a back staircase to the roof of the school. "Nobody knew exactly what the heck was going on, so a bunch of us went up to the roof and were watching, and it was just pure bedlam," remembered Father Maurice Carlton, who in 1967 had only recently taken his vows as a monk. He had graduated from St. Benedict's with Officer Nazareta in 1958 and from the roof he looked on in horror as the neighborhood he knew so well came undone. He and the others inhaled the suffocating smoke of the arson fires and listened to the ricochet of gunfire. They watched as guardsmen parked a personnel carrier near the abbey church on the corner of High and William Streets. "There were bullets bouncing off the Greek church across the street," Father Maurice recalled. He couldn't tell exactly where the shots were coming from, but they were close enough to scare him and the other monks.

Governor Hughes was intent on putting down the riots quickly and, if necessary, brutally. After seeing for himself the violence in the Central Ward, the governor (who would go on to become chief justice of the New Jersey Supreme Court) dropped his usual self-restraint and called Newark "a city in open rebellion" and vowed to retake control. "The line between the jungle and the law might as well be drawn here as any place in America,"[6] Hughes declared, playing up to the Johnson administration in Washington that had threatened to send in federal troops if the governor couldn't restore order on his own. His shocking language reflected the callous attitudes that would later be blamed for having made the riots inevitable.

Constant reports of snipers kept the skittish national guardsmen on edge. Choking on the heavy smoke and deafened by screeching sirens, they fired thousands of rounds at the housing projects blocks away from the Benedictine monastery. When Newark police caught sight of the monks on the roof and yelled for them to get back before they too got shot, Father Maurice and the others scattered. "It did not take much of a warning," he said, "for us to get the hell out of there."

CHAPTER 4

A Community Divided

ST. BENEDICT'S STARTED the 1967–68 school year a few weeks after the riots. By then, the fires had all been put out and workmen were busy repairing some of the seven hundred stores on Springfield Avenue that rioters had trashed. But inside the monastery, Newark's angry summer had reopened an old fissure, one with origins in the community's founding. Was a city like Newark, and a street like High Street, a righteous place for a Benedictine abbey?

Father Boniface Wimmer, the determined German Benedictine who had founded the order's first monastery in the United States in rural Pennsylvania, had originally resisted the idea of establishing a religious sanctuary in Newark. "The parish has a fine location, but I am afraid of cities," he wrote in 1854 in his initial rejection of Bishop James Roosevelt Bayley's request to build a monastery in Newark.[1] By then, the city was almost two hundred years old. It was no bigger than 35,000 residents, but thousands of those were believed to be Catholics, many of them German, with more coming every month. Despite his doubts, Wimmer began the protracted process that eventually led to the establishment of a permanent Benedictine community in the city. The industrious monks quickly transformed their parcel of high ground above Newark's downtown core. In 1868 they opened St. Benedict's

College, the precursor to St. Benedict's Preparatory School. And in 1884, the land on the corner of High and William Streets officially became St. Mary's Abbey, named after the parish church and adjoining elementary school on what had become abbey grounds.[2]

The founder's apprehension about the city and its suitability for his monks was temporarily resolved, but the urge for serenity clashed with the Benedictines' legendary commitment to place. In the following decades, the monks purchased part of a grand Gilded Age estate in Morristown, about twenty-five miles west of Newark, and over the years developed a seminary there and a prep school for boys, called Delbarton, that competed with Newark for resources. By 1968, there were two separate communities, one urban and the other suburban, with two different missions, one focused on the disadvantaged and the other serving the privileged. Morristown assumed the title of St. Mary's Abbey, while the original setting on High Street was eventually renamed Newark Abbey in a show of its commitment to the city.

In that same year, as St. Benedict's commemorated its first century, Abbot Martin Burne issued an audacious challenge. Just a few months after the governor of New Jersey had labeled Newark "an American disaster," Abbot Martin said he wanted to increase the number of "able ghetto students," using a term for inner-city youth that was accepted in those times. Burne, a Newark native and former navy chaplain who had joined the March on Washington in 1963, was willing to go out on a limb for neighborhood kids he thought would benefit from a traditional prep school education despite prevailing racial stereotypes. He challenged the city's business leaders, as well as St. Benedict's alumni, to raise the money needed to cover the tuition for these students. Although his proposal was quite modest, amounting to no more than ten Black students a year, he anticipated strong pushback. And he got it.

Alumni doubted that the number of Black students could be increased even slightly without watering down admission standards and the school's college prep curriculum. Monks too were worried. At their own internal chapter meetings, they laid bare their fears of a growing white backlash by suburban parents who objected to using the money they raised for the school to bring in "unqualified" Black and Puerto Rican students. Some threatened to send their sons to competing schools. In that first September after the riot, fifty-six already-enrolled students had changed their minds and transferred out. Acceptance offers were rejected. Applications declined.

Not all the monks were ready to, as one put it, "hang the crepe yet," and they vowed to find a way to keep the school open. They planned to ask their Central Ward neighbors for strategies to attract more minority students. And until enrollment stabilized, they pledged to reduce costs in the monastery. The monks lived austerely, with few personal possessions, limited wardrobes, and sparsely furnished rooms. They agreed to take on heavier teaching loads to save the cost of hiring lay teachers. They eliminated six of the monastery's daily newspapers, cut back the money set aside for Christmas gifts, and limited themselves to two bottles of beer a day.[3]

But the problems ran far deeper than how much beer the monks imbibed. Some of the same men who had fought against abandoning Newark for the countryside a few years earlier now expressed doubts about the wisdom of remaining in the city. "The Blacks are talking of burning again," one of them ranted, according to the minutes of a chapter meeting. Several monks repeatedly expressed concerns about their ability to connect with the African American community, even if they underwent what they called "Black sensitivity training."

By 1970, only a handful of Black students from the projects had enrolled, yet alumni and monks alike fretted that the school was lowering its standards and watering down its curriculum to accommodate them. Applications continued to decline.

Newark itself was in turmoil. Investigators charged Mayor Addonizio and several other city officials with widespread corruption. During Addonizio's trial, he was heard boasting on secret wiretap recordings, "There's no money in Washington, but you can make a million bucks as the Mayor of Newark."[4]

Before the trial ended, Addonizio was forced into a runoff election with a diffident Black civil engineer named Kenneth A. Gibson, whose family had joined the Great Migration in 1940, leaving Alabama for Newark's Central Ward. Eyes across the nation were on Newark and the possibility that it would elect a Black mayor, the first major Northeastern city to do so. Gibson, backed by Amiri Baraka, Harry Belafonte, and other prominent Blacks, won a runoff election and took control of the beleaguered city.[5] Newark's Black majority now held political power, but the city they took over was in ruins. Gibson inherited a punishing budget deficit, substandard housing, record unemployment, a still-defiant police force, crumbling schools, aggrieved teachers, and a city with the reputation for being the worst in America. And the next few years would prove that neither Newark, nor St. Benedict's, had yet hit bottom.

* * *

Gibson was in his second year as mayor when Father Albert Holtz, a studious Benedictine monk, made his way from his room in the monastery to the new yellow brick school building that had been constructed in 1959 as a good-faith representation of the abbey's continuing commitment to Newark. It was around eight p.m. and, as usual, Father Albert was a bundle of energy and curiosity. Newark-born, he knew the city inside and out. He remembered being brought downtown as a child so his father could photograph him with the famous bronze of Abraham Lincoln in front of the old Essex County Courthouse just a block from St. Benedict's. As a prep student in the late 1950s, he sang first tenor in the all-state chorus and ran track. He watched the monks who were his teachers with a mixture of respect and awe and decided, by Christmas of his second year, to follow them into the monastery. Each monastery is self-governing, each monk a member of an instantly recognizable gang living according to a set of ancient rules that guide every hour of their lives. Much of what goes on inside is a mystery to outsiders, but one thing was clear to Albert. This downtown abbey was no mountaintop retreat. The men inside were not there to escape from real life. The city infiltrated the abbey walls every day and night.

Father Albert's mission that night in 1972 is long forgotten, but not what happened when he crossed a passageway connecting the old prep school buildings with the new addition and nearly ran into a short Black man in an army fatigue coat. The man's hair was braided in cornrows and he was immediately suspect because he was carrying a television monitor and a video camera from St. Benedict's audiovisual equipment locker. Father Albert pushed the burglar into the school's small library, and slammed the door shut, hoping to hold it closed until help arrived.

The young priest was about six feet tall, trim and fit, but he wasn't able to keep the door shut for very long. The man in the fatigue coat shoved it open and hightailed it down the passageway. Father Albert chased after him, and soon caught up. They grappled. The thief slugged Father Albert with a hammer, hitting his head hard enough to draw blood, then ran away. Father Albert was brought to St. Michael's Hospital down High Street, where doctors stitched the wound on his head.

Almost every monk, it seemed, experienced something similar in those days. Someone sneaked into the church and stole sacred articles. A policeman shot at a thief he was chasing down High Street and the bullet smashed through the window of a monk's room. One of the more frightened monks spoke up at a chapter meeting and shrilly told the others they should "sell the whole mess and get out before we all get killed."

Every dip in enrollment or bit of red ink on the school's ledgers triggered another existential crisis. Unlike other monastics, the monks of Newark Abbey did not bake bread, brew beer, or run a retreat house. The school was their sole mission, and if the school failed, the abbey itself would be jeopardized. The monks spent countless hours over many months debating their continued presence in Newark, with much of the angst recorded in a revealing contemporary journal that Father Albert kept.

"At present, I can't see us going on next year," Albert wrote, his cramped cursive penmanship betraying his inner anxiety. "It would be too much of a drain and strain on all of us, and wouldn't be very beneficial to the students—few people see beyond one more year anyway."

There was no escaping the gloomy enrollment figures, but a sizable number of the monks were jittery about more than the school's future. Like their founder, they were afraid of the city, afraid of their deteriorating neighborhood, and afraid of the young Black men that they'd been told were indispensable to the future of St. Benedict's Prep. The apprehensive monks feared that they didn't know how to teach kids from the neighborhood, nor did they think those students could do the work that St. Benedict's had traditionally demanded.

As the debate continued to tear the monastery apart, Newark hit what many consider its lowest point. The P. Ballantine & Sons Brewery, one of the largest employers in the city, and a powerful symbol of Newark's century-long dominance in that industry, was sold to Falstaff Brewers of St. Louis, which immediately shut it down, throwing 1,600 people out of work. The city council president called the closing "a major catastrophe." The *Newark News* did not cover Ballantine's demise because the paper then was embroiled in its own strike. It would resume publication for six months, then shut down its presses for good. The railroads that had made the city such an important commuter hub all declared bankruptcy. Unemployment in Newark reached 17 percent, almost three times higher than the national average, with no relief in sight.

The crisis over the abbey's destiny took a toll on the monastic community's spirit. Instead of a contemplative body of like-minded men seeking the divine through prayer and work, the community had become what one priest labeled "a loose confederation of sovereign souls." The men who believed St. Benedict's had run its course sat apart at meals from those who favored staying put. They traded accusatory side-ways glances in the hallways, and whispered unkind comments in the commons. The bickering spilled over to the abbey church, where monks from one side skipped the daily five o'clock mass when a priest on the opposing side was the celebrant. And most telling, during the moment of the mass where the faithful are supposed to share a sign of peace, monks from opposing positions avoided the fraternal embrace that, until then, had been the monks' traditional gesture of reconciliation.

Finally, the abbot called a vote to decide the fate of the school. It was done in the ancient practice of the Benedictines—a white ball or marble for a yes vote, a black ball for a no, yellow for an abstention. But he forewarned the community that even if the required two-thirds vote to close wasn't reached, he would shutter the school anyway. "What do I hope for? I don't really know," Father Albert confided in his personal journal. "What will (would) life be like in Newark Abbey if St. B's didn't exist? Does anything else hold us together?"

Twenty yes votes would mean the school would close. When the mar-bles were counted, there were nineteen white ones, ten black ones, and four yellow abstentions. Although the final tally fell short by one, the abbot declared, "In line with what I said in the last meeting—the school is closed."

The next morning, Ash Wednesday, the headmaster of St. Bene-dict's notified the faculty that the school would suspend operations in June. As hundreds of students started what they thought was going to be just another school day, they were told to head to the auditorium instead of their first class. The abbot sat on the stage as the headmaster broke the news about the school's final days. Sitting in one of the audi-torium seats was fifteen-year-old James Francis Curley, who, as Father Augustine J. Curley O.S.B., in 2022 would be elected the third abbot of Newark Abbey.

"I forget how he began, but it was very abrupt," the abbot recently recalled. The headmaster read the letter he was sending to parents. In three short paragraphs he outlined the struggles of the previous few years to hold down tuition while propping up enrollment. He made no mention of the deeper split within the community over race and the school's role in Newark. "The Board of Trustees meeting with the Monk-Faculty reluctantly accepts the sad fact that this June 1972, St. Benedict's Prep will suspend operations. I do hope you will remember the good that St. Benedict's has done over the years and pray that whatever the future holds for us, we shall respond to the grace God gives us."

In the days that followed, parents demanded a meeting with the monks. It was the kind of heated confrontation that took place at hundreds of Catholic schools (including my own) that were throwing in the towel. The parents were angry that the decision to close had been made without giving them a chance to raise money or recruit enough kids to keep the school going. "You can't close our school," they argued. His back against the wall, the abbot countered: "It's not your school. It's the monks' school." He contended that it would be irresponsible of him to risk the monks' security by keeping open a school that was already losing money, and seemed destined to lose lots more.

* * *

The last graduation from the original St. Benedict's Preparatory School was held June 9, 1972. The next day's edition of the *Newark News* (which would permanently cease publication a few weeks later) reported that the 127 seniors "filed solemnly out of the auditorium," a sad, final graduation for a school that had meant so much to so many in the city. "God be with you Benedict's men," was the headmaster's final sendoff.

Shortly after that last assembly, a Liberty moving company van pulled up to the monastery on High Street and loaded up the furnishings of a dozen or so monks who were determined to flee Newark. The abbot in Morristown had decided to welcome all who chose to live and

work there. None of them are still alive, but a history of Delbarton
and St. Mary's Abbey in Morristown describes those who packed their
things into the van that day as having "lost all faith in conducting a
school in the Central Ward of Newark. The kind of school and mission
they were accustomed to used to serve white suburban youngsters and
families," which is an accurate description of the exclusive prep school
that Delbarton was then and remains today.[6]

In the weeks after the school closed, the local CYO basketball
league held some of its games inside St. Benedict's cramped 1920s-era
Shanley Gym, which is topped by a steeply banked wooden running
track. Most of the players were Black kids from around Newark. One
team, St. Bridget's, boasted a talented young player who made up for his
modest height with explosive speed, gutsy ballhandling, and bull's-eye
shooting. Anthony Badger didn't mind walking the mile and a half from
his home on Brenner Street down the wreckage of Springfield Avenue
to the gym because it meant that instead of playing on the bumpy asphalt with a makeshift hoop at "the parking lot" near his home, he could
show his stuff in a real gym with plexiglass backboards, hoop nets, and
an electronic scoreboard. He didn't know much about St. Benedict's or
the dissension that had split apart the old monastery just a few doors
down from the gym. All that mattered to him was that Shanley's backboards had a square painted on them, and if he managed to put the ball
in the square on layups and jump shots, it magically went in.

CHAPTER 5

The Essence of Freedom

AFTER THE LIBERTY moving van rumbled down High Street, and all those who wanted to leave the city finally were gone, the monks in both Newark and Morristown experienced a shaky relief. The bitter split inside the monastic community had come to a regrettable yet somehow welcomed end. Had one side chickened out, while the other proved they had the guts to stick with Newark? Or had more than a dozen men grown weary of fighting with a bunch of unrealistic dreamers who were willing to take the whole monastery down with them?

Some of the younger monks in Newark felt victorious, but they weren't ready to sit back and savor their victory. There was too much to do, too many decisions to make. Taking stock of their situation showed them how much the standoff had cost. Just a few weeks earlier, they could have counted forty-one members of Newark Abbey's monastic community. But since the school closed, fifteen of them had departed, and two others had been granted authorized leaves of absence. Reality set in fast.

The Benedictines' storied independence meant they could expect no help to come from the archdiocese or any other part of the Catholic hierarchy. They had to figure out a way to replace the tuition money they had relied on from St. Benedict's, and their prospects were bleak. Of the twenty-four remaining monks, nine were elderly and two so young they were still taking classes to complete their degrees. Five were already working in local parishes. That meant just seven men could realistically look for paying jobs outside the abbey walls to bring in money to sustain the monastery.

In the stark light of their decimated monastic community, and the declining fortunes of their home city, even someone as supremely optimistic as Father Albert considered the unthinkable. In his journal, he wrote: "Is it madness to consider any alternative but dissolving the present abbey?"

The chance of succeeding with a new venture, or merely surviving as a community, were discouragingly slim, yet the monks were not giving up on the city, its kids, or the idea of opening *some* kind of school to serve Newark's shifting demographics. In the meantime, the monks who could work hit the pavement. Some found jobs as teachers or chaplains, but a few ventured far from what they had been trained to do. Edwin found work at a drug treatment center in Jersey City, and his classmate Philip taught religion in a Catholic grammar school in the morning, and drove a delivery truck for a paper bag company in the afternoon.

For a community based on communal prayer and work, it was a jolt to leave the monastery in the morning, work at individual jobs in different cities during the day, then return at night like regular commuters. Some started to wonder how they'd ever go back to being a true Benedictine community of prayer and work. They suspected that there was only one realistic way to achieve that goal. "Look, everybody knows we're gonna wind up saying, 'Let's run a school,'" one of the monks remarked at a chapter meeting. It was only September, less than three months after the old St. Benedict's had closed, but the way forward seemed clear. "So, let's cut the crap and start moving on the school."

That same month, Edwin and Philip were ordained as priests. As the youngest members of the community, and the most vocal supporters of the new school project, they took the lead, testing various ideas and theories. They worked closely with one of their St. Benedict's classmates, Paul Thornton, who had gone to Harvard after graduation and then, still a layman, returned to teach at the prep. And they consulted with alumni who worked in financial services. The monks may have taken vows of poverty and lived modest, even frugal, lives, but they knew that any new school needed start-up money.

By the first week in October, Father Ed announced at a chapter meeting, "We're runnin' a school here next year." Despite that brassy optimism, all they had was a bare-bones idea about starting some kind of educational venture. No details had been finalized, not even what the new enterprise would be called. They were acting more on faith than reason, but after so much self-examination over the last few years, they believed that starting a new school was the only morally acceptable option.

"While such a decision is really forced on us by the logic of our not having moved to Morristown in June," Father Albert wrote at the time, "still it is a crazy thing to try. We really must be nuts. Me most of all." One of his brother monks told him he was looking at it in the wrong way. Although they had left themselves with few realistic courses of action, their Benedictine values compelled them to stick with Newark and dare to open a new school to serve their neighbors. It might seem contradictory, he explained, but being forced by those values to take such uncertain steps was "the essence of freedom," a way of acting on their beliefs without being deterred by the predictable concerns over money, marketing, and precedence. In other words, they were free to fail because their vows precluded everything except daring to try.

They started with a few fundamental requirements for a new school. They thought it had to be small, at least at first. It would be all boys, as St. Benedict's had always been. But they didn't want it to be all Black. The students should reflect the population of Newark, which was majority Black, but also included a growing number of Puerto Ricans and other Latinos, and some whites. But moving beyond that basic framework would be difficult without a director, someone with the vision and drive to take charge of the project. But who?

Father Albert was the obvious choice. He had recently earned a master's degree in educational philosophy at Columbia's Teachers College in New York, and had years of experience in the classroom. But he was reluctant to take on the responsibility, and as was reflected in his writing, he wasn't fully convinced that a new school was feasible. Another monk who was trained in accounting declined to even be considered for the post. You'll need a good accountant, he told the others, forecasting the financial challenges ahead. Reopening the school would be an act of faith. Its leader would have to put aside the many legitimate reasons not to try it, and focus single-mindedly on the improbable but necessary mission. That required not an expert, but an idealist, a zealot even. The monks elected Father Ed, who was not yet twenty-seven, and who until that moment had spent more time in classrooms as a student than as a teacher.

The young man picked to run a school that did not yet exist, for students who hadn't yet been recruited, in a city that had just hit bottom, might seem to be an odd choice, a desperate last resort when all the older men understood that the mission was quixotic at best, doomed to fail at its worst. To understand their decision, it's important to know something about Father Ed's formation. Like all Benedictines, he had vowed to listen intently to God, the scriptures, and his superiors. He vowed fidelity to the monastic way of life, which prescribed both poverty and chastity. And as a follower of St. Benedict, he took one vow that set him apart from other religious orders. The Benedictines' vow of stability binds each monk for the rest of his life to the community where he professed his vows. Unlike parish priests who regularly are transferred from place to place, Benedictines live and work together in the same place for decades. And some never leave. [1]

Father Ed had pledged his life to Newark Abbey, and by extension to the city itself. He had come of age in the 1960s and his world view reflected the rapidly changing values of the time—heightened empathy for others, a deeper sense of universal justice, and abiding respect for the civil rights of all men. Add to that a city-block-sized chip on his shoulder toward the monks who had turned their backs on Newark, along with an Irishman's prickly attitude toward being told what he can and cannot do, and it could be said that the kid once known as Dennis Leahy, now Father Edwin Leahy, O.S.B., was an ideal choice to pull off an outrageous stunt like leading a gang of like-minded Newarkers to resurrect a school that had failed less than a year before.

Although Edwin's election seemed spontaneous, his superiors may have been subtly preparing him to take the lead in Newark. Although he had been reared in the nearly all-white New Jersey suburb of Woodbridge, and attended St. Benedict's when few of his classmates were Black, both he and Philip were sent for theological training to a Benedictine seminary in the Deep South while Jim Crow ruled without restraint. When they returned to New Jersey to complete their theological studies, they were assigned to live at Newark Abbey instead of Morristown. The abbot didn't consider their assignment part of any long-range plan for buttressing Newark's urban mission, but their presence there, after witnessing the segregation of the South and living with the racism that had triggered the riots in Newark, ultimately had that effect.

There were other signs that his role as leader of the new school was preordained. Just before Edwin arrived in Newark, a fellow monk lent him John McPhee's *The Headmaster*, an inspiring tale about Frank Boyden's sixty-six-year-long tenure at the helm of Deerfield Academy, the Massachusetts prep school he ran from 1902 to 1968. He couldn't have imagined it at the time he read the book, but Father Ed's tenure at St. Benedict's would come to resemble Boyden's personal voyage. Both were young men when they were selected to lead schools that were in deep trouble. Deerfield Academy was failing and seemed to be heading toward closure when Boyden, then twenty-four, was offered the job as headmaster. Both he and Edwin managed to assemble staffs that turned their schools around. Both would be considered eccentrics who rejected decorum, spent more time in the hallways than in an office, and reveled in keeping students and staff off guard with their shenanigans. And just as Boyden was described as likely to be the last of his kind—the genteel academic with a dry wit who created an institution in his own image—so would Edwin come to be seen as the last of a breed of headstrong men in black robes dedicated to the school they entered as teenagers and never left.

As that ruinous year of 1972 neared its end, most of the men at Newark Abbey agreed that although Newark was the right place for them to start their school, a change of scenery would help them focus on the many decisions they still needed to make. They traveled eighty miles to the remote upstate New York community of Yulan for a three-day brainstorming retreat at an old Catskill Mountain resort masquerading as the New Age Inn of the Spirit. They got to the mountains midweek and went to work right away, basing their planning sessions on a twenty-eight-page mini-study that Father Albert had hurriedly put together before he left Newark. At one point during their three days in the mountains, the monks took turns outlining their own philosophy of education. Albert offered a well-reasoned definition of pedagogical ambitions, then laid out a detailed approach for tailoring instruction to the monks' target community of Black and Latino city kids. Others presented their own ideas, which in many cases were based more on personal experience than formal theories. Then one monk's simple response stopped the conversation short. He explained that he didn't have much training in modern educational practices, nor was he up on the newest research or academic strategies. Important as those concepts might be, he believed the first commandment of teaching is, simply, "Just love the kids." Consider them for who they are and provide them what they need. And most of all, make sure they know that they matter. That what happens to them matters. That they are loved.

* * *

The monks returned from the Inn of the Spirit with two hugely different academic proposals for a new school that the entire monastic community would vote on. The monks rejected a trendy, outside-the-classroom concept in favor of a more traditional curriculum concocted by Father Albert. In subsequent meetings, the monks added to the basic framework, deciding such issues as having competitive sports (basketball yes, but the storied football program would have to go—too expensive and the incoming student body would be too small to field a team equal to the old St. Benedict's reputation in the sport). They hadn't finalized a name for their school, but were considering a range of options. They briefly considered calling it the Phoenix School, for obvious reasons, or the High Street Learning Center, before settling on a conventional name that still differentiated the new school from the old one. They dropped the modifier "preparatory" and called it simply St. Benedict's School.

They decided to run all their ideas for the new school by prospective parents who they hoped would be willing to risk their sons' futures with them. The monks were delighted when the parents enthusiastically supported Albert's proposal for a multiracial student body with a traditional academic focus and an extended school year that included opportunities for out-of-the-classroom project learning.

By Ash Wednesday of the year after the abbot officially announced that St. Benedict's was closing, the monks notified alumni and friends that they were going to open a new school on High Street in July. In an interview with *The New York Times*,[2] Father Ed described the restart as a "small, interracial school that will seek to face what we have come to recognize as some of the educational problems of our time." He told the reporter that the school would be called simply St. Benedict's and, he explained, would be an experimental alternative to what a heritage preparatory school offered. By necessity it would be smaller. By design it would be less expensive. And driven by the optimism of its founders, it would succeed by being nimbler than its predecessor and more open to adapting to the needs of its students.

He skirted the delicate issue of standards, and the lower expectations ascribed to minority students, but he tipped his hand by noting, "We're not going to shovel everyone into college." (However much he may have believed that in 1973, he and the other monks were eventually embarrassed into abandoning that goal. Around two years after the school opened, a parent rose at a meeting and asked why, if it had been good enough for the school to be called St. Benedict's Prep when most of the seats were filled by white kids, it wasn't good enough for the resurrected school filled with Black youths like his son to also be called prep? Hearing that, Edwin realized that his group may have been tainted by the same racism of lower expectations as the monks who left for Morristown. He decided to change the name back to what it had always been, St. Benedict's Prep.)

Edwin and Philip took on the task of recruiting Black students from their Newark neighborhood. In the prep school's last years, they had gotten to know the few Black students who were enrolled at St. Benedict's, as well as others who came to Shanley Gym for CYO basketball games. Anthony Badger remembers that after one of those games the young headmaster encouraged him and his teammates to apply to the new school that was going to open there in the summer. Tell your parents, the monk said, and we'll be in touch.

Anthony was then in the eighth grade at one of the academies in Newark that Dominican nuns ran for gifted minority kids. The sisters encouraged Mildred and Willie Badger to attend an early planning meeting with the monks. The Badgers didn't say much at the meeting, but Father Albert noted that they "seemed interested and concerned." After interviewing Anthony, the monk described him as outgoing, well-spoken, and, at five feet seven, possessing an impressive jump shot.

On a Saturday afternoon in early spring, the monks held an open house for prospective students and their parents. Those who showed up got an unwelcome reminder of just how divided the city of Newark remained nearly six years after the riots. Amiri Baraka's Committee for a Unified Newark occupied the building on High Street next door to the school. On that afternoon, three white men picketed the building to protest Baraka's controversial proposal to build affordable housing in what then was the predominantly Italian American North Ward.

Sensing the potential for trouble, Newark police parked seven patrol cars in front of St. Benedict's. Outside Baraka's building, Black teenagers tried to shout down the protesters with a repeated chorus of "Whites go to Hell!" that the visiting parents couldn't help but hear.[3]

As Newark's public schools started their long summer vacation, the monks took care of the final details of their experiment. The first day of school was set for Monday, July 2. Parents were pleased with the extended calendar because it kept their sons from getting in trouble during the months away from the classroom. The early start would also give the monks a chance to assess the students' abilities and then adjust the curriculum for the fall and winter terms to address areas where they felt the boys hadn't been adequately prepared for high school work. According to their plan, the year would end with a spring phase given over to special projects. The monks had decided to insist on proper written English on all papers and assignments, but they were willing to let the kids use street slang for class discussions.

Finally, after a challenging year in which they had gone from uncertainty about remaining in Newark to planning a school unlike any other in the city, they were ready for the new St. Benedict's to rise on the battered remains of the old school. Newark Abbey had witnessed a divisive struggle that had threatened its existence and tested the sacred vow the monks had taken to stay put. Those who left had not looked back, glad to finally be free of the city's foreboding entanglements. And those who remained understood that if the experiment about to unfold did not succeed, Newark Abbey's own future would be at risk.

The night before the formal reopening, Albert and Edwin swept the classrooms and hallways clean one last time, taking on the task themselves because they had not hired a janitor. Their brother monks were already calling them the odd couple; Albert finicky about details, ever ready with a well-thought-out plan; Edwin hot tempered, impatient, driven by a vision of service and a deep-seated need to prove he is right. Albert looked to Edwin for fire; Edwin to Albert for reason.

Together, along with the talents and insights of many others, they had managed something that even to them seemed almost miraculous. The intense effort had exhausted them beyond the point of any philosophical reflections. With brooms in hand, they both simply agreed that it had been far easier to close a school than to open one.

The next morning, Anthony Badger and eighty-eight other boys filed into the cafeteria of the 1959 building that had demonstrated the old St. Benedict's allegiance to Newark. Even the school's modest tuition was out of reach for Anthony's family, which he described as being "rock-bottom poor." Willie Badger had recently abandoned them, and without substantial help from the school, there's no way Anthony could have attended. But as it did for most of the students, the school provided the Badgers with substantial financial aid. Later, they'd also give Anthony a work-study job helping out on the old telephone switchboard.

To get to school that first morning, Anthony walked past the old German cemetery, down the scorched remnants of Springfield Avenue's stores, past the corner where Richard Nazareta had nearly lost an eye and the spot where Amiri Baraka had his head bashed in by a Newark cop, to the broad brownstone stoop at 520 High Street that is still the main entrance to St. Benedict's. About two dozen other Black and Latino boys were in that freshman class, along with a handful of white students, including Tom Leahy, Father Ed's younger brother. The upper grades were a mix of returning students and new recruits willing to risk their futures on the dreams of a few white monks in Black Newark.

That first day began with convocation, just like every day since. Mayor Gibson was there to put into perspective what the Benedictines' decision to remain in Newark meant for his city and its people. The reopening was one of the few positive things he could point to during his time in office. "To open an education institution in Newark is an important occasion," Gibson told the hundred people who'd come to the school to celebrate St. Benedict's rebirth. "But to reopen one after it had closed, as we are doing here today, is a great deal better."[4]

That the monks were white and determined to stay in predominantly Black Newark sent a message about the possibility of overcoming the racial divide that had devastated the city and jinxed its future. Today, the reopening has taken on greater significance in the story of the city's survival. Richard Roper, who worked in the first Gibson administration, and later held a range of public policy and academic positions at Princeton University and the Port Authority of New York and New Jersey, said that St. Benedict's reopening gave the city a huge boost at what was a critical moment in its long history. "That an institution perceived by the city of Newark as one of its strengths was on the verge of moving out, but instead made a conscious decision to remain in Newark and build its future in the city, had a tremendous psychological impact."

If 1972 had marked a nadir for St. Benedict's and Newark, this day in 1973 when the school was born a second time represented a striking symbol of faith in the city, and one of the significant moments of its spiritual rebirth. As the speculative new school that a bunch of street-wise downtown monks had started in a roughed-up city prospered, that spirit of renewal spread throughout its neighborhood. The nearby campuses of Rutgers, the New Jersey Institute of Technology, and Essex County Community College boldly remade themselves. Essex County renovated and expanded its justice complex a block away from the school. In 1983, High Street itself underwent a transformation as it was renamed in honor of Dr. Martin Luther King Jr. Downtown, construction got underway on the first new office buildings in decades, although to make them viable they were linked by skybridges to Penn Station so commuters never had to walk on city streets.

But by 1986, the state made the pivotal decision to build the New Jersey Performing Arts Center—envisioned as the city's Lincoln Center—in downtown Newark without skybridges. The project, completed in 1997, decisively transformed the perception of Newark as a dying city to one that still had a lot of life, where an institution like St. Benedict's Prep could not only hang on, but grow, build, and thrive for decades to come.

CHAPTER 6

Let the Bodies Hit the Floor

HALF A CENTURY after that first opening day, Rey led another group of freshmen on the initial steps of their journey to becoming members of the St. Benedict's community. As senior group leader, he was in charge of initiating the newcomers into the school's cherished customs and traditions. And as his father's son, he wanted to make sure they understood the difference between doing what is right and taking the easy way out.

Unlike other prep schools where getting through the admissions office is the biggest hurdle to getting in, at St. Benedict's being admitted is only the first step, and a relatively easy one. A graduate's recommendation for a wayward nephew, or a note from the uncle of a girl who's struggling, can be more important than a transcript in being accepted. It's what freshmen do, and don't do, once they set foot on the property that ultimately determines their membership in the community. And that grueling process begins with the freshman overnight, which this year bore the marks of what was quickly becoming Rey's hardline leadership style.

In the overnight—a long-standing tradition on King Boulevard that has recently been adopted by some public schools in Newark—incoming students are holed up inside the school both day and night for an entire week. They are immersed in St. Benedict's rich heritage, memorizing its strict student honor code, and learning its many rites and rituals while older students push them to the brink of exhaustion. The conditioning starts the moment they arrive. They have to surrender their precious cell phones, and they don't get them back until the week ends. They eat, sleep, and study inside the school, cut off from their parents and outside friends who are enjoying their long summer vacations.

The pandemic had canceled Rey's own overnight in 2020, reducing the formative bonding experience to an asterisk for his class. He felt that missing the opportunity to build camaraderie and acclimate to the school's unique reality had tarnished his own first year, adding immeasurably to the way he initially rejected the St. Benedict's way. He was determined to make this year's induction memorable for the 125 beginners by imposing a blend of strict discipline and intensive belonging, bolstered by persistence, patience, and unconditional commitment.

One of the freshmen, thirteen-year-old Raúl, showed up at the doors to St. Benedict's knowing almost nothing about all the conflict, chaos, and controversy of the school's past, and focused solely on how he was going to survive his first year on King Boulevard. Several of his cousins had attended St. Benedict's before him and they warned him that the school was too tough for a puny kid like him. With his bowl haircut, thin arms, and knobby knees, he could be mistaken for one of St. Benedict's middle-division students. His cousins told him that upperclassmen act like tyrants during the week-long basic training, and then they relish giving freshmen—especially half-pints like him—orders throughout the year until the nightmare ends with the hellish, compulsory backpacking trip in May.

If that weren't intimidating enough, they told Raúl that if he somehow made it through the first year, he would start the second by getting pushed—fully clothed and blindfolded—off a platform at the deep end of the school's pool. It would be, they'd warned him over and over, the worst four years of his life.

Now that the school year was getting underway, he was determined to prove his cousins wrong.

The ordeal had started on the Sunday afternoon before the first convo when the freshmen—some of them, like Raúl, so small they looked like they couldn't reach a light switch, others already tall enough to vie for a spot on the varsity basketball team—lined up outside the William Street gate, loaded down with backpacks, duffel bags, and, for a pampered few who didn't realize how much taunting it would cause them, pillows from home. "They showed up like prey coming into the trap," gloated Kaleb, an upperclassman from Jersey City who was a key part of Rey's leadership posse. Most of the guys running the overnight were seniors, but Kaleb, a supercharged Black and Latino teenage musical maestro, was in his third year at St. Benedict's. He'd been on the fast leadership track for a while, moving up quickly from freshman counselor in his second year to leader this year of the Prof. Blood group, named after the long-time basketball coach memorialized in the portrait hanging on the gymnasium wall. He admitted that he hadn't possessed much discipline when he started at St. Benedict's, and he didn't expect the freshmen to show much either. But he was determined to whip them into shape.

It didn't take long for Raúl to realize that his cousins hadn't exaggerated the school's toughness. There was plenty of yelling, not just from the student leaders, but—Raúl was surprised to learn—also from volunteers from the U.S. Naval Academy who got in his face while he was forced to do endless pushups, squats, and burpees. The worst moments were the early-morning wakeup calls, especially when Rey initiated them with headbanging heavy metal music played loudly enough to rattle the rafters. It was part of his plan to break down the freshmen before building them up, but Raúl didn't let anything Rey threw at him get under his skin. Hardship was nothing new for Raúl. He was reared in Newark by an Irish American mother whose reliance on alcohol and drugs tore the family apart. His parents divorced when he was five, and he'd lived with his Ecuadorian father and his *abuela* ever since. To make a fresh start, they'd moved out of Newark and into neighboring Belleville, a blue-collar town similar in many ways to Newark before the riots. Until recently, most of its residents were white. Now, just over half of the town's population of around 39,000 is Latino. And another 6.5 percent is Black.

Not all freshmen make it through the overnight with the kind of determination Raúl possessed. Stories of those who shriveled under the pressure are part of Benedict's lore, but none is more legendary than the tale of Leon McBurrows, '82, who lived a few blocks up the hill from St. Benedict's. Leon was big enough to play football, and tough enough too. He had to be tough to defend himself. His father was a by-the-book Black army veteran originally from Georgia who, while serving in Korea, had married a Japanese nurse and brought her back to Newark. "Mixed culture, mixed race, living in Newark, that could be a struggle at the time," Leon told me. His folks were determined to give him a good education, and they were intent on getting him into St. Benedict's. But the school did not have a football team, and that meant Leon had no interest in going there.

Still, family and friends had convinced his parents that St. Benedict's was the right place for him, and that's where he wound up in July 1978. Things went downhill right away. It was still high summer, and all his friends were enjoying their vacation while he was forced to spend all day and night in a school he didn't want to attend. He hated everything about it. Sleeping on the floor of the old Shanley Gym that reeked of sneakers and sweat. Upperclassmen shouting in his face. Belting out a version of Yale's "Boola Boola" fight song and other hokey numbers he'd never heard of. By the middle of the week, he'd had enough. He had his eye on an exit on the east side of the building that opened onto a vacant lot. Leon figured if he jumped the cyclone fence around the lot, he'd come out on Springfield Avenue, with only a few city blocks between this hell and his home.

At five the next morning, with the rest of his class still asleep, he and a co-conspirator tiptoed over to the door. If I can't make it, Leon told his friend, let me back in.

"Once I hit the field, I was gone," he recalled. He jumped the fence, then zoomed past the Essex County Hall of Records, over to West Market Street. From there, it was a straight shot several blocks home. There was almost no traffic that early in the morning, but as Leon ran, he noticed a black car circling around and pulling up next to him.

"Where are you going?" It was Father Ed, who'd been tipped off about the attempted escape. Leon was in tears, sobbing that he was never going back to St. Benedict's. The headmaster encouraged him to give the school a second chance, but Leon was hearing none of it, and he took off again. When he reached home, his mother ignored his pleas not to call his father at work. Leon figured he was in for a whooping, but his father didn't raise a finger. "You go where I tell you to go," he stated calmly, the unspoken threat enough to petrify Leon. Minutes later, they were sitting in Father Ed's office, where the old sergeant sternly warned both of them that he never wanted to be called in for such foolishness again.

Rey had heard about Leon and plenty of other freshmen who had freaked out during the overnight. He was intent on making this year's version a reflection of himself, and that meant he wanted it to be tougher than any other, more honorable and laced with more integrity than ever before. "Pretty good" had never been good enough for him. "Perfection" had become a standard, not a goal. And as leader, he intended to demand as much of others as he demanded of himself, an ends-justifies-the-means kind of guy, with lofty expectations and a low tolerance for failure.

Rey and his team yelled a lot, exhorting the beginners to shape up, move over, and get going. "The fear they instilled in us was crazy," recalled Finn, one of the small number of white students in that freshman class. He had followed his older brother Gavin to the school after trying the St. Benedict's Student-for-a-Day program, which let him experience convocation and the camaraderie fostered by the group system before deciding. That's all it took.

"At first it was shocking," he said, speaking of the overnight. "I don't think anyone expected it to be the way it was. And then it brought everyone together . . . even though all of us barely knew each other."

Father Ed's involvement with the overnight was limited to giving one of his pep talks, overwhelming the newcomers with tall tales that entertained, enlightened, and sometimes confused them. The beginners didn't realize it, but he etched for them a thumbnail version of the four pillars that make up St. Benedict's approach to education. They'd hear the same things in an infinite loop over the next four years, and though they initially may not have understood his message, they would come to feel the impact of his words. First of all, he told them, "we create community" where individuals are accepted as they are, with all the history of their past lives that they bring with them. Acceptance into this community, he cautioned, is not automatic. Here, the colors of St. Benedict's—the traditional garnet and gray, as well as the black that visually ties them to the monastic tradition—can be worn only by those who've earned the right.

"Second, we're going to pay attention to your heart as well as to your head." Speaking from his fifty-plus hard years of experience, he told them that most of what he's seen as poor grades has nothing to do with how smart students are in class, but how much turmoil they go through when they leave school. St. Benedict's, he told them, will tend to their hearts as well as to their minds.

Third, St. Benedict's creates leaders. Neither the monks nor the lay staff will do anything for the kids that the kids can do for themselves. "Eventually, this school will be run by you. Pay attention now so you can learn how to do it when it's your turn." And finally, he made it clear that although academics are an essential part of any education, textbooks and grades may be less important than experience and character. The next four years will be tougher than anything they've ever done, he warned them, so get ready to work hard. And he encouraged them. "We've had guys dumb as rocks go through here," and they made it. "Look," he admitted, presenting them with the first instance of his self-deprecating humor, heavily tinted with reality, "if I could make it here, anybody could."

The headmaster's message hit home with Michael, a Black kid from Newark with dreads, a gregarious smile, and, in his own words, a big ego, who had turned fourteen two weeks earlier. He had one younger brother and two sisters in the elementary and middle divisions, and he'd been at St. Benedict's since the fourth grade. During his years in the middle division, Michael dressed in gray and sat cross-legged on the gym floor during convo, looking up at the senior group leader with a combination of intimidation and admiration. "Sitting on the floor, to me, it's humbling, but at the same time, you have a goal," he said. He was responding even then to the sense of belonging that the school fosters and makes manifest in the black hoodie, which has to be earned. "Getting your black is the ultimate goal because you don't want to be on the floor anymore." He'd seen student leaders come and go and was accustomed to following their orders, so the overnight was not as tough for him as he thought it was for those who didn't know what to expect. For them, he figured, "it was probably horrific."

By midweek, Rey had decided to jack up the overnight. He awoke at 4:30 a.m., while the freshmen were still snoozing in the big gym, and blasted the screaming and heavy percussion of Drowning Pool's "Let the Bodies Hit the Floor," shocking the drowsy teens awake and no doubt redoubling their longing to go home.

Rey then ordered them to grab their stuff, go downstairs, and get changed. Half-awake and thoroughly disoriented, some of them probably plotted their own escape to match Leon McBurrow's. Rey marched them to the smaller Shanley Gym to practice the "Alma Mater," with Michael's spirited singing leading the way. Eventually, as a group they got everything right, but Rey made them do it over again. And again. "That's kind of the point," he told me later, "to grind on their nerves. You can't let them succeed at whatever they're doing, so that's reinforcing the idea of struggling together. And at some point, you have to realize it's bigger than yourself, bigger than what you're doing. You've got to do for the other person as well, and make sure they're doing for you."

Many of the freshmen were street hardened, and the message that Rey, Kaleb, and the others were selling, well, they weren't buying. Some thought that all the gabbing about brotherhood was BS, especially the endlessly repeated "Whatever hurts my brother or sister hurts me." That's nothing like what they learned at home, or in their neighborhoods. When leaders weren't looking, they reverted to the basic law of the street, where you pushed or got pushed around. When Rey found out what was going on he pulled the bullies aside. "So, you think you grew up on a rough block?" He got in their faces the way he would in the neighborhood. "So did I. You've got to leave that behind if you want to be here." Later, Rey told me, "A lot of these kids come from Newark and places like this where community and actually sacrificing for the other is a foreign concept." He recognized the pattern from his own neighborhood: There were laws, but they could be broken if it meant getting what you want.

By midway through the week emotions were raw, and Rey was intent on turning up the pressure. He ordered the freshmen into the gym for yet another song session. "This shit sounds so weak," he complained, even though the beginners were putting everything they had into singing the by-now familiar songs. "What am I doing wrong?" He pretended to be talking to himself, pacing the hardwoods before picking up a folding chair. "You guys aren't getting it and we're almost out of time." He launched the chair across the gym.

Then came the moment for him to deploy his ultimate threat. Call their parents, he instructed his team. Tell them to pack for another week. Nobody's going home. When Finn heard that, he panicked. Although he was already totally invested in his new school, he dreaded prolonging his agony in the gym. It turned out to be more bluster from

Rey. He had no plans to extend their stay. He was simply trying to get the freshmen totally dejected so he could then build them back up. He marched all of them to one of the athletic fields that had been built on the urban renewal land Leon McBurrows had raced through. Now they are mirage-like patches of green amid the asphalt and concrete of the city.

"Everyone was really hyped," Rey recalled. "It turned out to be one of the most magical nights because it started raining and everyone was enjoying themselves and they started to get what it was. That's when, I think, everything clicked. Here they were, kids who were struggling yet persevering, and then motivating other kids to do the same."

Rey believed that the whole point of the overnight was "breaking them as individuals and then building them up as a collective." It was an idealistic goal, in keeping with St. Benedict's core beliefs, but not every freshman accepted it. Before the year ended, several would decide that St. Benedict's wasn't for them and transfer to another school. But for those who stayed, the week would come to represent the first steps in their growing personal awareness that they were becoming part of something bigger than themselves. "It brought us together," Finn told me, "because we knew we couldn't do it alone."

* * *

Rey's role as the most important person under twenty-one at the school came naturally to him. He oozed confidence, from the cut of his shoulders to the swagger in his walk. When he was at the podium, everyone looked up to him, but few had any idea how reluctantly he had arrived at the school in the summer of 2020. He'd just graduated from the century-old Ridge Street public school in North Newark, which had undergone a transformation from being mostly Italian American in the 1970s to primarily Latino today. Instead of running through the streets with his friends, he was stuck at home, thanks to the pandemic, watching a weird kind of assembly on YouTube with old white guys in black robes talking to the camera about brotherhood, honor, and sacrifice. Going to St. Benedict's hadn't been his idea, but his Puerto Rican mother, Ruth, had insisted. She knew he was a good kid, talented enough to belong on almost any school's basketball team as well as kicking ass on a debate team—a rare double in Newark. On the court he looked unbeatable, and in a debate he could drop his Newark street slang and argue like a university English major. He had a lot going for him, but his mother was afraid of how the city could trap even smart kids like him.

Rey's family had already tangled with the seedier side of Brick City and lost. His Cuban father, Thomas, had dropped out before finishing high school to open a barber shop. But as the years went by, and Rey and his siblings came along, cutting hair didn't bring in anywhere near enough to support the family no matter how hard he worked. So, like many others in this city where living below the poverty line was as common as waiting for a city bus, he had a side hustle, peddling dope, sometimes from the back of his shop, other times out in the street. In 2013, he was nabbed in a 2:40 a.m. traffic stop on Rt. 78 in Bernards Township, a wealthy suburb in central New Jersey. It began with a burned out brake light on his 2006 Nissan Maxima, but the police quickly found that he was driving with a suspended license, had several outstanding traffic warrants, and had stashed a small amount of marijuana in his pocket. The suspicious cop got a search warrant and, checking behind the front seat, found twenty-five bricks of heroin that, in total, weighed close to a pound.

As a non-violent drug offender, and a young parent, Thomas was sent to court-ordered drug rehab instead of jail. For a while, he was able to keep Rey and his other children from knowing anything about his brush with the law. But soon he got into even more trouble, and this time there was no keeping secrets. Rey remembered that it was the weekend of his mom's birthday. He was just seven and early that Sunday morning, he heard a commotion outside his bedroom door. Before he realized what was going on, an interagency drug SWAT team rushed into his room and started turning things upside down. "Thankfully it was only me and not my other siblings," Rey told me, mentioning his older sister and two younger brothers, who were staying with their grandmother. He said the police waved guns in his face and ordered him out of the room. He saw his mother sobbing hysterically, while his father was lying flat on the floor, his hands cuffed behind his back. "I was pretty confused, but then I started to think about it, and it clicked. I mean, I wasn't oblivious to it. I grew up around drugs and stuff like that, so I'd seen it." He didn't know exactly what his father had been up to, but he had noticed that his father sometimes left the apartment at two or three in the morning, a strange schedule for a barber. "I wasn't dumb. I saw things and I always questioned it, but I knew my place."

His father was one of thirty-one men and women busted in raids in seven North Jersey counties that Sunday morning. He was charged with conspiracy to participate in an illicit drug ring that authorities said sold around $1 million in narcotics during the three months of the investigation. There was no rehab this time. Thomas spent the next sixteen months in state prison, leaving Rey and the rest of his family to figure out how to get on with their lives.

There's no science to determining how the actions of a parent will shape or screw up the lives of their children. Sometimes they lay down a rutted path that entraps the child. Sometimes they flash a yellow sign warning them to take a detour. His father's arrest was a pivotal moment for Rey that has stayed with him, and guided him, ever since. "So that happened. I mean, learn from it, right?" he told me during a long talk in the Trophy Room at St. Benedict's. For six years after the raid, he lived with and tried to make sense of where his pops had gone wrong, and what his father's actions portended for his own future. "So it was, for me, from seven to thirteen, it was just kind of soaking it in, understanding, and then kind of deciding, what do I want to do with myself? Do I want to stay in that environment and be a part of it myself and perpetuate those things that we do here? Or was it something I wanted to change?"

Initially, he resented his father for not resisting temptation, and he blamed his mother for covering up and enabling him. He was angry, and he vowed to never walk the same path. But since arriving at St. Benedict's, the school's spunk and spirit had slowly seeped into him so that he eventually replaced his anger with a hard-earned empathy. He understood that his father had been born into a kind of life that he wasn't able to evade because he didn't know any better. For him, like so many others in Newark, the city provided him with enough dark alleys to hide from all responsibility. "I kind of learned to just not hate them for it," and instead to focus on improving his own life, Rey reasoned. "So, what now? What's next for me?" He was sure that he was not like his father, and he felt that becoming senior group leader proved that. "St. Benedict's helped me figure that out, because if it wasn't for Benedict's, I think I'd be here [in Newark] for the rest of my life."

CHAPTER 7

Another Break-in

WHILE REY WAS running the boys freshman overnight, Lucia—
Loo-CHEE-ah—his counterpart in the girls division, was nowhere
in sight. She too had been brought up on the streets of Newark, but
that's where the similarity ended. She boasted that she'd grown up at
St. Benedict's—and she meant it. Father Ed had known her so long that
he called her Chi-Chi. She was a standout, smart, strong, an athlete
and an academic star, one of the first two dozen girls to have been at
St. Benedict's for all four years since the girls division was launched so
improbably in 2020.

Lucia wasn't at any convocations that first week because she was in
Lisbon, Portugal, attending the World Youth Day of the Neocatechumenal
Way, a conservative Christian movement founded in Spain in the 1960s
that encourages sacrifice, intense prayer, and a revival of early Christian
formation. Lucia's family and several others at St. Benedict's are adher-
ents. "It provides an answer for me when there is none," is how she described the Way when I asked her what belonging to it means to her.

The Way is as much a part of Lucia's personal history as is St.
Benedict's, and everyone excused her for missing the start of the fiftieth anniversary year. She returned from Europe in time for the girls
freshman overnight, which began after the boys completed theirs. The

girls—who were a third the size of the boys division—struggle constantly to match the energy of their counterparts, and they often feel overshadowed. They were reminded of their secondary position every time they walked into their classrooms in old St. Mary's Hall, the cramped, uncomfortable building from the mid-nineteenth century that once housed an elementary school. Their classes are separate from the boys', and except for Fridays and special occasions, they hold their own convo, not in the gym but on the grammar school's ground floor. There were only 160 girls in the entire prep division, plus another 40 middle schoolers. They participated in fewer sports than the boys, they had set no championship records, and there were no photographs or banners of standout girls hanging from the walls of either the big or small gym.

But the girls could stand toe-to-toe with the boys in at least one arena: the improbable heroism of the story of their founding.

One of St. Benedict's greatest strengths, going back decades, has been its ability to keep the past alive through tradition and storytelling. The reincarnated school's bold history is usually retold with reverence reserved for a reading from the New Testament. And now the story of how the girls division came to be is honored with a similar origin story, one that is visualized in paper posters the girls made that do hang on the walls of St. Mary's Hall.

Their genesis myth begins in February of 2020, when an email went out to the parents of the students enrolled at Benedictine Academy in nearby Elizabeth, N.J., a traditional Catholic girls high school run for nearly one hundred years by the Benedictine Sisters of the Saint Walburga Monastery. For most of those years, the academy shared little with St. Benedict's Prep except for the saint in its name. In 2016, the same year *60 Minutes* broadcast a laudatory report on the boys school, describing it as "rare and successful," the sisters asked the monks in Newark to share some of the secrets of their success. Dr. Glenn Cassidy, a biracial 1990 alumnus who'd taught at the school for three decades, was put in charge of responding.

Working with Benedictine Academy, Cassidy helped build a student leadership structure that resembled the one the boys had. At the outset, the girls were not given equivalent power to run aspects of their school, but the principle of never doing for students what they can do for themselves was established as a goal. The girls studied *The Rule of St. Benedict*, selected their own leaders, and held their CliffsNotes version of daily convocation. The prep school's counseling department helped the girls deal with the same issues of depression, loneliness, and trauma that were common among the boys.

Invigorated by the changes, the girls felt empowered. But nothing could reverse the familiar and deeply troubling trends of declining enrollment, rising tuition, and the dwindling number of nuns available to teach. In New Jersey, small schools like Benedictine Academy also have to compete with large regional Catholic high schools that draw students from a much wider area, and can charge more for tuition. Never a big school, Benedictine Academy had been hemorrhaging students for years, and by 2020 enrollment had dropped to below 120.

That's when the school's principal sent parents a gloomy email message announcing that the sisters had reached the difficult but inevitable decision to shut Benedictine Academy. She wrote that more than one thousand Catholic elementary and high schools around the country had been shuttered since 2010, and that in Elizabeth alone—where there had until recently been fifteen Catholic elementary schools that referred girls to the academy—only two still had the lights on.

The senior group leader at the academy was a no-nonsense seventeen-year-old from Elizabeth's Portuguese/Brazilian community named Sabrina Reves—Sabrina, she says, like the teenage witch in the old television series. Earnest and reserved, Sabrina had already been accepted at Rutgers University, but the demise of Benedictine Academy, where she'd been for four years, and where she hoped her younger sister would follow, upset her deeply. Sabrina had studied St. Benedict's Rule, and she was familiar with the way the boys at St. Benedict's had been taught to take

responsibility for the things that mattered to them. Their maxim that res-
onated most with her was the one about selflessness—whatever hurts my
brother hurts me. She sensed that it should hold for her and her sisters as
well. But what could they do? They were a handful of teenage girls used
to holding their tongues and being respectful of adults. But something
had changed since they'd learned about student empowerment, and they
refused to accept the closing without a fight. It was obvious that the nuns
were not going to help. The order itself was shrinking, their financial obligations were overwhelming, and they had already made up their minds
to get out of the business of secondary education while they could.

The girls realized that their most likely allies were at St. Benedict's.
Earlier that year they had invited the boys team to Elizabeth for an in-
formal lunch in the academy's boardroom and had made friends there.
Sabrina and a handful of other girls called in sick one morning, explaining that they needed a mental health day because they were so distressed
about the academy closing. Without seeking anyone's approval, they
squeezed into a yellow Ford Focus that was older than they were, and
drove to morning convo in Newark.

For any girl to be present at convo then was unusual, and their skirts
turned heads. Following convo, the girls moved to the boardroom down
the hall from Father Ed's office, sat around the long conference table with
the boys leadership team, and got to work. The girls were looking for a
way to align with the prep without surrendering their own identity. They
believed the best way to achieve that would be for the schools to join as
co-institutional partners, with separate classes, separate activities, separate
physical locations but with shared Benedictine ideals about community
and service. Ideally, they hoped that St. Benedict's could buy or rent the
academy's building in Elizabeth, if the nuns agreed. If not, they believed
there was enough room at Newark Abbey for the girls to move there.

The boys leadership team didn't object to the girls' plan, but they
knew that no matter what was said about how students run St. Benedict's, only Father Ed had the power to make a decision like this. As

the meeting dragged on, the boys senior group leader coaxed Father Ed into the boardroom.

"He just kind of looked at us and he was like 'What is this?' and he sat down," Sabrina remembered. She gave him a copy of the girls' proposal, and told him to read it before saying anything. He asked questions that showed how skeptical he was about the idea they had brought to him. "Where do you think I'm going to put you?" he asked. How, he wanted to know, could he realistically bring girls onto the property when St. Benedict's had been an all-boys school forever?

"I was like, you *have* to," Sabrina said. She then repeated one of St. Benedict's many aphorisms, the one that says it's not always about what you want, but about what the community needs. "He looked at me then and he was like 'How do you know that?' I think that really got to him because he seemed kind of shocked when I said it."

The girls pressed their case before the highest authority they could find. They arranged a Zoom meeting with Father Elias Lorenzo, O.S.B., who had long been involved in Catholic secondary education in the area. They hoped he had a soft spot in his heart for the academy because he'd taken his vows at St. Mary's Abbey in Morristown, Newark Abbey's offshoot. But Lorenzo had a lot on his plate. Pope Francis had just elevated him to the post of auxiliary bishop of the archdiocese of Newark.

Still, he agreed to speak with the girls. They took that as a hopeful sign, but they did not get the friendly reception they hoped for. "He basically told us, 'Yeah, that's not happening,'" Sabrina recalled. The nuns had other plans for the Benedictine Academy building. Besides, there were only a few weeks left in the school year, and even if space and funding were found, there wouldn't be enough time to get everything ready for the next school year. It's time to move on, Bishop Lorenzo said, and he offered to host a farewell pizza party for them after the final bell rang at the academy.

Father Ed had been on the Zoom call with the bishop, and he understood immediately how tone deaf his pizza party offer was. He recalled how he and his co-conspirators in the monastery had faced the same kind of dismissive resistance in 1973 when their plan to resurrect St. Benedict's was still an untested idea. That riled his sixties contrariness.

No time to start a school? No space for the girls? Just move on? He knew it didn't make financial sense to take over Benedictine Academy's students—they couldn't charge enough in tuition to cover the additional costs, let alone pay for necessary renovations and expansion—and yet, he posted an announcement on social media seeking "pioneers" willing to try something new. He was aware that some alumni would consider it heresy to bring in girls. And he understood that he could not expect any help from the diocese, or the Benedictine sisters.

But he was convinced that starting a girls division was the right thing to do.

The day after he posted his "pioneers" announcement, health officials declared the coronavirus a full-blown pandemic, and schools everywhere stumbled into remote learning. St. Benedict's had people on staff who already knew enough about media to set up several digital town halls where Father Ed and Sabrina made the case for a girls division. Father Ed started one of the first meetings by quoting from *The Rule of St. Benedict*, which says that all visitors to the abbey must be welcomed. "The rule by which we live is openness to guests," he said solemnly. It didn't take long for the skeptics online to raise their voices. "Won't most of the girls be Black, and therefore not Catholic?" asked one alumnus. This was familiar ground for Father Ed, a repeat of the kind of objections critics had raised in the 1970s. The reason for doing this, he answered, was simple: We're Catholic, and being Catholic means being open to all.

"How about the culture of the place?" asked another. Girls on the property would be a huge distraction, the caller stated, regardless of whether the change was to be coeducational or co-institutional. In the end, the school just wouldn't be St. Benedict's with girls there.

Negative comments poured in. "This is a big mistake," someone wrote. Bringing in girls would "change what St. Benedict's Prep has been."

"Prove it," Father Ed shot back.

With more than three hundred people signed up for the Zoom call that night, questions poured in. "How can you afford it?" one asked. Father Ed had a quick answer. "This may be a revelation to a lot of people, but we couldn't afford to do it on July 2, 1973, either," bringing up the day the school hit the reset button. "This is a test of faith, brothers and sisters," he preached. "You also might say it's a test of stupidity."

How different would this scene have played out if, instead of a seventy-five-year-old baby boomer with a lifetime habit of deferring to the will of God, it was a lay headmaster trained in finances and educational theory making the decision about bringing girls into the all-boys school? How much more weight would be given to the impossibility of getting everything ready and paid for in a few months than to simply listening with the ear of your heart?

"The abbey has to stand for something," Father Ed stated firmly, as though issuing a challenge. Sustaining a physical presence in the city should have meaning, just as the walls and fences around the property have always meant that what goes on inside is separate and apart from the rest of daily urban life. "We are here to be a sign that it's possible to love in a different way—to accept the other way the other is, and in this process these gifts come to the surface and surprising things happen."

Having the power to design, shape, and run an institution unhindered by outside control has endowed Father Ed and his confreres with a remarkable coolness toward risk taking, the "essence of freedom" that impelled them to go against the tide and reopen the school half a century ago. And age hasn't tempered their boldness. The monks and the board of trustees eventually approved a multi-year trial run, after which they would look at the numbers and review the pros and cons of a girls division. It turned out to be the girls' good fortune that they pushed their radical proposal during the pandemic when classes were held remotely and the buildings on King Boulevard were empty most of the time. Father Ed would have preferred to keep the girls in the academy's own building in Elizabeth, but the nuns were carrying serious debt, and the building was one of their only liquid assets. Not long after the nuns announced the closing of Benedictine Academy, they sold the building to the city of Elizabeth for $5.5 million, and used the receipts to cover some debt and maintain Saint Walburga Monastery in Elizabeth where the remaining nuns continue to live. The academy's former grammar school's ground floor became a public school.

The monks looked at alternate locations for the girls, keeping an envious eye on a rubble-filled lot across the street that harbored depressing memories of 1967. But the private owner wasn't ready to sell, and the monks were reluctant to take on additional debt without knowing more about how well the girls could be integrated into the school. Father Ed estimated that they'd have to bring in eighty-five to a hundred girls at the outset to make the expansion work. A girls division was sure to draw from the academy's younger students, as well as from the Cristo Rey school in Newark, part of the national network of inner-city Catholic schools, that also was scheduled to close at the end of the school year. And then there were the girls who had dreamed of attending St. Benedict's but never thought it would be possible.

Girls like Kymberli, a natural leader who lived in East Orange and started at St. Mary's elementary school, on the abbey grounds, in the second grade, while her older brothers, Bruce and Benjamin, were enrolled next door at the prep. "I absolutely adored the school," she told me when we met in the boardroom one afternoon after class and before she ran off to work out with her crew team. Perpetually smiling, she is a charismatic young Black woman whose brothers used to bring her to convo and walk with her through the hallways. Enchanted by it all, she used to fill out applications she found online and fantasize that she was sending them to St. Benedict's.

She couldn't believe her luck when she heard that a girls division would be opening just weeks after she graduated from St. Mary's. The pandemic complicated her first two years at the prep, and delayed her

Appalachian Trail hike for a year. When she finally hit the trail, the weight of her backpack soon knocked her off balance and sent her careening into a tree. She lost consciousness for a few seconds, and when she came to, she insisted that she was well enough to continue. But the medics took her to a hospital where they confirmed that she had a concussion and, despite her objections, sent her home. Resolved to do everything her brothers did, she completed the hike as captain of her team in her junior year. This year, she was part of Lucia's leadership team, serving as freshman group leader, and helping the youngest girls find their way.

Lucia also reveled in the timing of the new division. When she said she grew up at St. Benedict's, it was more than a figurative accolade for the school. When she was an infant, her Italian American mother, Sara, and her Puerto Rican Italian father, Mario, joined the staff as adult supervisors of Leahy House, the sixty-bed dormitory on the property that was opened in 2000 for students from dysfunctional homes. Father Ed and the other monks watched her grow up. Even after her parents moved to their own home in Newark's Forest Hill section as their family grew (she is one of nine children), and her father was named director of admissions, he continued to bring her to work at St. Benedict's.

Like Kymberli, Lucia grew to love the school even though there was no place for her there. Then, even as she heard the exciting news about the opening of a girls division, she was concerned that her parents wouldn't be able to afford the tuition. She needn't have worried, because employees get tuition remission. An alumna of Benedictine Academy, Mary Ellen Harris, offered financial aid to dozens of students in both the girls and boys divisions. Lucia was one of them. Rey was another.

Michelle Tuorto, the associate headmaster for academics, had about six weeks to have the new division staffed and ready to go. In many ways, she is Father Ed's opposite. He is the visionary, the idea man who can see things as he wants them to be and, by the power of his own ambition, make them happen. She is a petite blizzard of curly hair and academic principles, a scientist by training who seems to never tire no matter how often the headmaster leaves the messy details of his schemes to her.

She caught a break when several experienced teachers and staff agreed to move from Benedictine Academy with the girls who were transferring. She then rearranged the curriculum and accommodated the girls schedule while sticking to the tight budget Father Ed gave her. On Monday, July 6, 2020, forty-seven years after the monks had overhauled the St. Benedict's of old, the girls division was formally launched. There were eighty-nine girls, the same number of boys the monks started with in 1973.

* * *

Three years later, on a warm summer Sunday afternoon in Newark, cars lined up along William Street to discharge the girls who hoped to become members of the St. Benedict's Prep girls division class of 2027. Waiting with her parents outside the chain-link fence, a small girl with large glasses was all energy and excitement, her shoulders bent under the straps of a bulging backpack, a pillow under her arm.

"Bye, Ma, I love you," Sheridan chirped as the gate opened on schedule and the line of girls shuffled in, trying their best to look brave. Sheridan's parents, Olivia and Damond, watched her enter the school grounds, hiding their concern about not seeing or hearing from her for a full week, but satisfied that they had made the right choice by sending her to St. Benedict's. Olivia was born and raised in Newark, Damond in Brooklyn. They now live in suburban Maplewood, less than ten miles from Newark. Maplewood is a racially diverse town with a progressive reputation, but concerns have been raised in recent years about racial inequality in the local public schools. Damond believed that white students got to take the most challenging classes while "African American kids were getting the bad classes, and not being pushed." That was one of the reasons he and his wife decided to send Sheridan and her younger brother Pierce to St. Benedict's. He admitted that he hadn't known much about the school, but what he did know about its history influenced his decision.

"Initially," he related, "it was primarily for Caucasians, and then after the riots, I guess Father had decided, 'Hey, why not service whoever we can service?' That was why I moved the children." Olivia described Sheridan as smart, self-motivated, and capable of doing well at any school. Still, she said, she should be challenged, and she didn't believe that their public schools would do that.

After Sheridan checked in, her parents reluctantly turned away and left for home. Other girls continued to say goodbye to their parents. Some got out of expensive foreign cars, while others trudged up the street with all their belongings in plastic bags. The thirty-nine new girls, all of them dressed in black slacks and plain white blouses, with black leather flats, made their way into the big gym. Most were the only ones there from their own elementary school in Newark or the eleven other cities and towns they came from. Some were quite shy. Some, like Sheridan, immediately assumed the role of friendship ambassador. Before the clamor spiraled out of control, the girls were told to line up in order from oldest to youngest without talking, relying only on the identification cards each wore on a lanyard.

Abbot Augustine, who the kids have called Goose since one Spanish-speaking student years ago pronounced his name in Spanish— Au-GOO-steen—had wandered over to the gym after dinner in the monastery. In his long black robe and halo of white hair that flowed into a gray beard reaching down to his chest, he is the image most people have of a monk. As we both watched from the sidelines, the girls silently lined up again, this time in reverse birth order. It was a scene of gentleness and simple fun that was so unlike what the freshman boys had been through a week earlier that the abbot seemed pressed to put it into perspective. "We've had to tone down the girls overnight," he said, almost apologetically. Where Rey had drilled the boys as though they were in boot camp, the same kind of routine had proved to be too harsh for the girls in previous years. "They were texting Edwin that they needed something for their hair," the abbot said. There were many other complaints, some that had led to tears.

Lucia had turned down the volume considerably. If grit had been the emphasis on the boys side, grace was her goal for the girls. The abbot watched as they got to know more about each other by grouping themselves according to the brand of toothpaste or cereal they preferred, and which fast-food restaurant was their favorite.

When all thirty-nine had put on pajamas, hair wraps, and fuzzy slippers, they sat on the cafeteria floor in front of the leatherette banquettes reserved for seniors during school lunch periods. They were introduced to Sabrina Reves, who narrated the origin story of the girls division. Father Ed made his way through the rows of girls to join her. "Most people around the world cannot imagine girls forcing something like this to happen," he said. Sheridan and the other beginners stared at him, still awed by this old man in his weird black robe who talked to them like an equal. "It's important that you realize the power that you have, especially when you work together as a group." Being at St. Benedict's, he told them just as he had the boys, is all about having a voice, and learning how and when to use it. And pointing to Sabrina he said, "It's important to do things that don't seem to be something you can do."

* * *

After a long week without their cell phones or their parents, the girls gathered in the boardroom to be grilled on the history of the school and of Newark Abbey, the next step in their initiation. Lucia was determined to be tough on the girls assigned to her. Sheridan was one of the first to face her. She looked nervous but she was actually bubbling with confidence.

"What does Ora et Labora mean?"

"Pray and work."

"Why are there ravens on the crest of St. Benedict's?"

"They represent the poison bread that ravens took from the saint's mouth."

"Sing St. Benedict's fight song, and sing it like you mean it."

Sheridan's "Boola Boola" rocked the room.

Finally, Lucia asked, "What is a Benedict's woman?"

"A Benedict's woman does not accept failure," she recited flawlessly, "acts with dignity, respect, and honor, attempts to share knowledge with her brothers and sisters, and respects all walks of life. Whatever hurts my sister hurts me. And whatever helps my sister helps me."

Lucia nodded, and with a voice brimming with pride and admiration, she declared, "Congratulations, Sheridan."

By passing the test, she had joined Finn, Michael, and Raúl in completing the first step in the year-long process of joining St. Benedict's community. She now had the right to wear the gray pullover that all freshmen and transfers wear for at least a year. If she managed to complete every other requirement, including the A.T. hike in May, she would be entitled to wear the black uniform that would identify her as a Benedict's woman.

Father Ed congratulated the girls, wearing a look of satisfaction at the results of what Sabrina and the girls had accomplished, something that Sabrina herself doesn't always fully appreciate. While she is attending college, she works in the facilities department at St. Benedict's. One day I stopped by her office on the edge of the cafeteria. She lamented that she sometimes doubts her own capabilities. But once in a while, when she is at the school, one of the young girls recognizes her from the posters on the wall at St. Mary's Hall that portray the history of how the girls division got started.

"Oh, you're the Sabrina who opened the girls division," the wide-eyed girls tell her. "That's so cool that you did that."

CHAPTER 8

Just Slightly Off-Center

AFTER SUFFERING THROUGH the pandemic-inspired mess of remote learning and YouTube-only convos in their early years at the school, Lucia and Rey were determined to make their term as student leaders the year that St. Benedict's regained its spirit. In many ways, they seemed to make a perfect pair, two kids from Newark, both of them smart and talented, with a real sense of the school's mission. For nearly a year they also were a couple, although it wasn't a normal high school romance. They never went bowling or to see a movie. Lucia's uncompromisingly strict father and the rigid constraints of the Way made it impossible for them to meet outside of school, so they made the best of their time at meetings and school-sponsored galas where they could pretend they were on a date. Because he'd known her so long, Father Ed had asked Lucia if she felt she could be a co-equal to Rey as leader while also being his girlfriend, and without hesitating she had answered yes. "Benedict's was home for me way before Rey, so it's way more important. We always agreed that if there's any problems with us, school comes first."

As captain of the girls volleyball team, she could spike the ball and protectively guard the net, but at five foot two, she was at a disadvantage at convo and other school events whenever she had to push past guys who towered over her. But she possessed enough confidence and energy to project a presence far larger than her diminutive stature. She is a planner, the attentive kind of person who uses a color-coded agenda and can be relied on to show up at meetings with talking points written out, along with the typed-out minutes she took of preceding meetings.

Rey didn't have to worry about convincing anyone he was in charge. He seemed made for the position, at least his version of it. While many other guys had afros or shoulder-length hair, he kept his just an inch longer than military cut, with a ruler-straight line across his forehead. His waist was trim, his back ramrod straight, his self-confidence as evident and easy to read as the Benedictine crest on his black hoodie. His goal as leader was to restore the school's unique essence and bring back some of the discipline that had been lost during COVID. Stuck at home, students had discovered how easy it was to sign into a class then slip away. And once every exam became a take-home test, studying seemed to become optional. Many students had developed bad habits that could cost them dearly if they didn't break out of them.

As they planned the year ahead, the leaders each had their own priorities. "My goal is to make sure that the girls division is staying around for more than four years," Lucia told me the first time we spoke days after she was selected leader. Alumni concerns about the school's culture hadn't materialized in large measure because the girls controlled their own space, had their own classes, and on most days held their own convocation. Kaleb let me know that some boys did regret having girls around, and problems sometimes divided the separate leadership teams. But he said that during their joint convos the disputes usually got resolved so effectively that "you can't tell if we had problems or not." While most students didn't have much contact with the other division, the girls I interviewed all seemed to be keeping track of what the boys were up to. The boys generally acted the way teenage boys usually do in the presence of girls: consistently goofy, giddy, or oblivious.

Rey was concerned by the way remote learning seemed to have

robbed students of the chance to work together, threatening the sense of community that propels the school's success. Even when students were allowed back on the property, social distancing and face masks kept them apart. Kids were just not interacting with each other, Rey believed, because "everyone was so used to being attached to a device."

Dr. Ivan Lamourt, a 1982 graduate who now leads St. Benedict's large team of counselors, said that during the pandemic he saw anxiety, depression, and loneliness rise among students who were also dealing with dysfunctional families, addiction, and abandonment at home. Their phones had become a lifeline, and when they returned to in-person learning, teachers struggled to keep them off their devices during convo and in class. At lunch, Lamourt saw tables of boys in the cafeteria staring at their screens instead of talking to each other. And what most disturbed him and Father Ed was the way phones undercut the afternoon meetings of the smaller multi-year groups that are supposed to keep students from falling through the cracks. Once freshmen are drafted into these groups, they stay there all four years, up to and including the day they graduate. Being bunched together this way gives everyone an additional, strong, identity, and it provides younger students the daily chance to mix with and learn from upperclassmen, and vice versa. Rather than belonging to a homeroom, students identify with their assigned group, named for an important figure from the school's past. Decades later, alumni will still boast that their group was, and is, tops. But Rey's own experience with group meetings during the pandemic didn't inspire any of that loyalty. Although the guys in his group still discussed scripture and competed against other groups in sports and academic competitions, for most of the thirty minutes they met every afternoon, they never let go of their phones.

But that was going to change. At a faculty meeting a few days before classes started, Lucia and Rey stood before teachers and staff to proudly announce that they'd solved the phone problem. While other schools wrestled with what to do about the devices, they'd decided that group leaders at St. Benedict's would simply collect all phones before convo and store them in a faculty office until the day ended. Period. Full stop. Lucia and Rey basked in their achievement briefly before being subjected to a punishing lesson in group dynamics. Although teachers had complained that phones were a growing nuisance, they immediately started to pick apart the proposal, as has happened at many other schools. What happens to students who need their phones to monitor their diabetes? the school nurse wanted to know. How are parents supposed to get in touch in case of an emergency? asked another. What about a student who gets sick and needs to call home? The student leaders tried to respond to each objection but soon got twisted up by all the possible scenarios they hadn't considered. That's when Father Ed stepped in, his impatience poking through his composure. They could spend a week ironing out responses to every situation and still end up blindsided by something no one had yet anticipated. He urged everyone to move on, while keeping in mind that adjustments would inevitably need to be made, as they usually are whenever anything new is tried, especially when it originates with students.

"You've got to remember that this school is run day to day by students," he reminded everyone. "There are going to be messes. If you're not able to deal with messes, then maybe this is not the place for you."

Besides blaming phones for dampening St. Benedict's community spirit, the student leaders were upset that discipline had taken a holiday since COVID hit. Lucia was especially upset by the way dress code enforcement had grown lax, and lateness had become habitual. Since the lockdown ended, a herd of stragglers showed to convo after eight o'clock almost every morning. Boys and girls waltzed in with their shirts untucked or their skirts hiked up too high, and nobody said a thing.

Lucia and Rey were determined to put things right. At the same faculty meeting where they laid out the new phone policy, they announced that they were going to make sure the dress code is strictly enforced by imposing immediate consequences for any violation, no matter how small. They would follow the student handbook like a Bible. Polo shirt not tucked in? Hair dyed an inappropriate color? School ID not visible? Under their zero tolerance approach, the slightest infraction would be enough to bar a student from attending convo. "Last year everything was so lenient that no one cared," Lucia stated at the meeting, her voice a bridge between faculty and students. This year, she warned, would be different.

To enforce the new rules, the leaders proposed another radical change. Tardy students would not only be kept out of convo, they'd be held back from their first class. Show up late more than seven times, and they might not get credit for the course. If it was a required course, they'd have to take it again. Michelle Tuorto supported the changes and predicted that lateness would decrease substantially which, over time, it did.

Lucia and Rey weren't done reshaping the school. Discipline was key, and to keep people in line they wanted to bring back detention, or jug as it is known in Newark (some students imagined jug standing for Justice Under God, but it's just an old term from Father Ed's generation). They envisioned it being used as an intermediate step after a verbal admonishment and before outright expulsion for minor disciplinary infractions, like acting up during convo.

Father Ed stood at the back of the room during their presentation, and he didn't like what he was hearing. "Father Mark would be spinning in his grave if he saw them bring back jug," he told me, speaking under his breath while Rey was still outlining the new policy. He was referring to the late Father Mark Payne, who is credited with designing the school's distinctive emphasis on student leadership. Father Mark believed it was better to encourage the right actions, rather than punish bad behavior. "I spent plenty of days in jug and it didn't change a damn thing," the headmaster whispered, referring to his days as a not-so-stellar student at St. Benedict's. "Our kids see nothing but negativity. We shouldn't be adding to it." Despite his reservations, he did not to stand in Lucia and Rey's way.

* * *

For the teachers at the meeting, Lucia and Rey's presentation was an impressive demonstration of student initiative, as well as a stark reminder that St. Benedict's was no ordinary school. "The student leaders have been responsive to your needs in a way I've never seen," remarked an associate headmaster. Teachers, relieved that the troublesome phones would be banished, seconded him, and the kids in charge beamed.

For Rey, this had also marked a personal milestone. The overt expression of his will in front of Father Ed and the entire faculty was just the first step in his inner struggle to counter the negative influence of his father and the city where he had been reared. The Sunday morning raid at his home years before had left an indelible impression, and being at St. Benedict's—and serving as senior group leader—had changed his expectation of discipline in others, as well as in himself even though he had started out being dead set against attending the prep.

While Rey was still at Ridge Street, one of the city's traditional pre-K–8 elementary schools, his mother worried that the seedier side of the city might someday entrap him just as it had his father. She wanted something different, something better, for her children. When Rey was old enough to start thinking about high school, her concern intensified. "High school can make you or break you," she told me over Cuban espresso one Sunday after church. She knew that the Newark school district was so dysfunctional that the state had taken control, and run it, from Trenton, for twenty-five years. There'd been some modest improvements over that time, and a few selective public high schools in the city had earned better reputations than others. But even if Rey qualified for a seat in one of those schools, his mother didn't trust what would happen to him after school. No matter how often she'd warned him to stay away from trouble, she'd found him hanging around with kids she knew were headed in the wrong direction. She searched for an alternative school they could afford but came up blank. Then a coworker told her about St. Benedict's.

At that time, she worked as a teacher's aide in an early childhood learning center in Newark's Ironbound section, a neighborhood separated from the rest of the city by railroad tracks and the Passaic River, and invigorated by an influx of Portuguese and Brazilian immigrants. A coworker, Giovanni Bonilla, '08, mentioned to her that he and his younger brother had gone to St. Benedict's. All she knew about the school was that it was for boys only, and those boys came from rich families. Bonilla told her that there are a few families like that, and they help by paying full tuition, which makes it possible for families like hers to send their sons. And he told her that the monks would keep Rey out of trouble, as they had him and his brother when they were students.

Ruth kept his advice in mind and in 2020, when Rey was in the eighth grade, she made him apply to St. Benedict's even though he had his heart set on going to Newark Technology High, a selective school that several of his friends planned to attend. That was the year of the COVID lockdown, and after schools imposed remote learning in mid-March, he spent the rest of the school year at home with his computer. That same month, he learned that St. Benedict's had offered him a generous financial aid package, including the same scholarship Lucia also would receive.

"Give it a try for one year," was how his mother got him to abandon the idea of Newark Tech and attend St. Benedict's instead. Still, he fought it. Within days of his eighth-grade graduation, he had to sit in front of his computer as a watered-down version of convo streamed on YouTube. Freshman overnight was canceled. He tried out for the freshman basketball team without realizing that there would be physical tryouts despite the pandemic. He hadn't dribbled a basketball since the lockdown began, and he'd lost a step or two. He didn't make the team.

That first year at St. Benedict's was one long struggle for him, and he hated it. He resisted all the school's efforts to pull him in. Nonetheless, he stuck with it. He gravitated toward faculty who were alumni, men like history teacher Jared Boone, a Black man who'd been senior group leader in 2013, and who embraced the belief that the person you are can become the person you want to be. Rey also admired Bonilla, who by then had joined the St. Benedict's staff. Bonilla watched as Rey gradually entered the school's powerful orbit, transforming himself from resister to convert.

Now, when Bonilla sees Rey at the podium leading the school through convo, when he watches him raise his hand and quiet the entire gym, he's glad that he played a role in getting him there and keeping him from bailing. "I see him all the time and I tell him, damn man, I knew you were going to be a perfect fit for this school," Bonilla said, a smile of obvious satisfaction crossing his profile, "but I didn't think you were going to be *this* perfect." He applauded Rey's take-control attitude as leader, and watched with admiration as he proposed and then implemented changes that, to him, "made Benedict's return to what it used to be when I was in school here."

* * *

While the veteran faculty at that first meeting greeted the new rules on phones and lateness with varying degrees of relief, nine newly hired teachers struggled to understand what exactly they had gotten themselves into. Students laying down policy, and the headmaster siding with them over faculty objections? Not to mention that there was still a full six weeks of summer to go, but they'd have to start teaching in a few days. Bobby Hastie was one of the puzzled newcomers. A compact twenty-four-year-old cross-country runner from suburban Robbinsville, in central New Jersey, he'd done some substitute teaching in the Philadelphia suburbs but never in a city like Newark, or a school like St. Benedict's. He was one of the first teachers hired under Father Ed's unorthodox new scheme for determining whether faculty candidates were what he liked to describe as being "just off-center enough" to put up with the school's unconventional approach. He favored hiring alumni, confident that their experience as students had steeped them in the peculiar appeal of the place. The roster of current teachers includes many with the year of their graduation appended to their names. And many, including Cassidy and Lamourt, have racked up decades-long tenures that rival the stability of the monks, a testament to the orbital pull the place exerts on some. But manpower and mission aren't always that well aligned. A number of recent hires chafed against the last-minute schedule changes and the many additional duties St. Benedict's imposes on teachers. They stayed for a brief time, then either decided not to return, or Father Ed had to tell them St. Benedict's was not for them. Routine academic hiring practices hadn't been sufficient to determine if they possessed the distinctive (or off-the-wall?) character needed to support the school's singular mission. Candidates didn't have to be Catholic, or hold a drawer full of degrees. But they had to be willing to live with St. Benedict's deeply rooted quirkiness.

A few weeks earlier, the school had notified Hastie that it was seriously considering his application for a position teaching math in the boys division. But first he'd have to come to Newark for what was called a preliminary candidate assessment and evaluation to identify what the note he received described as "confident candidates who are creative, collaborative, resilient, and innovative, with the ability to encourage, enrich and empower a community that bridges the gap between people and provides its students with opportunity." The screening was Father Ed's way of assessing how likely somebody like Hastie was to put up with the creative disruption of what he and the student leaders continually set in motion, and why at St. Benedict's, "plan" is considered a four-letter word.

Hastie also received a cryptic set of instructions, with a mandatory gear list, the word "**MANDATORY**" in capital letters, bold and underlined: backpack, water bottle, large garbage bag. So far, nothing out of the ordinary, though perhaps unorthodox for a school interview. Then, Hastie told me, it got weird:

One dollar and ninety-two cents ($1.92) IN EXACT
    CHANGE!
Three quarters
Six dimes
Nine nickels
Twelve pennies

The peculiar list continued:

10" x 10" sheet of white paper
One shoe other than the ones that the candidate is wearing
12-inch piece of string
Extra pants and socks
Towel

"You can't make this shit up," Hastie exclaimed during a break in
that first faculty meeting. He described the eccentric screening he and
the other candidates experienced as a combination of initiation ritual
and obstacle course. On the day of his evaluation, he was teamed with
a St. Benedict's student, and together they faced a series of challenges
utilizing items from the gear list. Some were straight forward, intended
to test the candidate's ability to follow directions. The $1.92 had to
be tallied in the exact denominations outlined on the list. Same thing
with the 10" x 10" sheet of white paper, which had to be cut from a
larger sheet in advance. The single shoe? That became a prop for the
candidate-student team to come up with offbeat uses for the shoe besides wearing it. Hastie conceded that being creative is not his strong
point. All he could think of was using the shoe to swat a bug. Others
suggested using it as a pillow to sleep on, a vessel for carrying water, or
a weapon for self-defense.
    The biggest surprise came when the candidates were brought to
the school's twenty-five-yard-long indoor pool. There they were given a

challenge unlike any they'd ever faced in a job interview. Candidates and students were put in teams of four and given a task that would test their commitment to the school's philosophy of giving up what you want for what the group needs, even if what you want is to not be scared out of your wits. The mission was to retrieve a twenty-five-pound barbell weight plate from where it had been placed at the bottom of the deep end of the pool, coax it to the surface, and then ferry it across the entire length of the pool, all in less than five minutes.

Problem Number One: A bathing suit was not on the gear list.

Problem Number Two: The deep end of the pool is *deep* at thirteen feet.

Problem Number Three: The mission required every member of the team to participate.

Hastie had already competed in a triathlon, was a practiced swimmer, and was young enough to accept the challenge right away. But how to get the others involved? And what did this have to do with teaching math? He didn't have answers, but he was curious and willing to see it through to the end.

His team devised a simple strategy: Hastie would dive in and push the weight close to the surface, where a student who was treading water would attach it to a rope the team had made by tying their own clothes together. The others would then tug the weight across the pool to the finish line. When it was time to put the plan into action, Hastie kicked off his shoes and jumped in, still wearing his jeans. "I took a deep breath, swam down with my eyes open, located the weight and grabbed it with two hands, then pushed up from the bottom," he recalled. He struggled when he was still three feet from the surface, but managed to hand it off to the student on his team, who attached the clothes line. The others took over and pulled the weight across the finish line. In all, it took just under two minutes.

After they dried and changed, the candidates were brought back to the boardroom and seated in what's called the vulnerability chair, where students and staff grilled them about their professional teaching experience. Then they were asked to describe their happiest moments, and greatest heartbreaks.

"They learned a lot about me," Hastie told me. They had learned that he might not have imagined creative ways to use a shoe, but when it comes to teamwork, he was willing to put himself out front. He said he learned a lot about St. Benedict's too: "I found out the soul of the school."

Eventually, Tuorto interviewed him in the traditional way, and outlined expectations and salary. A brand-new teacher, just out of college, is paid $50,000, with 2 percent cost of living increases yearly after that. (The Newark Board of Education offers a starting salary of $67,000 for a teacher like Hastie with a bachelor's degree.) Besides a full classroom load, Hastie had to take on at least one student activity as team coach or club adviser. He would be expected to attend daily convocation, and partake in the afternoon meetings of a student group. He might even be asked to hike the Appalachian Trail with the kids.

The day after he jumped into the pool, Hastie received a text directly from Father Ed.

Bobby,
   We want you on our team. Michelle will be in touch on Monday with details. Counting on you. Looking forward.
                                    Edwin

Hastie was hooked. Everything from the spirit he felt during convocation to the brotherhood he experienced working through the challenges with his teammates, convinced him that he had found the place where he belonged. "While I was sitting there in the gym, I could feel the love they all had for the kids." He hadn't encountered that in any other school he'd been in. It was, he said, the most authentic demonstration of caring and brotherhood that he had ever experienced, and he wholeheartedly wanted to be a part of it.

CHAPTER 9

A Championship Season

DURING THE FIVE-WEEK summer term, Lucia and Rey worked hard to get the kinks out of their new disciplinary systems. Diabetes turned out not to be an issue; the school nurse made sure kids kept track of their levels without their phones. And most parents survived without calling their child during the day. Over the course of the year, compliance with the tough new phone policy would vary because students themselves enforced the new rule, and it isn't easy for some teenagers to go all drill sergeant on their friends. A few would give in to peer pressure and occasionally allow their pals to hold on to their phones. But on the plus side, kids were interacting more, they were paying closer attention to teachers during class, and afternoon group meetings had once again become enriching interchanges.

As the fall semester began in September, it was accompanied by the full interscholastic sports schedule. Except for football, St. Benedict's competes in most other sports along with a few, like fencing, crew, and water polo, that other urban schools don't offer. Athletics is an integral part of the school's commitment to building community. When the athletic director sends notices excusing athletes early because "they are representing us," in a scheduled match or game, he subtly reinforces the message that everything at St. Benedict's comes back to brotherhood.

They put special emphasis on losses, painful though they may be, because they believe that real heroes bounce back after a defeat.

Lucia looked forward to her final year on the volleyball team. As captain, and one of the most competitive players, she was heart and soul of the team. She loved the sport, and she'd already decided to try to find a way to continue playing when she got to college. Rey, on the other hand, was sitting out wrestling season with a stubborn back sprain that just wouldn't go away. Besides, he was so busy as senior group leader, editor of *The Benedict News*, and an active member of several other groups, that sports had become less important to him. He'd even left home and moved into Leahy House, which meant he was on the property all day, every day, to make sure things were running right. He didn't plan on wrestling in college, and had his heart set on entering one of the service academies, maybe Annapolis. The midshipmen volunteers he'd gotten to know when they accompanied freshmen on the Appalachian Trail, and later in the pool during the rigorous water challenge, had impressed him deeply. They understood what it meant to be disciplined, to live by the rules, to wear uniforms that demand respect—things that meant the world to him.

At St. Benedict's this year, one sport was king above all others, and losses existed only in the hypothetical. The Gray Bees' soccer team had been dominant for decades, producing such stars as Claudio Reyna, '91, who led the team to a perfect 65–0 record over three years and was named the Gatorade National High School Soccer Player of the Year. Reyna went on to play for two U.S. Olympic teams and compete in several World Cups. His classmate at St. Benedict's, Gregg Berhalter, coached the U.S. Men's National Soccer Team for five years from 2019 to 2024.

This year, St. Benedict's soccer team was enjoying unparalleled success, going undefeated the entire season. In fact, since 2016, the school had won more than one hundred matches without a single loss, a seven-year win streak that made them one of the winningest teams in the nation and earned for one of its stalwart players, midfielder Ransford

Gyan, the same honor as Reyna—designation as the best high school soccer player in the country.

The 2023 season ended in a classic matchup between St. Benedict's and its prep school rival, Pennington, whose own chance at going undefeated had been wrecked by an earlier loss to the Gray Bees. Pennington was desperate for revenge. The winner of the match would not only decide the New Jersey state prep school championship, but in a real sense crown one of them the best high school soccer team in the country.

St. Benedict's doesn't hold traditional pep rallies. It doesn't need to. School spirit gets whipped up during convo, and soccer gets everyone excited. After all, Rey and the rest of the seniors had gone through all four years without ever having to say the words "Our soccer team lost." On the morning of the big game, convo began with the usual routine of readings, reflections, and prayers. On the piano keyboard, Dennis Lansang, a Filipino MD from Jersey City who left pediatrics to teach high school chemistry, played Jersey Club dance music, the aggressive high-speed electronic beats that originated in Newark at the turn of this century. It always lures kids onto the floor to show off stiff-armed robotic moves that get the whole gym worked up. Brett, the soccer team's co-captain, took the mic, beaming with a self-satisfied smile. And why not? All season long he'd come to the podium to announce the previous day's victory, acknowledging his team's inevitable march toward yet another win, another championship season.

Rey joined him at the podium and led an enthusiastic round of "Boola Boola." Secretly, he was thinking about the plan he and Lucia had hatched earlier that week. They'd been in school since July, and there were no holidays scheduled until Thanksgiving, weeks away. Not yet having fully tested the limits of their power to run the school, they wondered what would be more appropriate than a day off once the soccer team was crowned National Champion for the fifteenth time? He would blast an email to everyone in the boys division before the game started, remarking on the high energy at convo and looking forward to giving Pennington another beating. He outlined the plan for a day off, but conditioned it on everyone keeping up their energy and carrying the team to victory.

The big game was played at Roberts Stadium in Princeton, a gorgeous soccer pitch that had opened a little over a year earlier. More than one hundred Benedict's students piled into three school buses for the trip. Music blared, and at the back of one of the boys busses, Rey and other seniors held a spoken-word competition where someone suggested a topic for a poem that they all improvised on the spot. They riffed on the theme of how sweet it would be to wear a national title ring.

It was a chilly November evening, with the temperature in the big stadium hovering at around 40 degrees. Kaleb and the drum line kept everyone from thinking too much about the cold and focusing instead on the thrill of winning another championship. Both teams fielded elite players from foreign countries as well as sought-after players who had transferred from other schools, a growing trend in the state that is changing the way soccer, basketball, and football are played. Most people gave St. Benedict's the advantage because of Ransford, who ran like a sprinter, turned like the needle on a compass, and never ran out of gas. Originally from the West African nation of Ghana, Ransford was not yet in high school when a St. Benedict's graduate from Ghana convinced him to come to Newark. During his COVID-fractured freshman year, while most other students were sent home, Ransford lived at the Leahy House dormitory. Despite his superstar status, he eagerly joined the St. Benedict's community. He hiked the Appalachian Trail, competed in group games, and consistently landed on the honor roll. He was still there as he warmed up for the biggest game of his life thus far.

For the first eight minutes of the match, the teams battled to a draw. Pennington, ranked twenty-fifth nationally by the United Soccer Coaches, seemed to be holding its own against top-ranked St. Benedict's. But at the eight-minute mark, the Red Hawks pulled ahead. It was a wake-up call for St. Benedict's—they'd rarely lost the lead all season. Within minutes,

Ransford tied the score, bringing the noisy crowd to its feet. St. Benedict's quickly added another goal to pull ahead. That was when St. Benedict's fans started thinking, *Yeah, we got this*. Pennington made some replacements, and tied the score at 2–2 before the break. Both teams went back to the locker room determined to regain the lead.

During halftime, St. Benedict's drum line kept spirits high, and the concession stand kept stomachs full. When the game resumed, Pennington showed all the signs of a team that wanted to win more than its opponent. The Red Hawks scored once, and then added a second goal to pull ahead 4–2. The mood of the St. Benedict's crowd iced over. "But we fought back," Rey recounted. "We reminded each other that that's what we're here for, to keep the team alive." St. Benedict's next goal brought the score to 4–3, but that was all they had, and for the last fifteen minutes neither team managed to put a ball into the net.

After the whistle blew and the game ended, Pennington was jubilant, St. Benedict's fans blue-screened. The drums were stilled as the stunned crowd filed out of the stadium and onto the buses for the long, sad, ride home. This time, there was no music on the buses, and no poetry.

Rey was sullen, but more than the shocking loss had changed his mood. During the game, St. Benedict's students had exchanged text messages the way they often did at sports outings and other events. Those who were at the stadium as well as students who were watching the live stream posted comments after good plays and bad, and texted plenty of trash talk. Rey was used to it. What got under his skin were comments he read about Ransford and the other West African players. He'd heard this type of racial slur from opposing teams. But these nasty comments had come from the St. Benedict's side.

The group chat that ticked him off most had started with petty comments from members of St. Benedict's rowing team. In the texts they resented the money that the school spent on scholarships for Ransford and several other African players. That money could have gone to other teams, they groused, teams like theirs. Then someone in

the chat responded, "Yeah, send them back to Africa." As they continued, their tone grew darker. Stung by the loss, and disappointed because
they believed they wouldn't get the day off that Rey had promised, combined with jealousy over the soccer team's prestige, they crossed a line.
"Send the n . . . ers back to Africa."

Everett was a third-year student on the rowing team who'd been
on the text chain from the beginning. He and the other rowers couldn't
be at the stadium because they had practiced that afternoon, so they
watched the live stream during their workout. After practice ended,
Everett caught the rest of the game at home. That's when he said the
negative texting started. "One of the people in the group used the hard
R and that's when I was like, 'I'm just going to stop,'" he explained when
I asked him how the texting had turned so intolerant. In school, Black
kids casually sling around the N-word with a soft A as the last syllable
when they are among themselves. But it gets amped up into an insult
when anyone else uses it, especially when it carries the hard R ending.

Sitting in the back of the bus, Rey put the disappointment of the loss behind him and focused on the disconcerting messages. Restoring Benedict's
spirit had been his mission since the school year began. The texts seemed
drawn from the same kind of me-first individualism that had weakened
the school during the COVID lockdown. Moreover, they were disturbing
reminders of the ignorance and racism that had led to the school closing
in 1972. He feared the texts could contaminate the whole school, so he
notified Father Ed and the dean of the boys division, David Rodriguez, '96.

When the buses pulled up, Father Ed was waiting in the lobby.
He demanded the names of the boys involved in the racist texts. There
were five: Everett, who is white; one student from Haiti; and three
others from Ecuador and Mexico. Although Blacks and Latinos had
tangled in some of Newark's public schools, St. Benedict's was largely
free of racial tensions, and the school's Honor Code abhorred intoler-
ance. The morning after the game, the entire school gathered in the

big gym for the gloomiest convo of the year. Some students had heard about the texts, but everyone knew that their unbeatable soccer team had been beaten. Even Kaleb, usually as bubbly as a shaken-up can of Coke, struggled to animate the "You Go And Conquer!" affirmation he usually led. Realizing the kids were depressed, Dr. Lansang belted out a composition the Rev. Winstead might have written for days like this. "Stay up. Don't let nothing get you down." Then it was time to address the reason everyone was down. Brett, the soccer team co-captain, took the mic. Two of his teammates stood beside him.

"We announce our victories and our defeats." Brett was straight-faced, bordering on grim. He was proud of the team, he said, and of the support the school had shown. "At the end of the day we play for you guys and the badge on our hearts represents our school and our community." He had both hands around the mic, which he held upright on top of the podium. He needed self-control and focus for what he had to say next. He paused a moment, twiddled the mic, and squinted slightly, as if he'd walked into a cloud of smoke.

"But with defeat comes negativity, and I want to touch on the fact that negativity shouldn't come from our own community, especially racism." He straightened up then, but kept both hands on the mic. Next to him, his teammates kept their hands shoved deep into their pockets, checking the ceiling or examining their shoes as if they couldn't bear looking at the crowded bleachers, knowing that out there were the texters who had written such hateful things.

"You're allowed to talk about the game, what we did poorly, but racist comments are unacceptable." Against the back wall of the gym, Father Ed was pacing. When Brett said, "This is just a lesson learned," the monk stopped short and stared at him from behind, suggesting there was another lesson still to be learned.

* * *

After classes ended that day, Lucia and Rey sat as they often did in the admissions office near the main lobby, where her father was director. Both of them were bummed out by the loss, but Rey was especially worried that all their work to revive school spirit was in jeopardy. Since the school year began last summer, he'd been pushing everyone to give 100 percent, just as he had been giving his all. And yet. He was a spirited young man with a complicated, multidimensional character that was still in formation. The temptation to test the limits of his power as leader was too strong for him to ignore, and here was an opportunity, if he could just figure out the right way to approach it. He couldn't make a day off feel like a pity party because the soccer team had forfeited the big game. That wouldn't work. But if they framed it as a reward for everyone's hard work since the summer, who could argue with that? "It's not like we're doing any less as a community just because we lost the national title," Rey reasoned. He and Lucia talked it over and decided to go ahead with the unscheduled holiday. But they knew they'd have to run it by Father Ed first. They put together a plan.

"Rey suggested that I ask Father Ed, and since he and I have a closer relationship, he would respond to my ask a little better than Rey's," Lucia remembered. She strode confidently into the headmaster's office, where the sign over the door announces Authorized Access At All Times. "Very calmly, I asked him how he was." The priest was quiet long enough for her to mention how the loss had amplified the burnout they all had felt before the game, and obliquely raised the idea of a justified day off. "That put the idea in his head," she said, and as that idea was sinking in, they launched part two of their plan. Rey casually entered the office as if he happened to be passing by without knowing Lucia was there. Oh yes, Rey affirmed when the headmaster asked his opinion, a day off was valid. "We take for granted that excellence is the norm around here." A day off would remind everyone that their hard work hadn't gone unnoticed.

Father Ed suspected he was being played, but he went along with the ruse and added his own twist. "It's not me who can approve a day off," he told them. He took out his cell phone and gave them the number of Kevin Harris. "Call him."

"When they called, I was in my office," said Ralph Kevin Harris, St. Benedict's, '78. He is vice president of Local 3 of the Laborers International Union of North America, which works with the building trades in Newark and throughout northern New Jersey. "They said, 'Father Ed told us to ask you if we should give the kids a day off because the soccer team lost.' I said I'll call Father Ed right now, and they said, 'Do it.'"

Although Lucia and Rey didn't know it, they were the ones being played. This was one of Father Ed's oldest routines, and Harris had been in on it for years. It goes back to his own time at St. Benedict's, in the class that was a year behind Anthony Badger's. The school was small then, and it was a struggle getting everyone to buy into the notion of an eleven-month school year with few holidays. Whenever the question of taking a day off came up during convo, the headmaster would look toward Harris, who even then was ready to play along. "He'd say to me, 'Ralph, do you think we should have a day off?' And I'd say, 'Nah, not today, Father Ed. We didn't deserve it today.'"

It was a classic bit of Edwin-inspired myth-making and a part of St. Benedict's tradition—once you enter the community, you're in it forever unless you mess up. Having Lucia and Rey make the call was also a strategic move on the headmaster's part, what Rey with a toothy smile and awkward laugh referred to as a "side quest," but that the priest intended to be yet another test of how much students were committed to working for what they wanted.

After Harris spoke with the leaders, he called Father Ed. "You ain't never changed a bit," he told the headmaster. And taking an easier line than he had so many years before, he agreed that the kids deserved the day off. The following day, Lucia and Rey scheduled an after-class convocation and made the announcement, notifying everyone—teachers hearing it at the same time as students—that because they all had worked so hard and had gone through so much since the summer, and stressing that it was not consolation for losing the championship game, Monday's classes were canceled.

* * *

Regardless of how it was packaged, having a day off eased the sting of losing the soccer game. But when classes resumed, a disquieting buzz coursed through the school. Outside of the soccer captain's curious few words about how racism was an unacceptable reaction to losing a game, no one had publicly addressed the ugly group chat. During convo, Everett and the other texters sat in the bleachers as if nothing had happened, even though a lot actually had transpired.

The morning after the game, Father Ed had called all five texters into his office and lectured them about loyalty and how being part of a team—especially a rowing team—meant sticking together, win or lose. He looked at them, especially the ones from immigrant families, and shook his head. Don't you know there are people right now saying the same thing about you, wanting to send you back where you came from? Using the N-word like that must mean you don't know American history and therefore can't understand how much what you said can hurt.

The headmaster came down hard on them, but he also kept in mind that they were teenagers, individuals who—as he said many times— have partially formed brains that lead them to do, and say, stupid things. He ordered them to apologize to Ransford and the other African soccer players, and find out from one of the history teachers the significance of the words they'd texted. "We're like, okay, that's fine," Everett recalled. "We'll take the punishment. We went to class. Then they took us out of class, I think, like thirty minutes later." They were sent to the front office and learned they'd been suspended for the rest of the day as well as the next. They were told to come back on Monday morning, even though it would be a day off, and see Father Ed.

The five texters spent an uneasy weekend worrying that Father Ed would expel them. He didn't. He told them he'd allow them back on Tuesday, but he suspended them indefinitely from the rowing team. The rowers were relieved, but only until they received an email from Rey. He didn't think Father Ed had gone far enough. In his view, the texters had not acted like members of the community. And following that reasoning, he thought that they should be treated as if they no longer belonged to it. The headmaster urged Rey to let it go, but as senior group leader he worried that other students would think the offenders had gotten off easy, and that would encourage them to follow their example. The only way to address the wrong that had been done, and prevent it from happening again, was for Everett and the others to lose their membership in the community, and the privilege of wearing their black hoodies that went with it. Rey decided that they should be forced to wear shirts and ties, which is what they wore their first day as freshmen, before they had taken the first step to joining the community. Getting a taste of what it's like to be an outsider again would compel the rowers to work hard to earn their way back in. Rey added one final condition. The five would have to apologize—not just to the soccer players, but to the entire school.

When he told Father Ed what he'd decided, they locked horns. The headmaster agreed that what the rowers did was offensive and immature, but he feared that outing them publicly could do more harm than good. He saw that Rey was intent on laying down the law, but he thought publicly shaming them by taking away their colors was overkill. Then, as he had done when the leaders wanted to revive detention, he stepped back. If Rey's move backfired, there'd be some cleaning up to do. But a lesson would be learned all around.

At a subsequent convo, Kaleb again gave the school's affirmation of personal integrity, ending with a rousing "You Go And Conquer!"

Lansang put on a Jersey Club recording and then stepped out from behind his electric piano, attempting to fire up the school by giving his own rendition of a Jersey Club dance. The former physician put his spirit into it, but his fifty-eight-year-old hips never managed to catch the beat. Finally, the big gym quieted down. Rey sauntered over to the podium and conferred with Father Ed. Everett, wearing a long-sleeved black shirt and black and white striped tie, came forward, and the other four rowers, all in their shirts and ties, joined him as he raised his hand for quiet.

Everett stiffly read his apology to the soccer players and to the entire school. "What I said was wrong and there is no excuse for it. I would like to apologize to my group, friends, and team. I have made all of you look bad." He went on to say that the language he used in the texts was "hateful, inappropriate, and unnecessary," and that being white, he realized he has a duty to speak up when he hears others using that kind of language. Finally, he said, "I am not asking for anybody to forgive me immediately. I am asking for a second chance to be able to earn your forgiveness." The other four texters read their equally sanitized apologies, pleading both insensitivity and ignorance. The first-generation Haitian acknowledged that it was ludicrous for him, as both an immigrant and a Black man, to have sent those texts. "I have a responsibility to educate myself," he said, and in language that sounded more like it was written by artificial intelligence than a contrite teenager, added, "and immediately correct the people around me whenever they partake in regressive behavior."

Afterwards, I sought out Ransford to ask if the apology had cleared things up for him. Despite his national fame and the college scouts who tracked his every movement, he remains quite shy. "Once they did it in front of the whole school, that was enough for me," he said, smiling as if none of what happened had been a big deal. "When you're down, you can say some words that you don't really mean." He spoke quietly, his voice a note above a cheery whisper. "They didn't really mean it that much. And them standing in front of the school to apologize for that, that's enough."

And after a brief pause, he admitted that losing the game, the last of his scholastic career, hurt more than seeing what was written in those texts. "I don't really pay attention to that." He smiled. "I'm cool. I don't care."

Everett and the others attended special classes on racism and Black history until the fall term ended. Rey made them wear their shirts and ties for a total of around five weeks. By the time Everett and the other rowers were allowed to wear their black again, basketball season was in full swing, and Ransford had accepted a full soccer scholarship to Clemson University.

The soccer texts proved to be the biggest test so far of Rey's leadership style. It was his chance to show how tough he could be when the school needed someone to be tough. Headstrong and confident in his own ability to make the right decisions, he was willing to go against the headmaster's guidance, believing he knew better than the old monk how letting the texters off too easy could impact the rest of the school.

The entire episode became a flow chart to understanding how Rey leads, making up his own mind and then plowing ahead, ready to ask forgiveness but not permission. "A lot of times, no one's ever going to be fully satisfied with the decision you make," he told me. "Everyone's got their opinions, but as long as you act with the right intent, in the best interest of the community," you'll be okay.

CHAPTER 10

Listen with the Ear of Your Heart

ONE WEDNESDAY MORNING in early November, Father Ed carried a paperback Bible into the only class he still teaches at St. Benedict's. A crucifix hangs on the wall of the classroom on the ground floor of Bishop Joseph Francis Hall, one of the newest buildings on the property, along with a large digital whiteboard that the headmaster uses about as little as he uses the teacher's desk that he pushed against the back wall. Sheridan, the self-confident freshman who had so impressed Lucia with her command of school lore, was one of about two dozen girls who settled into their desks for the class this morning, a required course for all freshman. She took out her notebook and sat, pen in hand, ready to take notes, while many of the other girls kept their desks clear. Some had their eyes on Father Ed as he began the familiar story of Moses and the burning bush, one of his go-to lessons. Others inspected the finish on their fingernails.

This morning's class was a chance for Father Ed to once again ask the familiar questions that he says are inherent in that Bible story. It was his way of making the sacred scripts relevant to the youths sitting before him: What day was Moses out there? What time? How many others would have rushed off to more important things, like tending to their flock, instead of absorbing the wonder of what was happening in front of them?

"You've got to take the time to look for God's presence," he told the girls. The extraordinary happening in the ordinary. Any day. Any time. It's all around you, if you look for it. I've heard him tell that same story many times, in many different settings, and the points he makes are always the same. God's presence made those few yards of ground beneath the bush holy. In a similar way, the ground on which the abbey stands in the heart of Newark is made special by their presence—not just the monks but also the teachers, the staff, and especially the students, who come from near and far, from cultures familiar and cultures complex and foreign, who put aside their differences to walk and sit shoulder to shoulder, to watch out for each other, and to learn the way to a life worth living. And, he often adds, the need for that brand of accord has never been greater.

Because he now spends so much time raising the staggering amount of money it takes to run the school, the former biology teacher isn't in the classroom much anymore. But he has reserved for himself what he considers a crucial course for freshman girls. It is officially listed as Religion 1, but he hates that name. Instead, he calls it Transmitting Faith, and like his homilies at convo, each class is an improv performance, presented with more passion than planning. It is as free form as any of his talks, but he hits familiar themes over and over. The repetition, he's told me, is deliberate. He believes that you have to teach like a grandmother, repeating the same thing many times, to have a real impact on these teens. He doesn't rely on videos or handouts. Just Father Ed laying it on the line for more than an hour with two dozen teenage girls who see him as headmaster, teacher, and, sometimes, grandfather.

During this morning's class, he referenced another Bible story he had discussed in an earlier session, and asked the meaning of something in that story. All he got from the girls were blank stares.

"Maybe when you get older like me you will remember some of this stuff," he grumbled.

In a roundabout way, that impromptu remark sparked a question, not about faith but about life. From the back of the room came a barely audible query. "How old are you?"

"I'm seventy-eight."

That stirred mocking chatter, and got a few of the girls to forget their nails and direct their attention to Father Ed. "What?" he deadpanned, knowing that, at the very least, he had the girls' attention. "Come on. You didn't have to react like that."

The class evolved into a freewheeling conversation that the girls knew, by this point in the term, had almost no boundaries. More questions came.

"Do you ever question your faith, Father?"

"Yeah, sometimes I wonder, Does God really exist? That's when faith comes in. You have to believe in spite of that doubt. You need to be open to that possibility. If you are, then faith is a gift."

His says his goal in the class is to apply the old lessons about morality and trust in these stories to the contemporary challenges the girls face. It's a long shot, but he tries. He doesn't ask, but he knows based on experience that more than half of the girls are not Catholic, just like the rest of St. Benedict's. No matter. As he's said many times before, St. Benedict's was resurrected not because its students would be Catholic, but because the monks are.

So how do they teach religion in a Catholic school where most students are not Catholic? At first, it didn't. After the fierce debate over whether white monks were equipped to teach math and English to Black and Latino teens, the monks worried that if they tried teaching religion in the traditional way, they'd be considered missionaries and not educators. Besides, they all had grown up in families that transmitted faith inside the home. Preaching in Black churches, and staying in touch with the pastors of St. James A.M.E., the Metropolitan Baptist Church, and other Black congregations, helped Father Ed understand how strong religious bonds can be within the Black community. He and the other monks reasoned it might be best to stand aside and let parents and grandparents take care of passing along their religion. But then, just as it had been a Black parent who embarrassed them into restoring the word "prep" to the school's name, an African American priest set them straight about religion.

That priest was Father Joseph A. Francis, the man whose name is on the building where Father Ed teaches his faith class. In 1976, Pope Paul VI elevated then Father Francis to the post of auxiliary bishop of the Archdiocese of Newark, the first African American bishop in the Northeastern United States. Given St. Benedict's mission in the city, and its physical closeness to the seat of the archdiocese in Newark, Bishop Francis took a keen interest in the school. When he found out that the monks had removed religion from the curriculum, he challenged them, asking what message it sends the Newark community if this school, run by monks, on the grounds of a Benedictine abbey, doesn't teach religion. "You'll share soup with us, you'll share bread with us, but you won't share the faith with us? What do you think we think when you do that?" Father Ed remembered him asking.

Stung by the bishop's remark, the monks made room for religion in the curriculum. They experimented with World Religions–type classes that included the study of the spiritual as well as cultural beliefs of other faiths. But as the mix of students at the school has grown increasingly diverse—many Black students are Protestants, some Latinos belong to evangelical or Primitive Pentecostal churches, and international students bring in their Hinduism, Buddhism, and Sikhism—finding common ground has become more difficult. Father Ed decided to avoid religion altogether and focus instead on faith, a theme he brings up whether he's speaking to students, alumni, or trustees.

Teaching religion, he told me, is a waste of time. "You start to talk about religion with people, and you get in all these fights and arguments, and that's what we're killing each other over. You rarely find people wanting to fight over faith." To him, it's only belief in the mystery of the divine, whatever name is given to it, that is important, even to the fourteen-year-olds in his class.

* * *

Opening yourself to the divine might seem a remote message to teenagers today, but it was foundational for a scrappy kid from suburban New Jersey who, from the time he was five, was enraptured by his Catholic faith and the mysteries of the priesthood. Father Ed grew up in a newly built split-level house in Woodbridge, New Jersey, one of the sprawling, mostly white, suburban communities spread out along the Garden State Parkway that runs north-south through the state. Before he took the name Edwin, for one of the monks he admired at St. Benedict's, he was Dennis Leahy, or Dee-Lay, as he was known to his classmates on High Street, a baby boomer with an Irishman's temper matched by a passion for high jinks.

He learned how to live a life of moral grace from his father, Bill Leahy, a loyal member of Operating Engineers Local 835, and a guy with a faith as strong as his heart was big. "My father was a collector, right?" Father Ed recounted. "My mother could tell my father, 'Bill, we need a loaf of bread.' He'd go get a loaf of bread. He'd come back with six guys. He met this one, met this friend, met another friend, like that."

Priests often were among those he brought back home. "There were priests in our house all the time, so I grew up with that." His father's religious devotion mystified him because he didn't know its source, but he never had any doubt about its strength. He saw his father on his knees praying every morning and every night. He attended mass regularly, and went to confession most Saturday nights, making sure he was the last one to enter the confessional. "This is before it was face-to-face and any of that kind of stuff. The priest would tell him, 'Bill, I'll be up in fifteen minutes,'" and they'd leave together for another dinner at the Leahy house.

Dennis attended the local parochial school, St. James, and then, as was expected of many Catholics at the time, he planned to go on to a Catholic high school. In the eighth grade, he took entrance exams for three of them: St. Peter's Prep in Jersey City, a well-regarded all-boys school run by Jesuits; St. Mary's in South Amboy, a coed school linked to the Sisters of Mercy; and St. Benedict's, which his father was familiar with because a neighbor's kid had starred on their football team in the 1930s.

What happened after he took those tests is another chapter of St. Benedict's lore, one Father Ed likes telling because it emphasizes the role of fate, as well as what he calls the will of the divine, in determining the direction of individual lives. St. Mary's accepted him based on his test scores and his grades. But St. Peter's did not, and he did so poorly on the mathematics section of St. Benedict's admission test that the monks also turned him down. "I think about this all the time," he told me. He was already admitted to St. Mary's, but his father went to the pastor of their parish and asked him to intercede with the monks in Newark on his son's behalf.

The letter that pastor, Msgr. Charles McCorristin, sent to the monks is preserved in St. Benedict's archives, one of those unassuming documents that end up changing everything that follows.

Dear Father Abbot,

At the recent examination for admission to St. Benedict's High School, five boys from St. James School took the test. Three passed and two failed.

Among the two who failed was Dennis Leahy, of Columbus Ave., Woodbridge. Why he failed seems to be just one of those things that is hard to explain. For the last two years he has been on the "Honor Roll" of the school, and I was very much interested in having him make St. Benedict's. The reason: I think the boy has a vocation. His parents are very anxious to give him all they can in the way of an education, willing to make the necessary sacrifices. He has an uncle a priest, and the rest of the family is of the highest character.

I wonder if you could do something for this boy and thus help to foster another vocation? The family and myself would be very grateful to you if you would.

Mr. Leahy's strategy worked. The abbot in Newark reversed the decision and soon Dee-Lay boarded the train in Woodbridge and got off less than an hour later in Newark. The way he remembers his first days at St. Benedict's—it's another vignette he often repeats—he walked down the main hallway and stood outside Room 12, where the realization came to him clear and strong that this old place with creaking floors and well-worn desks, with a black-robed monk standing at the head of the classroom full of boys like him, just steps up from one of the busiest streets in the heart of downtown Newark, this place that had rejected him but then had changed course and allowed him in, this was home. For him, the story is another example of the importance of being aware that the extraordinary can surface in an ordinary moment.

The prep school that Dennis Leahy entered in 1959 reliably turned out a stream of priestly recruits, boys like him who were enthralled by the life of community and service they witnessed up close. But he first had to survive the rigors of what was known then as a working man's prep school, juggling the time spent on books with the hours he devoted to playing sports and goofing off. He admits that he was a mediocre student and an athlete with more heart than skill. And even then, he was a hothead. Once, when playing doubles tennis, he got so angry at a missed shot that he smashed his wooden racket on a net post, venting his frustration but also forfeiting the match because he was left with nothing but splinters to play with. Incidents like that were early signs of the temper that erupted years later when he was an ordained priest and the school he'd adopted as his home practically on first sight was closed for reasons he detested.

His uneven academic record at the prep probably contributes to his unwillingness now to expel underperforming students. Faculty sometimes disagree vehemently with his decisions to keep students who have been disruptive in class, even some who have physically threatened teachers. Father Ed turns the tables and asks them if they are just trying to get rid of the kid and his emotional baggage so they can restore order. He is reluctant to ask any student to leave, but he's especially patient with freshmen because he's seen so many of them eventually turn things around, just the way Rey did. He pushes to keep them at least until they get to hike the Appalachian Trail at the end of their first year because that's the real test of whether, beneath the surliness and disobedience, despite the sullen anger and pent-up rebellion, they belong at St. Benedict's. He's seen stone-cold students who were emotionally dead come back to life. But even he acknowledged that sometimes students are so troubled that St. Benedict's can't help them. He never makes that decision by himself. He checks with faculty, counselors, coaches, and even other students, anyone who may have some insight that escaped him. When all else falls short, he turns again to *The Rule of St. Benedict*. In Chapter 28, Benedict advises that the last resort should always be prayer.

* * *

Father Ed came from a mostly white, suburban neighborhood, like nearly everyone else who attended St. Benedict's when he and Father Philip did. Both told me their awareness of racial inequality began at St. Bernard's, the Benedictine college and abbey in Cullman, Alabama, where they were sent for study. Although brief, their time in the Deep South provided the insight that kept them so invested in Newark when others in their monastic community were giving up on the city and its people. Like Newark Abbey, St. Bernard's was founded in the nineteenth century to serve what then was a substantial population of German Catholic immigrants. By the time Edwin and Philip arrived in the early 1960s, Cullman had gained the notorious reputation of being one of the "sundown towns" of the South, all-white enclaves where Black Americans were openly warned not to be caught on the streets after sunset.

The young monks saw that warning displayed on a billboard the day they arrived in Cullman, and they never forgot it. Nor could they ever blot out the sight of the segregated water fountains and lunch counters that were accepted without question for the whole time they were there. As children of the '60s, they couldn't shake the injustice they witnessed in the South. Nor, when they left that city where Blacks were banned, and returned to Newark with its majority Black population, could they ignore the true meaning of what they saw at home. It was just three months after the riots, and the streets around the monastery were still littered with debris, the nearby housing projects still seething with pent-up anger.

To this day, Father Ed openly criticizes the monks who left Newark because they wouldn't instruct Black students. But he also reserves some criticism for himself. Despite his sensitivity to the slightest hints of prejudice and racism, he'd gone along with the plan to intentionally drop the word "preparatory" from the name of the updated version of St. Benedict's, and all that such a change implied about the abilities of the students who had enrolled.

"I always ask myself why." When he told me this, it was clear that he was still wrestling with the implications of that word deletion fifty years ago. "I have this prevailing thought that if you're white and you were born in the United States, racism is a problem for you. You can recover, but the first step in recovery is admitting you've got a problem."

* * *

Father Ed let his faith class drift that November morning. One girl asked him who was the most offbeat student he'd ever taught, and that got him to reminiscing about one memorable troublemaker who'd turned a spray can into a flamethrower, and later handcuffed himself to a staircase. Then, as suddenly as he'd veered off into those distant memories, he declared that it was time to break for meditation. "Back straight. Feet flat on the floor," he instructed. Sheridan immediately assumed the position, but when a girl in the middle row slouched over her desk, Father Ed snapped at her: "You've got to do better than that." He told the girls to close their eyes and let everything else go. "Imagine a boat going down the river. Don't follow it. Acknowledge it as it goes by, then let it go."

The girls' shoes gradually stopped shuffling. Water bottles were put down. "Stop yapping," he grunted. At last, the room fell silent. But some of the girls wouldn't or couldn't keep their eyes closed for very long, and he let it go. They've told him that closing their eyes makes them feel vulnerable, and doing that voluntarily goes against all they know.

After a few minutes he asked, "What time do we finish?" He's told me several times that he did away with bells to signal the end of class because hearing them ring throughout the day is "like living in a pinball machine." Besides, he said, there's no need. Students won't ever let a class go long. One girl responded, "12:05." Minutes more to go. "Way too long," he groused.

At exactly 12:05, the girls started to shuffle out, and he asked two of them to stay behind. He admonished one for talking out loud and being disrespectful during the class. Then he called over the other. "I could tell from your face that something's going on." He knew that the girls' parents had split up. Where's dad, he asked. She didn't know. When was the last time you spoke to him? She didn't remember. He told her he recognized the depression she was feeling. When his father died in 1980, family and friends expected him to help them understand how to grieve. "It's a double jeopardy for those of us who dress the way we do because they think we have all the answers, relative to this life, the next life, everything." He managed to preach at his father's funeral, but he was so busy running the school that he never adequately processed the loss. The trauma resurfaced in 1982, and hit him hard. He took refuge in his room in the monastery, wrapped in a blanket like someone who was just waiting to die. He was thirty-seven. The only way he got better was by talking to somebody he trusted. For him that was a fellow monk. "So, talk to somebody," he urged the girl. "You can't talk too much. You deserve to be your best self."

The rest of the class had left by then. In the hallway, one of the girls who'd waited for him sidled up and asked for a dollar to buy an extra order of mozzarella sticks at the school's lunch line, using the same tone she might have used to wheedle an allowance from her grandfather. Although he can be overbearing when he's angry or frustrated, Father Ed remains approachable, especially to the girls. He squinted at her with an *Are you kidding me?* face. "They only give you five," she whined. He shook his head, then reached into his pocket and gave her a dollar bill.

* * *

With so many different religions represented at St. Benedict's, Father Ed has worked diligently over many years to forge alliances with other faiths. There is a constant interchange of students with the Joseph Kushner Hebrew Academy in Livingston, about fifteen miles from Newark, and the Noor-Ul-Iman School, in central New Jersey. He's created relationships with communities in Israel, Lebanon, the Netherlands, Bolivia, and Mongolia. He has hired openly gay teachers, and looked the other way when students and staff have disregarded Catholic orthodoxy on contraception and sexuality.

Just as the walls around the abbey are meant to set off what happens there as special, he says the continued presence of the school in

Newark's core after all that's happened there is a sign of the faith that he is attempting to convey. Every day it is a place of joining together individuals from the youngest student to the oldest monk, from the closest neighbor to those who come from India and Africa, those who worship Christ alongside those devoted to Allah, Yahweh, and the Buddha, all without the strife that has afflicted so much of the world for so long, all learning from and teaching each other.

"I wanted Newark to teach us. In order to do that, you have to listen," he told me. "You have to have a listening heart. The first word in *The Rule of St. Benedict* is 'listen,' right? With the ear of your heart."

CHAPTER 11

Brotherhood

AT THE END of a joint convo on a Tuesday morning in mid-November, Rey sauntered over to the podium to call for a round of applause for Father Ed on the anniversary of his being named headmaster in 1972. The priest surveyed the big gym, casting an eye over staff and students, especially those in the Gray section, and without cracking a smile threatened to throw out anyone who hadn't clapped for him. It was a typical Father Ed performance, an unrehearsed mixture of unabashed grandstanding and sincere gratitude. When he took back the microphone from Rey, he downplayed his milestone, telling the kids that nobody sets out to do something for fifty-one years. "Just a tip," he said. "Anything that you do, you do one day at a time." And you do it, he went on, with whatever talents you have, and with all of who you are, all of your history, however good or bad it might be. "Then let somebody else add it up."

Hundreds of kids listened to the headmaster's message, but few may have needed to hear those words more than Tareek, a third-year student from Newark with a track star's physique and an orphan's outlook on the world. When convo had started that morning he hadn't been anywhere near his own section—Gray. And he wasn't wandering the perimeter of the gym as he had developed a habit of doing. In his black hoodie, black slacks, and a pair of black suede shoes with silver buckles, he was standing awkwardly in the middle of the big gym looking lost and more than a bit scared. It was his turn to read the Gospel and it was a big test for him, combining two of the things he feared most: speaking in front of a large group and reading out loud.

From the time Tareek was in elementary school, he's struggled with printed words. He once was so fearful that his teacher would call on him to read out loud that he tore the pages from his book. Even now, he'd rather run a hundred laps backward in flip-flops than utter a single word in front of a classroom, let alone as large a crowd as a joint convo. He was still poring over a printout of the Gospel passage and studying it more thoroughly than he usually did his schoolwork when he was handed the microphone and told to begin.

"A reading from the holy Gospel according to Luke." He read with his head down, the microphone in his right hand close to his lips, the quiver in his voice revealing his reluctance to be there as well as his determination to get through his performance. The lines Tareek read were a condensed version of the story of the servants who, after they had finished a full day of tending the fields, were expected to serve their master dinner before eating anything themselves. It's a confusing passage, leaving it unclear whether the master is to be condemned or supported for demanding the servants perform their duties, and whether the servants should be satisfied to fulfill their obligations to serve without begrudging their master, or indignant because of the inferior status he kept them in. Tareek stumbled over a few words, got back on track, and finished without ever looking up. Most students in the boys division read with the same monotone, their voices dialed down low, their pace turned up too fast. The readings get assigned on a rotating schedule from group to group, and it was a coincidence that the passage that Tareek was assigned to read dealt with obedience and expectations, because what he expected of the school and what the school expected of him were threatening to ruin his time at St. Benedict's.

Tareek was one of the first students I met at St. Benedict's, and as I learned his backstory, and that of his younger brother Jokari, who was a year behind him, I was dumbstruck by how life had already kicked his ass from one end of Newark to the other. Same for his brother. I didn't expect to encounter so much hurt in anyone so young. Their early life was pockmarked by abuse, neglect, and indifference, a disconcerting saga that, even in the context of the misfortunes and adversity other Benedict's students face, seemed spectacularly cruel.

For long stretches of time when Tareek and Jokari were very young, their mother, Adlaide, was in and out of drug rehab, and while she was recovering her sons were shuttled off to live with their father, James, even though he was often unemployed and struggling with his own demon, alcohol. He brought the boys with him as he moved from place to place, depending on where he could get government housing subsidies, until his money and his luck ran out. As he sank deeper into drink, the state's Division of Child Protection and Permanency stepped in, placing the children in a series of foster homes in central New Jersey.

The cycle would begin anew when Adlaide left rehab. She regained custody of the boys and brought them to live with her in a cramped apartment in one of the rundown wooden-frame houses on South 18th Street in Newark's Clinton Hill neighborhood. She managed to make a home as best she knew how, finding bunk beds and a big-screen TV, and subscribing, for a time, to cable. They even adopted their own pet pit bulls, Honey and Lady. The kitchen on South 18th Street had what the brothers called a "coil stove," a battered electric range where they learned to cook simple things like pasta and hot dogs when their mom, who slipped into and out of using drugs, said she was too tired to make dinner for them.

"I will forever love my mom. I know a lot of the things that she did for me and my brother, and I will forever be grateful for her," Tareek told me one afternoon at school, his husky voice dialed down to just above a whisper. "The drug abuse was the part that I didn't like. She was always tired. Most of the time she slept. So, a lot of it felt like me and my brother were just kind of taking care of ourselves."

Both boys had missed a lot of school time as they were yanked from one foster home to another. When their mom enrolled them at the local Avon Avenue elementary school in Newark's South Ward, Jokari scored high on state proficiency tests, while Tareek was reading at a pre-K level and could only write simple sentences using what is known in the classroom as "creative spelling." Newark public schools then weren't equipped to do sophisticated physical or emotional testing, so his teachers could only guess that he was struggling with dyslexia and attention deficit disorder, compounded by years of neglect and the long-term impact of the traces of drugs in his mother's system when he was born. As he fell further behind, Tareek became more restless and withdrawn. And despite Jokari's better-than-average performance on tests, his biggest problem continued to be controlling his emotions. He could be as headstrong as he was cooperative, as rebellious as he was sincere.

State officials and outside consultants then were running Newark's public schools and pouring money and support into charter schools, which drew students and funds away from the district. More than a third of the city's students switched over to charters, with thousands more on waiting lists. To compete, district schools were encouraged to innovate, and Avon was considered one of the most successful. It was led by Charity Haygood, a young Black principal who had arrived in Newark in the mid-1990s as an enthusiastic and supremely optimistic Teach for America volunteer. She lavished personal care on the youths in her classroom, and as she moved on to administration, she continued to be involved in the personal lives of her mostly poor, mostly Black, students. In the neighborhood, she came to be known as the "visiting principal" who showed up at students' homes, sometimes to congratulate them with a balloon for a good grade, and empty-handed at other times to find out why they had failed another test.

After her staff flagged Tareek's learning difficulties, Charity took a

personal interest, bringing him to her office after school to play chess
and write simple letters. She kept an eye on Jokari too. He wasn't having nearly as much trouble with academics, but he sometimes became
moody and disobedient. When their mother relapsed into drugs, she
left the brothers unsupervised for long hours of the day and night. They
spent much of that summer in the streets, playing a chase game they
called "manhunt" until midnight or later, and sometimes smoking marijuana, even though neither was yet ten. They gravitated to an offbeat
neighborhood entrepreneur who paid them to sell fireworks and T-
shirts that he stored in the trunk of his car. He had designed the shirts
himself with the saying "The future is the future; the past is the past. You
are who you are because you choose your own path." With the money
he paid them, they bought food for Honey and Lady, and provisioned
the house when their mother hadn't bought anything for them to eat.

When things deteriorated further in the South 18th Street apartment, the boys went back to their father, who brought them to the
Hotel Riviera in downtown Newark, a notorious welfare hotel with
a lingering reputation for drugs and violence. The convenience store
in the lobby provided the snacks they had for dinner. He promised to
take them to Disney World when things got better. He described in
fabricated detail a house he was building for them in North Carolina.
The boys learned that promises are easier to make than to keep. An
uncle helped out by taking them in, but when their father resurfaced
with more promises they'd go back with him. When Tareek described
this period of his life, he used one of the longest sentences I ever heard
him speak, evidence of how interminable his childhood wandering must
have seemed to him. "We were with our uncle," he related one afternoon, "then my mom, then my uncle, then my mom, then my dad, my
dad, mom, dad, mom, then back to my uncle, then back to my mom,
mom, dad, mom, dad. And then . . ."

Tareek liked drawing and art, but printed words were like renegades
to him. Jokari kept his grades up, but his free-range attitude kept getting

him into trouble. Charity grew increasingly concerned. She arranged to get a tablet for Tareek so he could practice reading at home, and met with his mother to explain how he was to use it to do his homework. But she found out that he was using the tablet to play games. He kept falling further behind, and Jokari's behavior grew more disruptive.

As a teacher and principal in Newark for years, Charity had seen the signs of neglect many times before, and she had learned that nothing she or her staff could do at Avon would be successful if the boys' home life was perpetually unstable. The only way to know for certain, and to try to have some influence, was to see for herself. After school one day she visited the South 18th Street apartment. The rooms were dark because burned out light bulbs had not been replaced. There was mold in the bathroom and boxes everywhere as if they had just moved in, or were getting ready to move out. Although she'd seen worse conditions, there was no mistaking the signs that the boys weren't being properly cared for.

The chaotic situation came to a head one afternoon when the boys' uncle showed up at Avon and told Charity he was convinced that his sister, Adlaide, and his brother-in-law, James, couldn't properly care for their sons. He had his own challenges at home and couldn't do much more for them except call child services, which would likely place Tareek and Jokari back in foster care. Charity had them brought to her office. The brothers pleaded with their uncle not to call the state, insisting that they'd rather stay with their dad in the welfare hotel than be fostered again because "at least when we're with Dad we get to eat every day."

Seeing the anguish that the possibility of separation triggered, Charity told their uncle to go ahead and call child services, but since it was already late, she offered to bring the boys to her home in Newark for the night to ease the transition. It was a familiar undertaking for Charity and her husband, Ryan. Over the years they'd opened their Newark home to numbers of children.

That was in October 2017. Charity and Ryan thought they might be able to "stand in the gap" for a while, but that gap kept being extended.

With a safe place to sleep, ample food, and clean clothes, the boys' attitudes quickly improved, and so did their grades. It couldn't have been fun for them to live in a house where they weren't allowed out at night, and where the adults knew they were fibbing if they said they had no homework, but they got used to it. Charity continued to get reports about the boys' parents from their uncle, and she revisited the Clinton Hill apartment, which convinced her they shouldn't be sent back home. Then one day in early April 2018, a student from their old neighborhood rushed up to the brothers at the Avon school to tell them that he'd heard their mother had been shot.

While the boys were living with the Haygoods, a lovers' triangle gone bad had turned the squalid apartment on South 18th Street into a crime scene. One of their mother's old boyfriends, who was known in the neighborhood as Rah-Rah, had suddenly resurfaced. The thirty-one-year-old with dreadlocks and a dollar sign tattooed on his forehead was waiting to be sentenced on felony counts of theft, burglary, and making murderous threats stemming from a 2017 arrest. No one expected him to show up on South 18th Street but he did, and he found Adlaide in bed with a man who had been his friend since they were kids. According to the police report, Rah-Rah pulled out a silver-plated pistol and fired it three times. The first bullet hit Adlaide and passed through her right breast. The other two hit his old friend, once in the leg and the other in his lower back, shattering his spinal cord and leaving him permanently paralyzed. Police arrested Rah-Rah the next day and charged him with attempted murder. A jury convicted him of aggravated assault and possession of a handgun. He received the maximum sentence of twenty years in prison.[1]

Although the brothers hadn't witnessed the shooting, they were haunted by what happened, and how much worse it might have been. They don't like to talk about it, and when I asked them to tell me how they felt, both acknowledged that they try to block it from their minds. "One day, I think it might have been after school or something, it's really a vague memory to me, but I just remember hearing about it," Jokari told me, referring to the shooting. "I don't know if I was in a panic, but I didn't know if he was, like, coming for us next or something like that. And then I just wanted to know if she was okay or if she was going to die."

Adlaide recovered and entered another drug rehab program in New York City.

Charity and Ryan, a civil rights attorney who is director of the New Jersey Institute for Social Justice, a nonprofit in Newark that works on issues of equity and fairness, have kept the brothers with them since that first night in 2017. They have offered to legally adopt both of them, but while Tareek was eager for that to happen, Jokari was unwilling to permanently break the bonds with his biological parents, despite all that'd happened. Instead of adoption, the Haygoods have become what is known as kinship legal guardians. The brothers settled into the Haygoods' pleasant single-family home in Newark's Weequahic section, the formerly Jewish neighborhood immortalized by Newark-born novelist Philip Roth. The tree-lined streets and tidy single-family homes are a few blocks from where the brothers once sold T-shirts and fireworks. They stayed in touch with Adlaide. She even attended birthday parties and other family events. They said they hold no grudge against her, and genuinely love her. However, when their father tries to call, they don't always answer the phone.

As an inner-city principal, Charity understood how precarious the boys' situation was. Jokari was in danger of not realizing his obvious potential, while Tareek was at risk of never catching up. She and Ryan decided it would be best to keep Tareek at Avon, where she could stay on top of his progress. But Jokari was angry, obstinate, and disrespectful to his teachers, which put Charity in the uncomfortable position of being seen as disciplining him differently than other students. The Haygoods enrolled him in the prestigious Newark Boys Chorus School, where he was doing well until the pandemic forced the tuition-free school to close. When the Haygoods searched for an alternative, several of Ryan's colleagues recommended St. Benedict's. Although Charity had been a public school principal in Newark for a dozen years, she knew almost nothing about St. Benedict's except that it was a private school for kids who were not like the kids at Avon. She disapproved of the privileges she believed private schools and charters enjoyed over district schools. But then Ryan came back to her with what he had heard about Benedict's, especially the dedication of Father Ed and the deeply respected traditions the school embodies. St. Benedict's seemed to him to be a miniature version of Morehouse College, a historically Black liberal arts college in Atlanta that their older son Charles had attended.

"What attracted me to it was his whole focus, the school's focus, on it being student-run," Ryan recalled. That was music to his ears. "America can be a very cold place for Black people, especially Black men, and I want them to be ready for it. I like the philosophy of getting that started early because, although I'm not an educator, I've seen over the years with my wife's experience, that if the kid's not ready by the time he graduates from high school, then he loses a lot of years in adulthood just wandering."

Despite Charity's initial misgivings about private schools, they enrolled Jokari in St. Benedict's middle division to complete seventh and eighth grades. Unlike the Boys Chorus School, St. Benedict's was not free. And the Haygoods didn't qualify for financial aid. Jokari learned the school's traditions and legends, and he joined the school's Boy Scout troop. He managed it all well, although he bristled at taking orders from students who were barely older than he was.

Living with the Haygoods and following their restrictions and expectations helped Tareek prosper at Avon. He graduated from the eighth grade as the Avon school's valedictorian. But the Haygoods knew he'd face enormous academic challenges once he left the protective bubble of Charity's school. Tareek told them he had his heart set on going to Newark's Arts High School, across William Street from St. Benedict's, where he could focus on his love of drawing. They knew that the rigorous schedule and academic standards of St. Benedict's would challenge him, but their sense of fairness overruled everything else. "You can't make a king out of one son and a pauper of another," is how Charity put it. "So, if Jokari got the opportunity" to attend St. Benedict's, "Tareek deserved it also."

In this, his third year at St. Benedict's, Tareek was determined to break his own pattern of starting off strong and then letting things slide until he falls so far behind it's impossible to catch up. He was in good form through summer term and into fall. His best grade was an A- in creative writing and media. His biggest challenge was English III, where the heaviest lifting was reading and interpreting full-length books. One was Toni Morrison's *Song of Solomon*. "That book is tough," Tareek said, tilting his head away from me. He tends to avoid eye contact when he's speaking, preferring a kind of sideways glance, as if he were talking to someone standing just over my shoulder. He told me he found Morrison's classic work to be "a huge puzzle," that threw him for a loop when the teacher tested him on it. The other book in the syllabus was Margaret Atwood's *The Handmaid's Tale*. "Hard to read," he stated firmly, but this time with a sly half smile suggesting he might have gotten a little too comfortable, despite his promise to self, and hadn't read as much of the novel as he was supposed to.

He managed to not fail any class, not even Chemistry, where he struggled. Dr. Lansang, the former pediatrician turned chemistry teacher who also doubles as piano-playing cheerleader, tried to bring some of that same excitement to the chemistry lab where Tareek and two dozen others sat for an hour or more of first period science every morning. He kept Tareek seated at a desk alongside his own to limit his wandering. Lansang is a whiz with the digital whiteboard at the front of the lab. The formulas he tried to get across were far from simple, but with detailed explanations and repetition he managed to convey some understanding of the subject to his students. Tareek considered Chemistry his best class. "I don't have the best grade in there," he conceded, "but I enjoy going to that class the most." More than likely, it was Lansang's tender approach, his continuous encouragement, his elastic patience, and his positive, nonjudgmental attitude, and not the drill on molar mass that took up most of a November class I attended, that kept Tareek firmly in his seat.

That day was turning out to be a particularly good one for Tareek. He'd read the Gospel at convo without mishap, stood at the center of attention for the whole school to see, and here he was on top of the material in chem lab. When Dr. Lansang introduced the concept of hydrates and the process of removing water from them, he asked the class to consider how a clothes dryer works. What in a dryer removes the water? It was just nine a.m. and despite the singing at convocation, many of his classmates seemed ready to go back to sleep. But Tareek was all-in. "Heat," he volunteered. Lansang gave him a thumbs-up.

Not all school days turned out so well for Tareek. Sometimes he joked around so much during convo that Dean Rodriguez sent him to the Trophy Room to see Father Ed, and he ended up being sent to detention. Even when he wasn't getting into hot water, he somehow still found himself on the wrong side of St. Benedict's rules. He runs cross country in the fall, sprints and high jump in winter and spring. In early December, as the winter track season was getting underway, Tareek tried to promote a fundraiser for the track team. He fired off an email to the entire school that included a link to a crowd-sourcing page run by an outside fundraising company, and politely asked everyone to donate. The Haygoods were already on the list of supporters, as was Jared Boone, the history teacher Tareek admired. He wrote next to his pledge "Good job taking the initiative on this effort."

But within ten minutes of hitting send, Tareek's initiative was slammed shut, with a stern message from the administration that fundraisers administered by outsiders cannot be circulated inside St. Benedict's. He took the setback in stride, quietly absorbing the disappointment, and keeping his eyes on the upcoming track season.

Tareek endured all of the school's academic, physical, and emotional trials. He shed his sullen game face when he told me that he actually had enjoyed the freshman overnight so much that he wished he could do it again. He'd hiked the Appalachian Trail with gusto, serving as camp specialist for his team. When he was told to do something like preparing a campsite or pitching a tent, he listened carefully to the instructions and fulfilled his responsibilities, like the servants in the Gospel passage he had read at convo. He proudly told me that staff had complimented him for showing leadership on the trail, but when I asked him if he'd ever considered vying for a leadership position, he told me wasn't into that. Neither did he ever think of joining Jokari in Boy Scouts. "I don't like it at all," he admitted.

What he does like is running and jumping, and he's good at it. Track coaches watched him grow bigger, stronger, and swifter, and they expected him to do well in the upcoming season. But while being at St. Benedict's gave him the structure he needed, he rarely felt he was where he belonged. Knowing of his years wandering place to place, it hurt me to hear him say, "I don't really have a group of friends. I eat lunch by myself, sit by myself. I'm often just by myself. That's how you often find me too. I'm walking somewhere. I wouldn't really . . . I don't feel like I belong." I had seen him laughing with friends, so I knew that what he'd told me wasn't entirely true. And yet, the longer I knew him, the more I detected loneliness in his voice, a trace of alienation in many of his words. With brotherhood at the core of what St. Benedict's offers, Tareek's restlessness was a clear sign that something just wasn't working for him. He'd lived through more bad days and hungry nights than any adult would want to endure. He constantly confronted the negative effects of his history, and the trauma he lived through was etched on his broad forehead for all to see. And yet, he was there in the gym with the Gray section almost every day, and whenever I watched him at convo, I saw him singing, swaying, and putting his arm on the shoulder of whoever was at his side.

CHAPTER 12

Unknown Sons

A FEW WEEKS after his good day reading the Gospel at convo and outshining his classmates in Chemistry, Tareek walked into the library at 7:50 on a Monday morning wearing his black hoodie and smiling shyly as he greeted Dr. Lamourt, the school psychologist. Lamourt held out a box of Dunkin munchkins for the two dozen students who'd come to the weekly Alateen group counseling session. Before Tareek grabbed one for himself, he offered the box to several girls who'd straggled in. Rey was there too. Tareek sat in the chair next to Lamourt, who led off the introductions, acknowledging that someone in his family struggles with addiction, then asking the others to explain why they were there. When it was Tareek's turn, in a muffled voice he told the group, "Addiction runs in my family."

Most mornings at St. Benedict's begin with one of these group sessions taking place somewhere on the property. Each focuses on a single, broad and difficult social issue or condition that interferes with the students' ability to learn: depression, anger, grief, conflict resolution, family dysfunction, and the varied forms of addiction. While Alateen mixed boys and girls (at least for a while), most separate the sexes. The counseling staff can recommend that a student attend, as they did with Tareek, but some decide on their own to spend a half hour there, revealing their most intimate concerns, instead of being at convo that morning.

Although Alateen zeroes in on the gamut of issues that addiction causes, Lamourt opens most sessions with the same general question. "Any burning desires?" he asked. It's his way of getting teens to open up by raising whatever is on their mind before getting to the heart of the session. Oscar, a senior from Newark who looked perpetually worried, spoke up right away, revealing a fear that seemed remote to the others, but was all too real for him. He said he was fretting over his relatives in Guyana, where neighboring Venezuela was making warlike threats over territory and seemed poised to invade. "I'm obsessively worrying about it," he told the group. The room was quiet for a few beats, as if no one knew how to respond, before Lamourt jumped in and said, "As opposed to burying those feelings, you need to feel them and confront them. If you're not feeling what's really inside, you go numb," and that can usher in harmful behavior. He told the group that the problem with many teenagers is that they are all too willing to give up their power to control their emotions. Powerlessness, he warned, can lead to resentment. And resentment, if you don't check it, "can ruin your life."

Lamourt had them close their eyes and think about the reason they were attending Alateen. Then he read from an Alcoholics Anonymous text for families and friends of alcoholics. "'Forgiveness is no favor,'" he read, his hand now on Tareek's shoulder. "'We do it for no one but ourselves.'" He told them that forgiveness is a powerful tool whose strength is greater than the anger we feel toward those who let us down. That anger, he said, can feel like power, but in fact the only person you really can get angry with is yourself.

Tareek sat silently through the rest of the session, which lasted for about a half hour before the students had to run off to their first class. As he wrapped up, Lamourt asked everyone to form a circle. Tareek grabbed the psychologist's hand. On Lamourt's other side, Rey did the same. They all then recited the serenity prayer about changing the things that can be changed, and accepting those that cannot. Tareek helped put the chairs back where they belonged before heading to chemistry class.

There are lots of kids at St. Benedict's who, like Tareek, bear the burden of a past they did not create and do not deserve. Some are better at keeping it hidden than Tareek is, but in this post-pandemic, social media–saturated, influencer-directed age, they all have to figure out how to separate what's happened to them from what they intend to do with their lives. St. Benedict's makes sure students feel empowered enough to wrest control of their lives from their past. And though he doesn't always recognize it, even Tareek is surrounded by people who are committed to seeing him thrive. The counseling staff, the faculty, the leaders of the group and section he and Jokari belong to, all keep him on their radar, understanding that at times he simply needs to be allowed to wander, while at other times the best place for him is in the seat right next to the teacher or counselor.

*　*　*

Tareek and Jokari are poles apart in many ways, and they have experienced St. Benedict's quite differently. From the beginning, Tareek struggled to simply get there on time, with his uniform in order. While the responsibilities of taking down assignments, completing them, and then submitting them in the required form have been a constant challenge for him, they haven't fazed his brother, who can be meticulously organized when he wants to be. For Jokari, it's been much more of an issue of style and integrity, particularly when it comes to his relationship with student leaders. Starting with his time in the middle division, he's bristled when other students have told him what to do. He gets especially incensed by the ones who demand strict adherence to rules but then flout them, like those who wear air pods after they've been banned, or talk on cell phones they were supposed to have surrendered.

The way he flares up at discipline is surprising because Jokari is so involved in Boy Scouts that he's had plenty of experience taking and giving orders. As a second-year student, he was already a senior patrol leader of Troop 1973, and he was ready to make his bid for Eagle Scout, the highest rank in scouting, in his junior year. Tareek, on the other hand, could live happily without ever being in the woods again. One's passion is basketball; the other's all about running track. One can talk the ears off a pit bull; the other often is silent as a stone. Just about the only thing they have in common, despite their unfortunate past, is the sartorial compromise they reached when they both chose the same black suede loafers ornamented with a thin silver buckle across the vamp. In addition to looking dapper, the shoes have a smooth bottom that lets them choreograph nimble slides when they walk, projecting street cool or cocky disinterest depending on their mood.

But cool comes with a price, and early one morning in the middle of a long stretch of rainy days, Jokari came down a set of stairs at school and his loafers didn't grip the slippery stair tread. He flopped down several steps, twisting his ankle. The school nurse thought it probably was sprained. She wrapped it, gave him a crutch, and sent him to convo. He hobbled over to the gym, watched over the group of freshman boys he had responsibility for counseling, and made it to his classes on time. That part was easy. What worried him was that his swollen ankle might keep him from practicing with the JV basketball team after classes ended.

Jokari had gone out for basketball as a freshman and made the team. "He's one of those guys that you can count on," Coach Badger remembered, as usual focusing more on his players' character than their performance on the court. He thought of Jokari as a team leader, a young player who responded quickly to his emails and, when necessary, was willing to relay the message to players who weren't as diligent. He considered Jokari to be a consistent ball handler who usually showed up on time, ready to practice. And yet.

"You know, he hasn't invested it all, and I guess it could be a good thing he hasn't invested his life and time in playing basketball because

I could see it on the court last year." Jokari didn't get to start on the freshman team, but Badger made sure he got to play. What he saw was a smart kid who hadn't developed the motor skills to do what he needed to do on the court as instinctively as other players. "Jokari needed to have played more basketball in the parks and playgrounds, freewheeling games where he could have honed his instincts." When it came to making decisions on the court, "it's like his brain and his body are doing two different things," Badger said. "He'd pick the ball up and walk. You can count on it two, three times. And that to me is a disconnect. He's already thinking about what he's going to do before he does it, which is fine, but you have to have the motor skills to match what your brain is telling you to do."

Jokari had to put up with more disappointment on the court this year. Two of Coach Badger's freshmen were starting on the JV team, while Jokari warmed the bench. Still, the attraction of the basketball court was so great that he occasionally slipped into a hoop fantasy: He'd join a top-ranked AAU neighborhood basketball team over the summer, polish the skills that Coach Badger told him to work on, and come back next year to win a spot on varsity.

Jokari didn't miss more than a single practice because of his twisted ankle, and he didn't stop wearing his slick suede shoes. Neither did Tareek.

* * *

The brothers are just one year apart in age and grade, but I rarely saw them together, not at convo or the group counseling get-togethers. Tareek regularly showed up at Alateen, but Jokari never did. However, he was a mainstay at Unknown Sons, which Tareek avoided.

The Unknown Sons group was designed to help adolescent males cope with life in households where a parent is physically or emotionally absent. Dr. Sinclair Davis, a Newark native who wrote his doctoral dissertation on the impact that absent fathers can have on students' ability to learn, runs it. He keeps his sessions low-keyed but laser-focused on getting teenagers to open up and discuss emotional issues that others in the group can relate to. He seats them in a big circle at the back of the library, and encourages them to say sensitive, emotion-packed things to each other, the kinds of things they could never bring up outside the circle. It's a constant struggle to get them to break out of their reticence, and even several months into the school year, I saw him ask a question and be met with nothing but silent stares. When that happened, he'd look to one of the older students to take the lead. Often, that was Jokari.

"He's got a voice in the community," Dr. Davis observed. He believes the other students respect Jokari because of his ability to rise above his anger and speak passionately about his own experiences. "People listen to him because he's not perfect," he said. I couldn't imagine the freewheeling discussions about family dynamics that I witnessed here taking place at a traditional prep school, where perfection is preferred and imperfection shunned. Such candor is especially important for the younger students at Benedict's who need to hear that the difficulties of their own family are not unique.

Dr. Davis kicked off one meeting I attended by asking a provocative question: How do you feel when somebody compares you to your father or to someone else? One student answered right away that he didn't think it was fair to be compared with anyone. Another said it felt good when someone else compared him to his father, but not when his mother did it, because her comments are always negative. Jokari had come in that morning wearing a Gray Bee knit cap, and took a seat on the outer ring of chairs. Everyone turned to look at him when he said that he hated the "comparison thing" because it always implied that the people he's being compared to "are better than me." He understands that such comparisons are meant to motivate him to do better, but for him, it just doesn't work. "When they ask me why am I not like so-and-so, I want to tell them it's because I'm not that person."

Jokari has shared his past life so openly in these sessions that everyone was aware of the dark aspects of his history. They empathized with him when he revealed that even at times when there wasn't enough money in his house to buy food or keep the lights on, "I didn't compare my mom to anyone else."

"And what about your pops?" Davis pressed him.

His father was not unknown, but there was no mistaking the depth of Jokari's feelings. "I was always bitter toward him. I look at other people who had fathers in their lives and couldn't understand why mine was the way he was."

Davis's goal is to get the students to a place where instead of simply blaming their parents—those who are present and the ones who are missing—they take responsibility for their own actions. "If you've jammed yourself up, you've just got to own it," he tells them. You've got to talk through the issues that bother you, not just get angry and bottle it up. He asked Jokari if he'd ever talked to his biological father about his lingering resentment. When Jokari replied that he had, a classmate who'd probably confronted a similar situation in his own life was eager to know how he did it.

"I just called him and said we need to have an adult conversation. I told him to just let me get everything out before you respond. And he said okay." The other students looked incredulous. I could never do that, more than one boy whined out loud. Dr. Davis quieted them down and encouraged Jokari to continue.

"For me, it's mostly just saying what I have to say and not filtering it or making it sweet," Jokari said, looking around the circle. All eyes were on him. The turmoil in their lives had led each one of them there that morning, but at that moment Jokari, although not the oldest student in the group, seemed the one who had most been tested by life, and had survived with his dignity intact. "We're not the ten-year-olds we used to be."

CHAPTER 13

Your History Is Not a Mistake

AS THEY NEARED the end-of-the-year holidays, everyone had settled into a rigid routine of convo, class, lunch, group, sports, and home—and they were exhausted. The cumulative weight of the six intense months of unceasing demand for discipline, achievement, and just showing up and being counted, weighed down the kids so much that at convo, Dr. Lansang let the Jersey Club go long, hoping to drive out some of the negative energy. Several upper division kids popped and bounced for a long stretch, and the dancing did the job, maybe too well, firing up the gym so much that when Rey put up his hand, the chattering rolled on. That brought forth fury from Father Ed.

"When the hand goes up, you need to shut your mouth, period." He was talking to the whole school, but faced, as usual, the Gray section, where Tareek and Jokari were seated in the middle rows. It wasn't just the noise that bothered him. He's forever haunted by the specter of losing what he and so many others had built here, keenly aware of how delicate it all remains, even after a half century of existence, most of it by all accounts a remarkable success. The kids think St. Benedict's is eternal, but he and the other adults know different.

Convo continued with accolades for Kaleb and the rest of the Latin jazz band that had played to a packed auditorium the night before.

Jokari jumped down from the stands to grab the mic and humble brag that the JV basketball team had whupped Roselle Catholic 82–40. Father Ed congratulated St. Benedict's brand-new girls fencing team, another one of his attempts to tear down stereotypes. The girls had competed in their first-ever match, with fencers in all three weapons— épée, foil, and saber—and he wanted everyone to know about their singular achievement. "The girls have already done something in their beginning that the boys didn't," he said, recalling how when fencing started at St. Benedict's in the mid-1980s, the boys practiced with broomsticks in the cafeteria and only had enough fencers to compete in foil.

There was one other announcement, and it surprised a lot of people, including me. With classes ending, Bobby Hastie, the new math teacher and cross-country coach who had been so enthusiastic about joining St. Benedict's when I interviewed him at the start of the year, was leaving after less than six months on King Boulevard. One of the senior leaders thanked him for all he'd done for the school in the brief time he'd been there, and wished him luck going forward. Rey hugged him and handed him the mic.

Hastie, looking as bashful in the spotlight as any prep student, admitted that although he had not been there very long, the school and its students had impressed him mightily. "Thank you for everything, St. Benedict's."

What made his departure so striking was that the weird initiation he'd gone through with other new teachers initially seemed to have convinced him that St. Benedict's was absolutely the right place for him to be. He finally had a chance to combine his love of running with his passion for teaching, and to do it in a school where he could offer city kids the helping hand they needed. He'd been delighted to take over the cross-country team where he had the chance to coach Tareek and other runners. And he reveled in the free hand he was given to teach Kaleb and the others Algebra any way he wanted.

"I learned all through college about equity in education and how not everyone's on an equal playing field," he told me shortly after his departure was announced. His own background growing up in suburban New Jersey, attending St. Joseph's University—a majority white college in Philadelphia—and teaching in a Philadelphia suburb had so shielded him from the challenges of urban education that what his professors taught him about achievement gaps had seemed purely theoretical.

"And then I go to St. Benedict's and all that theory you talk about in school hits you in the face." He saw it in his Math class, where students who'd come from public elementary schools were unprepared to do basic work. He saw students who'd never learned how to study before arriving at St. Benedict's, and had never been forced to complete homework. And he found that the block schedule that condensed an entire year into one semester of seventy-five-minute classes made it hard for students like Kaleb to accumulate the skills they needed to advance in the subject. Those are the challenges many Benedict's students bring with them when they arrive, and teachers adapt their methods as they learn what the kids need. But it all takes time. On top of his classroom struggles, Hastie had been sorely disappointed with his role as cross-country coach. He was thrilled to be at the school where the Runner of the Year banner with Edward Cheserek's name on it hangs in the gym. But trouble started as soon as he took over as head coach and the school's athletic director made the man he replaced his assistant even though he had more coaching experience than Hastie. Conflicts over who was actually in charge arose almost immediately. The previous coach, who was not on the faculty at St. Benedict's, was let go. Tareek and other runners who were used to training with him were so disappointed that they quit the cross-country team.

But Hastie told me that the biggest factor in his decision to leave St. Benedict's was cultural. He found it difficult to accept the way the school tolerated disruptive students. "Discipline doesn't really get dealt with," he complained. Like so much else at St. Benedict's, its disciplinary rules defy the norm at other schools. Hastie had expected things to be different from the suburban settings he was used to, but he never imagined that what he considered serious classroom misbehavior would be ignored. He described several incidents that had pushed him so far over the line he didn't think he could continue to teach there. In one that disturbed him greatly, a fight broke out in Kaleb's Algebra class, one kid punching another in the face. After Hastie managed to break it up, he called Jesse Alexander, '81, the school's dean of students, who is six feet tall and built like a football lineman.

"One of the kids was like, 'Am I going to be suspended?'" Hastie recalled, "and Jesse said, 'Oh no, you're good. You just need to get that out of your system.'"

Alexander took issue with Hastie's version of what happened. "It was nothing violent," he told me. "Just a bunch of teenagers acting like assholes, and he wasn't used to it." He said he warned the students involved that if it happened again, the outcome would be different, and he had them apologize to Hastie. "Then I asked him, 'Is this good for you,'" he said, referring to Hastie. "I told him, if you don't accept it, we'll change it." He said that Hastie told him he was okay with the way it had been managed, and that's the way it was left.

As a young white teacher from the suburbs in a school filled with Black and Latino youths, Hastie had knowingly entered what for him was foreign territory, and despite his willingness to go along with the peculiar new teacher evaluation, he turned out to not be as flexible, or off-centered, as he'd initially thought. Alexander, who is Black, thought Hastie had overreacted, and that he might have been able to overcome his lack of cultural understanding had he worked there longer.

His students liked Hastie, but they too noticed that he seemed out of sync with some of the school's norms. When I talked to Kaleb about his Algebra class, he said it was obvious that Hastie came from a place far different from St. Benedict's. "I feel like a lot of things we do, if this was a normal school, would not fly." He quoted Father Ed saying that not every student is made for Benedict's, and Kaleb said it applied to adults as well. "Some people are made to be here for just one season."

By the time he gave his farewell at convo, Hastie had already signed a contract to teach in a wealthy suburb in northern New Jersey where just over 1 percent of the students in the district are Black, and close to 35 percent are Latino and Asian. He received an immediate 30 percent pay raise, along with better benefits and a guaranteed pension, for teaching in a privileged community where he knew that the rare fist fight wouldn't be overlooked. Still, he told me that even his fleeting time at St. Benedict's was long enough for him to absorb the school's offbeat character, and that made him feel like he was letting down kids like Kaleb and Tareek.

"I still believe in the mission. I understand why St. Benedict's exists and why people go there and how it's run. It just didn't quite fit for me, and being there didn't make me happy. It's a selfish decision, and that's a hard thing to do in the world of education, to make selfish decisions. But I did."

A few weeks after Hastie left, I asked Father Ed whether he thought his radical teacher candidate screening was effective, given how wrong it was in detecting Hastie's willingness to abide by the school's approach to discipline. The problem, the headmaster told me, was that Hastie, like most adults, wanted to solve things right away, so that any infraction leads immediately to punishment. But that approach doesn't necessarily help kids like those at St. Benedict's who carry around such heavy loads of emotional turmoil. For as long as Benedictine communities have existed, *The Rule* has provided a path to redemption that allows transgressors to earn their way back into the community. With the exception of drugs, gangs, and guns, the headmaster usually leaves the redemption door wide open, and so does everyone else.

The lesson of it all? "If you can't deal with the ugly," Father Ed told me, "then you shouldn't be here."

But because other first-year teachers who went through the same weird initiation as Hastie have proven flexible enough to align with the school's mission, at least so far, the headmaster is not ready to add the quirky vetting process to the list of the worst mistakes he's made over the last fifty years. According to Dr. Cassidy, who is the unofficial keeper of that list, Father Ed has pushed through some frightful hires over the objections of staff, and later regretted them. Then there was the time he accepted a grant to introduce Transcendental Meditation to the school, but students roundly ignored the classes. The worst decisions tend to be the ones Father Ed makes without consulting anyone else. He once organized a special experience for seniors similar to the freshman overnight, planning it on his own without consulting others. About two weeks before graduation, he brought all the seniors as well as a few alumni into the school to talk about life after St. Benedict's. The program ended at about 10:30, and the headmaster, whose monastic schedule gets him up well before dawn, called a lights-out. He had completely misjudged the willingness of the eighteen-year-olds to go to sleep on the kind of schedule they had followed as freshmen. He was the only adult member of the staff present, and after trying for an hour and a half to get the seniors to settle down, he gave up and ordered them all to go home. It was the only time Cassidy can remember when Father Ed was not disappointed that the students he kicked out of the school didn't fight to get back in.

* * *

I can't begin to count the number of times I heard Father Ed tell his boys, "Your history is not a mistake." Everything they lived through, everything they've done, comes together in who they are. And as he has discovered over the last four years, starting a girls division simply multiplied the occasions for him to repeat that admonition.

In early October, a group of second- and third-year girls, all of them members of the volleyball team that Lucia captained, were caught vaping inside the locker room after practice. It was one of Lucia's biggest disappointments as senior group leader because she had made trust one of her signature goals. The girls were her teammates. She was close to them, she trusted them, and she had hoped they trusted her enough to come to her about the vaping incident before the administration found out. They didn't, and that perturbed her. "I was like, 'How dare you do that when I have your back all the time,'" she harangued them. Three of the girls lost the right to wear their colors, while the other three kept their blacks but were temporarily prohibited from participating in volleyball and other activities. Natalia, a second-year student who pulls her hair back tight and lays simple edges on her temples, was one of the girls who received the lighter punishment because she was more of a follower than a leader in the vaping. Nonetheless, when her mother found out that she'd gotten into trouble at school, she threatened to switch her to the local public high school if she ever did anything like that again.

I talked to Natalia about it one day, and in a voice so muted I couldn't tell if she was sorry or embarrassed, she explained that she didn't have a good reason for vaping in school, which she knew was prohibited. It was not an atypical response for any teenager, including those at St. Benedict's. "Honestly, if you see something, you're going to want to do it. I'm from Irvington. I'm pretty sure you know how Irvington is. My brothers, they grew up around gangs and stuff. I don't really have a reason why I did it. I just did it." It might be chalked up to peer pressure, but what she told me pointed to something else, a dizzying challenge to individual character that many students at St. Benedict's confront daily.

Irvington is a densely populated city west of Newark with about 60,000 residents, more than 80 percent of them Black, like Natalia, with about one family in five living in poverty, mostly in rented wood-frame houses and dilapidated apartment buildings. It is a high-crime city with lots of violent gang activity. When her mother threatened to send her to Irvington High School, Natalia knew it represented more than simply a change of schools. She had already discovered that people treated her differently depending on where she was. Not only that, she had started to realize that she often took on a different persona, with a whole different outlook, as she moved from place to place, from home to school and back. Keeping track of her dual identities sometimes left her unsure about who she really is. "When you're around a certain set of people, you start to act like that set of people," she told me. After witnessing how the city had infiltrated her brothers' minds and clouded their futures, she said she hoped for something different. "At Benedict's, I get to be a good person, not really doing things I'm not supposed to be doing. Plus, they give you a lot of chances, and I love that."

St. Benedict's accepts the notion that teenagers are young enough to undo the mistakes they invariably make. Natalia believed that her brush with the school's disciplinary rules wasn't going to hold her back. She refocused her sights on becoming an assistant group leader in another year, and maybe doing something that nobody at St. Benedict's had ever done before, start a cheerleading team. But she knew that following all the rules of St. Benedict's, and living up to the expectations the school puts on students, would continue to be a challenge for her because none of that mattered to her friends in Irvington. Even though she wanted to get away from the environment that had already trapped her brothers, she realized that whether she liked it or not, being from Irvington is part of who she is, and that influences how people see her.

"When I'm here," Natalia told me as we talked at the property, "I realize that some girls look at me as a ghetto girl," with all the prejudices and ignorant assumptions that have been bolted onto poor neighborhoods in poverty-stricken cities like Irvington. But then, she said, when she's back home in Irvington, with her St. Benedict's skirt and black top, carrying her books and not hanging out on the streets, people there see her as a privileged and pampered, a "really prissy" outsider. It's not easy dropping one identity and pulling on the other as though it were a sweatshirt. And sometimes, no matter how hard she tries to keep those two versions of herself separate, the lines blur and one part bleeds into the other with consequences that can threaten her dreams.

* * *

Despite all the efforts at understanding, forgiving, and holding out second and third chances, every year some intractable students push Father Ed's empathy and patience to the limit. There's one final option for them, a last line of defense before the headmaster reluctantly asks them to leave. It's known as the Velvet Rope, after the red velvet barriers that theaters and opera houses use to control crowds. It's a catchy name for a bare-knuckles behavior modification program for recalcitrant teens.

Since 2004, the VR has been the most extreme level of emotional intervention at St. Benedict's. Functioning as the school's intensive care unit, students are directed there when group counseling and individual sessions have failed to straighten out their misbehavior or tame the emotional issues that are interfering with their ability to learn. First-year students who are still getting used to St. Benedict's ways are usually exempt from the Velvet Rope's harsh treatment. It's those who've already been through the overnight and hiked the A.T., who've sat through at least one full year of morning convocations, and who know Father Ed's edicts as well as they know the Reverend Winstead's songs, but still violate the rules, who warrant this extreme level of intervention. Getting referred to the VR starts with a heads-up from a teacher or administrator, a consultation with the counseling office, and finally, a decision by Father Ed, who despite his long-distance fundraising trips, his position as president of the Essex County Vocational-Technical Schools Board, and his priestly duties, insists on being involved in every decision that touches on his students' long-term survival.

The Velvet Rope is a voluntary residential program where students live at the Leahy House dorm for anywhere from six months to the entire academic year, depending on their behavior and their needs. The school covers the cost of their room and board. While they are in the dorm they are separated from the rest of the residents. They do not eat, study, or hang around with the others, and they lose all their phone and TV privileges. They are restricted to the Newark Abbey property at all times, including weekends, and when they are in their rooms, they must keep their doors open.

For students who are referred there, the Velvet Rope is as much self-help as reprimand. They first must sign a contract agreeing to its harsh terms. Some refuse because their parents object to them living away from home. And some don't sign because they believe they can set things right on their own. If they decline admission, they are advised that unless they change the behavior that triggered the offer, they'll be forced to leave the school.

On a night when I stopped by, I found Oscar, the introspective senior from Newark who told the Alateen meeting he was worried about Venezuela invading his family's homeland, sitting behind the Velvet Rope studying a history book, something he said was impossible to do at home. He told me that his mom, an immigrant from Guyana, often drank herself into a stupor that left the entire family in tatters. He had been diagnosed with ADHD, and there were times when he was so stressed out, he simply couldn't focus on anything long enough to understand it. His grades were abysmal, he couldn't get himself to do homework, and despite Lucia and Rey's tough new policy on being late, he couldn't get himself to convo on time. He was in his fourth year at St. Benedict's, but all of his issues had kept him from meeting the criteria for getting his colors. He still wore the same kind of gray hoodie he'd worn as a freshman.

The VR is designed to get to the bottom of what is causing all that harmful behavior. "In the beginning it definitely feels like you're in a prison," is how he described his first few days there. Working with the counselors, Oscar identified the reasons he was failing his classes and worked to alter his behavior. But it wasn't easy for him to change. Every time he forgot his homework, was late for class, or left his backpack in the hallway, he added extra days to his stay. It takes some students longer than others for the lessons to sink in.

For his first thirty days behind the Velvet Rope, Oscar had to report to the study hall in Leahy House after class every day. He was barred from the game room, the pool table, and the television in the communal area, and he didn't get to use his phone at all. Twice-a-week group counseling meetings were mandatory, as were individual sessions when counselors saw the need.

As VR students adjust their behavior to do what's expected, they start to win back privileges. Once Oscar accumulated 30 good days without backsliding, he was allowed to ask in writing for the privilege to close the door to his room. At 45 days, he could watch TV and have visitors. When he reached 60 days in good standing, he could ask to visit home. He'd have to accumulate 120 good days to gain back all of his lost privileges, and then go without a slipup until he accumulated a total of 182 days to request a discharge.

By the time I spoke with him, Oscar had already spent several months in the VR program, and had resigned himself to remaining there through the end of the school year. And that suited him fine. "I realized that all these people are trying to help me and not trying to kick me out of the school." He knew that he still lacked self-discipline, and that some of his worst traits were hardwired in his brain. Unless he changed, he'd only get into more trouble, so he planned to spend a fifth year at St. Benedict's. Besides aiding him academically, he felt the additional year would allow him to continue the counseling that had helped him reassess his relationship with his mother, and better control the things in his life that have been turning him inside out.

And the extra year would give him one last chance to finally earn his colors.

CHAPTER 14

'Twas a Wonderful Life

THERE WAS NO way that Lucia and Rey were going to let the year end without ensuring that one more St. Benedict's tradition that had been upended by COVID was fully restored. In line with a decades-long custom, the day after students had turned in their last assignments and suffered through their final exams, they held their concluding joint convo of the year in the auditorium, followed by a big-screen showing of *It's a Wonderful Life*. When the movie ends, Abbot Augustine, a Christmas card–perfect image of Santa in his red costume and flowing white beard, and surrounded by a troop of elves, customarily would make an appearance. Old-fashioned and hokey, yes, but it had become one of the events that alumni said they treasured most, even though when they were forced to sit through two hours and ten minutes of the hardly black and mostly white sentimentality, they had reacted like they were being tortured.

As the boys and the girls divisions filled the auditorium, recent graduates lined up against the back wall, bolstering the notion that this day becomes more endearing once it is a pleasant memory and not an irritating requirement. In one of the first few rows, Kaleb sat air drumming on his leg. He wore a sparkly red Santa cap, with his group's cell phones packed into a bag he kept on the floor in front of him. Dr.

Lansang took his usual position at the piano, and Rey stood at a podium in front of center stage, alongside an advent wreath.

As he looked out over the entire school settling in, Rey had plenty of reasons to feel proud. He and Lucia had revived school spirit and restored discipline. They had proved the naysayers wrong about their get-tough phone policy and tightened dress code. Students were showing up on time and in uniform, and the absence of cell phones seemed to have restored a degree of academic propriety to most classes. Teachers congratulated them for turning the school around. Even Father Ed was impressed.

A few minutes before eight, a long-haired senior from the boys division who would go on to be the class's valedictorian quietly handed Rey a note. It was from Robert Cygan, the new history teacher who'd been hired just before Father Ed's bottom-of-the-pool vetting process was initiated. Cygan, an attorney, had for many years taught history at La Salle Academy in Manhattan, a Catholic school for boys with some similarities to St. Benedict's. He wasn't present at convo this morning because he was still in Room 91, atop the athletic center. "See me in my room after convo," the note read. It then listed the names of several other students, including a few who were part of Rey's leadership team. They all had taken Cygan's U.S. History II exam the day before. Rey's gut flipped, immediately turning what had been a celebration of a job well done, the joyful cap on a successful first half of the year as senior group leader just months away from heading off to college, into a ready-to-burst catastrophe for himself, for his friends, and maybe for the entire school.

Rey's head was spinning. He didn't want to accept what he rationally knew was the reason behind the note. For a moment he tried to convince himself that the teacher might simply want to know how all of them had come up with similar answers, something he could easily explain away. But he didn't have time to think it through. Convo had to begin at eight o'clock sharp. He put on his game face, raised his right hand, and quieted the hall. Agitated by the note, his heart thumping in his chest, he knew that the only way he could get through the morning would be to continue being as tough and diligent as he'd been all year. So he issued a stern warning. Whether they liked the idea of watching the old movie or not, he lectured the whole school, they had better keep quiet and stay awake because, if he heard horsing around, or saw hoods pulled up over drooping heads, he'd stop the film and start it over, and he meant it. He gave the signal for the movie to begin, and as the rest of the school settled down, he sought the others Cygan had singled out. They all knew why they were being called in, though they were reluctant to admit it. They simply never thought they'd be caught.

Like every exam given at St. Benedict's, Cygan's U.S. History II exam carried boiler plate language on the very first page.

*******BE MINDFUL OF THE ST. BENEDICT'S HONOR CODE REGARDING ACADEMIC IMPROPRIETY!!!! ANY VIOLATION OF SAID CODE WILL RESULT IN A ZERO.*******

The honor code is one of the school's foundational documents, ingrained in everything students learn from the first hours of the freshman overnight through the day they graduate. "Benedict's men and women are persons of integrity," the code begins. "Trust is the virtue by which we build our community; violation of the community's trust is grounds for dismissal."

It is the honor code that keeps locks off all lockers. It is what keeps the property remarkably free of graffiti. Rey had invoked the code in October when he made the rowers apologize to the school for their texts about the soccer team. There's extra emphasis on the code during exam week, and teachers constantly remind students what is expected of them. The code says: "I will not cheat. I will not lie. I will not steal. I will report anyone who does." And yet, for years, there had been a persistent problem with cheating that the school hadn't been able to resolve.

In 2015, the student publication *The Benedict News* published an article on cheating that was as candid as it was disturbing. "There is an honor problem at this school," one unnamed student told the author of the article, stating boldly that cheating is widespread, inattentive teachers who "are not good enough at catching students" are to blame, and students are continually finding ways to get "better and better at cheating."

While the students in the auditorium watched *It's a Wonderful Life* with escalating impatience, Rey and the others nervously crept up to Room 91. When they'd all gathered there, Cygan informed them that one of their classmates had observed them cheating on the two-page exam that was worth 15 percent of their semester grade and, bound by the code of honor, had reported them. Rey and the others immediately denied it. Cygan let it stand, indicating only that he was obligated to kick the issue up to the administration to determine who was telling the truth—the student who came forward, or Rey and the others.

After leaving the classroom, Rey sent the other students back to their seats, while he sought out Dean Alexander. He knew that, as dean of students, Alexander had dealt with many student screwups, but he hoped that, as an alumnus, he'd have a sympathetic ear. Rey found him outside the auditorium and briefed him on what was happening. Alexander listened, then told him what Rey didn't want to hear. He needed to man up, admit that he'd cheated, and take the consequences. Dispirited, Rey then sought out Tuorto, who told him the same thing. As the movie rolled on, he called the others out of the auditorium so they could figure out what to do. Like the students in the 2015 article, some of them believed that the teacher had made cheating so easy, so tempting, that he had practically invited them to cheat. They had believed that Cygan would probably sit behind his desk and read a newspaper the whole time they were taking the test, which is what he did. They had no sophisticated scheme to circumvent the honor code. It was merely a series of peculiar circumstances that let them think they could pull it off without getting caught. Room 91 is so cramped that the last row of desks touches the rear wall, leaving little room for any teacher to circulate. When the heat comes up in winter, the room turns into an oven, making the uniform black hoodies uncomfortably hot. Rey had asked for permission to remove his hoodie and finish the exam in his undershirt. After Cygan agreed, several other students also took off their hoodies. Some put them on the floor alongside their desks. But Rey and his friends kept them bundled on their desktops, effectively screening their workspace from the teacher's gaze, and giving them ample cover for hiding the phones they placed on their desks. Student leaders had exempted themselves from the controversial phone policy they pushed through at the beginning of the school year because they said they needed their phones to communicate last-minute schedule adjustments and handle other duties.

Besides Rey, Brett, the soccer team co-captain and section leader for transfer students, also was accused. So was Rey's good friend Riley, another section leader. Both were "enforcers" that Rey had personally picked to help him carry out his tough-love rehabilitation of the school after COVID. They had used their phones to answer some of the fairly simple questions on the test. In one section, they had to identify a historic figure like President John Adams, and explain the legal precedent of *Marbury v. Madison*. But instead of answering from memory, they Googled Adams's biography. They found a summary of the Marbury case, editing it to comply with Cygan's directive to "be concise but not pithy or perfidious." In another section of the exam, Brett typed the essay question about the novel *1984* into an artificial intelligence program and then copied the computer's response.

Cygan was new to St. Benedict's ways, but he rightly believed that the honor code made it unnecessary for him to even be in the classroom during the exam. "I told them all along that they're just a few months from being college freshmen," he explained, "so I'm going to treat them like college freshmen."

The other students looked to Rey to tell them what to do, and Rey had to peer inside himself for the answer. Lying to the history teacher he barely knew hadn't been difficult. But it had been impossible to withhold the truth from Tuorto or Dean Alexander, who knew him well. And though Dr. Lamourt wasn't on the property that day, Rey knew he could never lie to him about the exam. The Latino psychologist had become like a second father after many one-on-one counseling sessions when they tried to unravel his complicated relationship with his father, and the way that relationship dictated how he viewed all authority. How could he tell Lamourt that, like his father, he'd taken the easy route instead of doing what was right?

"I could have definitely lied my way out of it because when I'm the senior group leader, a lot of people hold my word to be the highest," Rey told me when I asked him to explain what had happened. He sounded like the cocky street kid he had tried so hard to conceal. "But what kind of man do I want to become if I keep falling down a rabbit hole of lying and things like that?" He talked to the others who had been accused and told them he planned to turn himself in, and encouraged them to do the same. At first they balked, insisting they'd be able to sustain their denials. But they were already so spooked that Rey knew they'd eventually break, and that would only make things worse for them all.

After the movie ended, he made the long walk back to the history teacher's room. The others followed.

* * *

When school resumed in the new year, Rey and the others were called before the honor code committee, composed of teachers and students and chaired by Susanne Mueller, dean of college placement and career development. Seated around four tables in the library that they had pulled together, the committee prepared for the uncomfortable task of questioning the cheaters one by one. "This is not an interrogation," Mueller reminded the other members. The students had already owned up to cheating. The committee's principal task was to determine appropriate punishments for them, especially the leaders who so often had lectured their classmates about doing the right thing. They worried with good reason that the leaders' blatant violation of the honor code would have a corrosive effect on the rest of the school if it appeared that they got away with cheating because of their positions. But punishing them so severely that they could no longer lead could plunge the school into chaos.

The students who cheated sat behind closed doors until they were called to the table. Each told a comparable story about concealing their phones behind their hoodies. Each had an excuse for why he hadn't put in the time to study for the exam, which the adults agreed didn't appear to be all that challenging. Most had decent grades going into the final, but they coveted an A to cap their college applications or to win a scholarship. Several said that they had gotten used to using their phones to answer exam questions during remote learning, and they had simply continued, an excuse that gained them little sympathy from the committee.

Char-lotte Searcy, a sharp-tongued English literature teacher in the girls division who'd taught at Benedictine Academy until it closed, bristled at the students' accounts, her disdain for the breach of leadership ethics apparent with every question she asked. "Why would you do this if you were already getting a good grade in this class?" Searcy, who is Black, filled the role of antagonist, speaking to the seniors, most of them Black or Latino, in a tone teetering between skepticism and disparagement. "You would have passed the test even without answering some questions, and passed the class even if you'd failed the exam. But you cheated because you were arrogant and thought you wouldn't get caught. Right?"

She reserved her toughest questions for Rey.

"Did you ever think of the impact that getting caught would have, not just on you but on the school?" Searcy asked.

"No," Rey responded. "In the moment my thinking was very cloudy. I wasn't clear at all, so thinking of everyone else wasn't part of what I was doing." He explained that he already had a solid, though less than stellar, 3.0 GPA, and had done well in several quizzes in the history class. But he wanted to ensure that he got an A or an A- in the class because that would boost his GPA and help his college applications stand out.

"What did you think is the worst that could happen if you did get caught?" she asked.

"Get a zero on the test."

"Did you ever think that you could get expelled?"

He hadn't, and when Searcy asked why, he stared at the table for long seconds, trying to figure out how to answer without making things worse. "In the time I've been here, no one's been expelled like that. That's not what the school does."

"Well, I guarantee you that if you were in college, you'd be called before a committee just like this one," Searcy told him. "They'd listen to all your sob stories and nod their head, uh-huh, uh-huh. Then they'd kick you out and they would not refund any of the tuition you'd paid. Guaranteed."

Rey told the committee that he knew from the beginning that turning himself in was the right thing to do, but he was afraid of the consequences.

"What were you afraid of?" Searcy asked.

He said he had been so immersed in his role as leader that he'd neglected his studies. He was no longer just a kid from North Newark. He had become the young man who ran morning convocation—senior group leader, the ideal St. Benedict's man, a man of honor, of honesty, of integrity. If he confessed that he had transgressed the honor code by cheating, he felt certain he'd lose all that. The leader who had forced the entire school to rewatch the entire first hour of *It's a Wonderful Life*, who had insisted that Everett and the other rowers wear shirts and ties as evidence they no longer belonged to the community, who had endlessly reminded everyone what St. Benedict's expected of them, would be stripped of his title because he was a cheater. Because, just like his father, he had believed the rules didn't apply to him.

"My style as leader has been to be very hard on the community. I expect the highest from everyone. And I failed to live up to my own standards." It sounded like he was using the language of the psychologists he admired to analyze himself. "I don't think that me holding everyone to the highest standard is a problem. It was me holding everyone to the highest standard and not applying it to myself. That's the problem."

"And how did that make you feel?"

"I felt like a fraud."

Just then, Father Ed stalked in, his eyes wide with anger.

"Seven adults," he sputtered. "Exactly what I told people not to do." His eyes darted around the tables as the students stared with something between surprise and fright, while the adults sat slack-jawed. The optics—seven adults aligned against Rey in the hot seat—infuriated the old headmaster. Because the odds are already against these kids, he objected to anybody making them feel outnumbered, no matter what they'd done. "Exactly what I told people not to do," Father Ed repeated. Then he turned and walked out without explaining or excusing himself.

Such outbursts were not uncommon, and more than one teacher told me that Father Ed sometimes admonishes them as if he can't distinguish between students and staff. While some said they simply have gotten used to his manner, Mueller had a different take. "He's a disrupter, and if you know that, you know how to deal with him." A few minutes later, Father Ed stalked back in. "This should never have happened," he sputtered, jaw jutting out, his eyes small behind the black-frame glasses he often wears. "Figure out how it happened and fix it, or I'll name new members" of the committee, the clear inference being, "and fix it myself."

Mindful of Father Ed's position on how the committee ought to proceed, Mueller had invited Rey's good friend Noah, who headed the White section, and other students to the meeting to balance the number of students and staff. But by the time the headmaster popped in, a few of those students had left, and additional teachers who were not part of the committee had asked to sit in. Mueller accepted responsibility for the mix-up, sent Rey back to the adjacent quiet room, and moved on quickly to the question of consequences for the cheaters. The adults decided—and the students at the table, including Noah, agreed—that those with earlier honor code violations on their records should flunk the course, which would force them to take it over. The others, like Rey, who were before the committee for the first time, would fail the exam.

The more consequential question was what to do about their positions. Because student leadership is a central tenet of St. Benedict's, how could Rey demand that others adhere to the same code he had violated? Noah, who'd been quiet throughout the questioning, spoke up. Tall and soft-spoken, with an aw-shucks gene woven deep into the fabric of his character, he'd been at St. Benedict's since the seventh grade, which gave him a deep understanding of the influence student leaders have on the rest of the school. When he finally spoke, he asked how the school could run if Rey and the others were stripped of their titles and responsibilities. But then, he wondered, if they retained their positions, how could anyone else be convinced to follow the code? Half the year was already over. Who would replace them? And why would anybody take orders from whoever replaced them in those positions? It was a lot for him to take in, a quandary with no acceptable solution. His eyes teared up and he buried his face in his arms on the table. For a full minute, nobody said anything, leaving space for Noah to recover, his consternation and bewilderment lingering over the table.

In another minute, Mueller asked what the other students at the table thought should happen to the cheaters, and they took a harder line than Noah, agreeing that there was no way for the school to move forward unless the cheaters were forced to step down. The question then was, for how long? Searcy argued that if it were up to her, she'd expel them for cheating. But since it was clear the school wouldn't do that, she favored removing their leadership titles for what remained of the year.

"I'm not in favor of crucifying them," interrupted Father Mark Dilone, associate headmaster. What they did clearly was morally wrong, he went on, "but something can be learned from the experience." The others agreed. "What Reynaldo does next is most important," Mueller remarked. Even without his title, she said, for the sake of the school, and himself, "he needs to lead by example."

They then debated whether the students should be forced to make a public apology to the whole school. The irony of the moment didn't escape them; it was Rey who not only had stripped the rowers of their colors, but forced them to apologize at convo for their abhorrent texts. Father Mark felt that removing the texters' colors had been an overreaction, and their public apology hadn't seemed sincere. In the end, the committee recommended that the cheaters keep their hoodies but, significantly, would have to remove the Benedictine crest that is sewn on it, just above their heart. The final decisions were up to Father Ed.

Over the ensuing weeks, Robert Cygan, who had been so disappointed by the cheating that he'd considered resigning, recorded zeros for the cheaters and made everyone else in the class take a new version of the final. This time, he stood near the back of the room where he had a clear view of the top of every student's desk. And on the cover page of the new exam, along with the honor code warning, he instructed the students to have nothing on their desks "but pen and parchment."

* * *

Over the next few weeks, there was no announcement about the leaders stepping down, no public apology given for their violation of the honor code. During convo, Lucia remained steady in her role as senior leader, while Rey sat in the bleachers with the group he'd belonged to since he was drafted into it as a freshman, the only outward sign that anything had changed being the blank space where he had removed the crest from his hoodie. It was Noah who walked up to the podium. Father Ed had asked him to step in for Rey. He'd known Noah since he entered the middle division, had watched him grow and become more confident each year. He had been impressed by the leadership skills Noah showed during the WILD (Wilderness Inspired Leadership Development) orienteering project at the beginning of his third year, when student teams learn to make a fire, build a shelter, and find a cache of food that had been hidden in the woods. Noah had so quickly and successfully guided his group through their challenges that adults started seeing him not as the insecure middle-schooler he once was, but as the levelheaded, calm-under-pressure leader he'd become. And that was exactly what Father Ed believed St. Benedict's needed at this moment.

Rey and Noah traveled similar paths, both seeking a way to emerge from the long shadows cast by their fathers. Rey needed distance from his father's involvement with drugs and the street. Noah had spent years wondering what it would be like to be close to his father, only to end up as determined as Rey not to follow in his footsteps.

For most of his life, Noah had no contact with his father, a Black man who'd been incarcerated for long stretches at a time. Home for Noah was suburban Madison, about thirty miles west and a world away from Newark, with his Italian American mother and her family. Like Rey, Noah's path to St. Benedict's was made possible by an alumnus who strongly recommended the school to his mother, Mary. She enrolled him when he was entering the seventh grade and unsure of who he was, a mixed-race kid growing up in a classy, mostly white suburb. Although he had friends in Madison, none of his classmates had any idea that his father was in and out of prison on various charges, including illegal possession of a gun. At St. Benedict's, Noah not only found others who looked like him, but many who hurt in the same way.

He was just a boy when he first set foot on the property, confused about his identity, and unhappy to be brought so far from home. His mother wanted him to try St. Benedict's for two years while she finished her degree at Rutgers Newark, just down King Boulevard, and he agreed. He wore his gray hoodie and sat on the gym floor as the seniors led convocation, never imagining himself one day being the center of attention.

By the time he moved up to the prep division, he was lanky and athletic. He poured his energy into basketball but was cut from the JV team. The disappointment was deep enough to tempt him to leave the school. But just as Rey had become close with Dr. Lamourt, Noah bonded with Dr. Davis, the counselor who heads the Unknown Sons group. Over the six years that they met in group sessions and private therapy, Dr. Davis helped boost Noah from a shy, confused teenager to a self-assured young man who dreamed of being a soldier or a sailor. Noah heard almost nothing from his father until earlier this year, but by then he was too angry, too disappointed, to let him into his life. Noah thinks of himself as an understanding person, but too much time had passed for him to be willing to restructure his life to let in the father he barely knew.

Even-tempered and hesitant to judge, he told me he hates having to put his foot down, but is ready to do so when it counts, whether in his personal life or at St. Benedict's. "You have to understand that not everyone responds to the same things. Some people respond to yelling, some people don't. Some people break down when you yell at them, some people don't."

He thought there should have been a formal announcement of the transfer of leadership from Rey to him, but since it didn't happen, he simply did what he'd been asked to do. He knew that although many students were aware of Rey's transgression, there was still a lot of confusion about how the honor code was being enforced, whether the change in leadership was temporary or permanent, and why there seemed to be such a difference between the way Rey and the other cheaters were being treated and the public display that the texters on the rowing team had been put through.

What was clear to him was that the community understood that he never sought the position he'd been thrust into, and that made all the difference. "People understand that I didn't ask for this. I didn't stab anyone in the back to get this position. It's just what happened."

At most convocations during the first half of the year, Rey had been visible and very much in charge. Noah preferred to let individual group leaders take turns out front while he stood against the wall, hands in his pockets, quietly keeping an eye on things. Their individual leadership styles reflected the differences in their personalities. Rey listened to heavy metal when he worked out, while Noah almost always had a chess game running on his laptop. Noah already had his driver's license, and a car that he drove to Newark every day. He lived at home in Madison and watched *Jeopardy!* on TV with his grandparents, who lived nearby and encouraged him to dream big. Rey had never learned to drive. He walked the same streets that had imprisoned his father and constantly reminded kids like him that if you can't score on the basketball court or on the street corner, you're nothing. It was St. Benedict's that taught him that he had a future of his own to seek and shape. This year had promised to be the culmination of all his hard work, a platform from which he would make the leap out of Newark and into his future self. Losing his leadership position shook him and his dream, but he was determined to not let it defeat him.

"Ever since the situation with my dad, I've always been adultified in my life," he told me. "And so senior group leader was normal for me, I had so much responsibility on my back." The tough, confident leader I had watched rule convo and mete out punishments, who stood up to the headmaster when he questioned his decision to strip the texters of their colors, had been stretched too far. He'd grown up too fast. "A big part of me just wanted to be a kid."

In the absence of an official announcement, rumors about what happened to Rey continually swirled around the school. "When I first heard it, it was a little bit like a whisper," Kaleb recalled. He worked with Rey on the admissions team and other activities, admired his leadership skills, and respected him enough to have asked him to write a recommendation for his own leadership application for the following year. When the rumors about his cheating kept spreading, and getting louder, Kaleb prayed they weren't true, but eventually, he said, "my heart kind of broke."

On the girls side, Sheridan, Kymberli, and Natalia heard gossip about cheating, but what actually happened remained a mystery. Lucia knew all the details but one—she couldn't understand why Rey had done it. When I asked her about it, she said it'd been difficult for her because she not only shared the leadership with Rey, but they had also studied together, and it was clear to her that he knew the material. "We speak so much about integrity and doing the right thing, and we've had so many conversations where it's like, 'No, we can't do this because of the position that we're in.' You have to take accountability for that. And for me, it was like, 'How can you do that?' And I was confused. I'm still confused."

When he was brutally honest with himself, Rey admitted that he'd had plenty of time to study for the history exam. But instead of reading *1984*, he'd watched a video summary online the same morning he took the test. Throughout the year he'd become steadily more distracted about his schoolwork and simply let it slide. Being leader took precedence over everything else. In the end, he'd given so much to the school for so long that he convinced himself he'd earned a free pass to an A in the history class. He went so far as to believe that because of who he was he deserved to be allowed to cheat, "which was stupid," he admitted, "but I just wanted a sense of relief."

When he told his parents what he'd done and what had happened to him as a result, they were gravely disappointed. But after he'd undergone therapy sessions with the school psychologists, Rey tried to get his mom and dad to understand that, however contradictory it might seem, being stripped of his post could turn out to be one of the best things that ever happened to him. Without the responsibilities of leadership, he'd be able to focus on what he'd done wrong, not only on the history test, but the way he was living his life, and the way he was thinking about his future. Even without the title of senior group leader, he could continue helping the school. It would take the same kind of perseverance that Father Ed and the other monks showed when the future of the school had been in doubt, and he was convinced he had it in him. He would stay on as editor of *The Benedict News*. He would continue volunteering with the admissions team and helping Dr. Cassidy explain the school to visitors. "The big thing for me is not letting myself disappear," he told me, "because if I let myself disappear, then I think I prove everyone right, that it was the right decision for me to have senior group leader taken away."

CHAPTER 15

Doing It Wrong

ALONG WITH HIS gift for rousing a crowd with this voice, his beat-banging skill on the drums, and his willingness to fill in for Dr. Lansang on the keyboard, Kaleb possessed a dramatic flair that he showcased in school theater productions like Derek Walcott's allegory *Dream on Monkey Mountain*, where he hammed up the role of the villainous Corporal Lestrade to admiring cheers from the audience. Several times a year, he also starred in presentations before visiting educators who came to Newark to get a taste of St. Benedict's complex operation and its non-traditional methods. He was front and center, when Catholic school educators from around the country, many from the Midwest, spent an early fall day on the property hoping to discover the secrets to St. Benedict's success.

These conferences are organized by Dr. Cassidy, who heads the Fr. Mark Payne Institute, which Father Ed established to help spread the word of what is happening on King Boulevard. After a brief introduction, Cassidy—everybody on the property, including students, calls him Cass—helped himself to the breakfast spread laid out for the visitors while Kaleb, Lucia, Rey, and other students outlined the familiar four pillars of St. Benedict's: community building, student leadership, emotional health, and experiential learning. When the floor was opened for questions, Gregory O'Donnell, director of the Principal Academy, a training program run by the University of Notre Dame's Alliance for Catholic Education, wanted to know how the pillars had been planned, prepared, and implemented in the rebirth of the school.

Cass almost choked on his bagel. He looked up from his seat at the head of the long boardroom table and spoke with the earnestness of a Boy Scout taking an oath. He wished he could tell the visitors that the monks had followed a carefully researched and scientifically designed plan, but it simply wasn't so. "We're famous for putting wings on the plane as it goes down the runway," he said, using an expression that logs plenty of miles at St. Benedict's.

It wasn't until the deluge of requests for help poured in after the national television appearance in 2016 that Cass had to look backward over what the school had already accomplished and attempt to synthesize the methods and insights that made it all work. In other words, he explained, they had started with the four pillars without even knowing it. Self-examination decades later helped them identify the concepts that have been the foundation of St. Benedict's since its 1973 makeover.

With the help of Kaleb and the other students, he laid out in detail how each of the pillars worked, starting with the core aim of building community, a goal that has been central since the very first convocation. It is a message that is poles apart from the self-centeredness of so much of modern society. The concern for each other that is evident in the way attendance is taken every morning at convo is the essence of monastic life transferred to the prep school, and it is a feeling that the presence of the monks reinforces every day. Their enduring commitment to the city and its people, to their students, wherever they come from, and to each other over the decades, manifests the stability of their lifelong vows in a way that gets transferred to their students.

The next pillar—never doing for students what they can do for themselves—wasn't given a formal structure until the late Father Mark Payne introduced his Boy Scout–inspired leadership chart a few years after the reopening. The eleven-month school year and the experiential learning that combines classroom work with practical leadership, survival skills, and critical thinking were inherent from the start, although they've gone through much refinement. Also there from the beginning of the new school was the understanding, often expressed by Father Mark, that "ninety percent of academic problems are non-academic," meaning that most educational challenges stem not from a lack of intelligence but from the emotional heartache kids grow up with, the inescapable parts of their lives that scar and deform their character. It has taken time for St. Benedict's counseling department to grow robust enough to address those needs adequately, and now some 40 percent of the school's students come in for help.

Cass let the students respond to most of the visitors' follow-up questions. They asked Kaleb how much control students actually have over school operations. With a brace-filled smile that makes him hard not to like, he described the decisions about dress code and cell phone use that Lucia and Rey had introduced at the start of the year, and he roundly approved of them. Cass likes to tell visitors that what they see when they visit on days like this is unvarnished and unrehearsed, and it's true. But Kaleb and the other students who work with the institute are so invested in the school that they rarely lift the curtain for the outsiders to see any downside. So he didn't tell them that when convo runs long, student leaders are responsible for adjusting the daily schedule, launching urgent emails to teachers and staff about changes only after convo ends, which leaves students confused and teachers, whose plans are wrecked, steaming. He talked about the honor code and the lockers without locks, but didn't mention that within a few weeks after the school year starts, emails routinely circulate as kids look for the book, bag, or a charger they suspect was taken.

Kaleb's strong attachment to the school kept him from telling visitors any of that. To him, St. Benedict's is a marvel, and so is his presence there. Living in Jersey City, about a dozen miles east of Newark, he hadn't known much about the school before he applied to high schools. He liked several others more, but only St. Benedict's accepted him. He started in 2020, along with his older sister, Kasia, who transferred in when Cristo Rey—the Catholic high school she was attending in Newark—closed. Right from the start, Kaleb adapted to the rules and routine of St. Benedict's, and his leadership skills shined. He was selected captain of his trail team, became a freshman counselor in his second year, and this year he served as leader of the Prof. Blood group, a position usually reserved for seniors. He made no secret of his desire for a higher leadership position next year, perhaps even senior group leader—if all goes well.

In a school as diverse as St. Benedict's, identifying a typical student can be like capturing a firefly, but Kaleb comes close. He works hard in his classes, without always achieving the grades he'd hoped for, but he's got other talents and interests outside the classroom where he excels. He's a natural showman, devoted to his music and his Pentecostal church. And leadership seems to suit him. Father Albert, who is faculty moderator of Kaleb's Prof. Blood group, has been mentoring him. "He shows a certain kind of class," Albert says. "He gets up in front of the kids and gives orders and he can get away with it. He'll put his hand up, and guys do have a way of listening to him, I think, because he's so genuine." He's sincere and mature, but still a kid. During their daily meeting one afternoon, the group was getting loud, many of the students joking around instead of doing schoolwork. When Father Albert caught Kaleb air drumming with his drumsticks instead of trying to restore order, he offered words of advice: If you want to be respected as a leader, he whispered, "ditch the drumsticks."

Kaleb's mother is Honduran, his father, who was born in Jersey City, African American. Three generations of Kaleb's family now live in the downtown Jersey City row house that the family owns, and his cousin, Derek, a freshman, lives so close that he is often in the house as well. Strong religious connections run through many of St. Benedict's families, most often to faiths other than Catholicism. Kaleb's father, Rashon, is pastor of the Church of God in Christ, a Pentecostal denomination in Jersey City, and he admires Benedictine values. For him, there's no putting a price on the kind of education Kaleb and his sister have received at St. Benedict's.

"Financially, it can be a bit burdensome," Rashon told me over a plate of arroz con pollo one afternoon in the cramped kitchen of their second-floor apartment. He is an accountant with a corporate bank that specializes in international finance, which allows him to work from home. St. Benedict's provides some financial aid, but now that Kasia is in college, it still costs them close to $10,000 a year for Kaleb to attend. "I've seen how Kaleb interacts with people," he told me. "It's a benefit that will far supersede the price tag or the value of a dollar."

Besides serving as group leader and performing on stage, Kaleb loves his music. At church he sings in the choir. At school he plays the quad in the drum line, performing at soccer games and the annual Monkfest celebration in August. And he's a standout percussionist with the school's Latin jazz band. But his most stirring performances come during convocations, when he leads the affirmation of self-worth and courage with the rhythm of a band leader and the spirit of a revivalist preacher.

When the visiting educators wanted details about tuition, Kaleb gave them the stock answer: $16,000 per year on average, but many parents pay no more than $6,500, with the school making up the rest with a prodigious fundraising effort that brings in the $1 million a month in private donations necessary to keep the school afloat. When they asked how involved parents are in the school, Cass took the question and laid out another peculiarity of St. Benedict's. The school generally does not engage with parents except when there's trouble. After parents sign on to the St. Benedict's approach, he said, they willingly step back and leave most things to the school and the students themselves. Parents had no input to radical changes like Rey and Lucia's new phone and dress code policies.

Once the visitors learned about the unusual school calendar, with its summer session and the experiential learning term bookending two traditional but accelerated fall and winter terms, they started tabulating days, which led them to ask about meeting instructional time mandates. As an independent school, St. Benedict's is not tied to state testing requirements, nor does it have to meet the state's 180-day school year threshold. Still, the school year averages nearly 195 days, with few holidays or breaks, along with the rare days off that students and Ralph Kevin Harris conjure up.

When the discussion turned to admissions, Lucia's father, Mario Gallo, laid out standards that few other prep schools have. "What we look for is a heartbeat," he said. He was trying to make a key point about the applicant's aptitude and willingness to do what it takes to join the community. All that is true, but the school acknowledges that it isn't set up to admit students with mobility issues. The staircases and long corridors, space-restricted bathrooms, and lack of ramps and elevators in the old buildings, make it impossible for students with physical challenges to enroll, a deficit the school is mindful of and hopes to address when money is available. St. Benedict's also doesn't have the staff to teach special needs students, although the counseling center administers testing that can detect a student's emotional challenges and, as it did for Tareek, recommend that teachers keep them close and allow them extra time for exams.

But for most applicants, Gallo said, what matters most is "the desire to be here." Referrals from alumni strongly influence admissions decisions, whether or not the families can pay the tuition. "It's all about opportunity," he said, and has little to do with what's on a transcript. When C or D students are surrounded by people who care, he told the visitors, they can suddenly become A students.

* * *

In late January, another group of visitors from all over the country came to the property. This time they gathered in the library near the statue of the Virgin Mary that was rescued from the 1854 anti-Catholic riot that laid waste to the original St. Mary's church. Catholic educators and public-school officials from as close as a Newark charter school to as distant as a Catholic school run by Benedictine nuns in Kentucky joined a few monks and teachers to pick at the muffins and fruit salad before the meeting got underway. Cass called this symposium "We're Doing It Wrong," a curious title for a session intended to highlight St. Benedict's achievements, but he explained that what he meant to get across was that the "We" in the title referred to everyone except St. Benedict's. "After decades of focusing increasingly on quantitative analysis of high stakes test results, we still have a large and growing achievement gap, because we—everyone but us—focus too much on that and not enough on the heart." The symposium would highlight the fundamental tenet of St. Benedict's—the belief that there's more than one way to teach kids. "There's too much focus on numbers," Cass said, "and not enough on people."

After having their fill of bagels and pastry, the educators—about eighty of them—were brought to the big gym, where they were separated into color-coded groups, much the same way that St. Benedict's organizes its students in order to help break down barriers and make it easier to share ideas. The bleachers were still empty when Lucia came forward and, with her trademark cheeriness and unabashed sincerity, explained a few things about how the school operates, starting with the raised hand. To perform it correctly, she told the visitors, your hand should reach just above your head, and your elbow should be unbent. She then demonstrated a perfectly raised hand. The visitors would soon see for themselves how effective the hand is at St. Benedict's.

Lucia then introduced Noah, calling him "one of the senior leaders," but not specifically "senior group leader." It had to be awkward for her. She and Rey were still technically a couple, and both of them still held out hope he'd be allowed to regain his leadership position. But there'd been no official announcement yet of the substitution, or how long it would last, which by default left Noah in charge. This morning, he simply identified himself as a member of the wrestling and baseball teams, and stressed how important the school's group system is to sustaining a compassionate community.

When it was Father Ed's turn to brief the visitors, he started by explaining that St. Benedict's goes its own way. "There are four things we do better than other people," he said, and went on to present his own interpretation of the four pillars. He said that the school's overriding mission is to teach young people to resist the idea that individual wants are more important than everything else. "They have to understand the reality of the other," he stressed, pacing with the mic in his hands. Once their perspective is trained outward instead of inward, young people "begin to understand the suffering of the other," which enables them to form a durable community.

He emphasized the idea that emotional challenges lead to the academic underachievement that beleaguers urban youth and frustrates the adults attempting to teach them. Classroom failures have less to do with pedagogy and far more to do, he said, with issues of the heart. "Our experience tells us that when you tend to kids' hearts, you can reach their intellect." That important job, he says, is the responsibility of Dr. Lamourt and the half dozen professional psychologists and therapists in the counseling center, which is located in the symbolic heart of the property, roughly equidistant from the classrooms, the monastery, the playing fields, and the abbey church.

He then confided to the visitors that giving kids a say in how a school is run is a dangerous idea, a notion they surely shared, though not for the reason he gave. "It's dangerous because you're dealing with people who are mentally impaired." He could see shock registering on the adults' faces, and reveled in it. "I'm seventy-eight," he boasted. "I say whatever the hell I want." Then, with the candor that Kaleb had avoided, he conceded that giving teenagers responsibility for setting schedules and planning events often leads to the threshold of disaster.

"They don't think the way we think because their brains are not fully developed." And, he acknowledged, they will make mistakes. It's a process he encourages, knowing that mistakes can be effective teachers. And empowered students become confident and capable adults.

Father Ed wasn't finished shocking his guests. "School is overrated," he said, throwing out the declaration like a challenge to the teachers and administrators in front of him. He described how he's had to call lots of parents over the years to discuss their son's failing grades. At times he's leveled with them, conceding that despite the academic setbacks their son encountered, he would find his way. "I have to tell some of them that he'll be all right—once he finishes school." He went on to say that so much of what St. Benedict's students learn comes outside the classroom. There's the A.T. hike at the end of freshman year that many of the visitors already knew about. But most weren't aware that since 2021, the headmaster has worked with a private leadership development group called Victory Road that has coached corporate executives, law enforcement and military officers, actors and athletes, all over the country. Together, they have created unique adversity challenges to augment what the upper grades had already learned about toughness and leadership during the backpacking project in their freshman year. One series of challenges takes place in the woods at the start of third year. It was this survival, orienteering, and team-building experience that Noah excelled in, impressing Father Ed enough to make him Rey's replacement. The other is a hardcore water-survival skills test for second-year students that would shock the adults later in the day.

As the headmaster finished up, students filed into the gym. The visitors were then treated to a spirited joint convo, replete with the boys and girls divisions singing, dancing, and sermonizing. When prayers ended, Kaleb strode confidently to the podium like a TV game show host ready to give away a fabulous prize. "Turn to the person next to you and say, 'I love you. You're worth it.'" As everyone in the bleachers followed his lead, student guides sitting with the visitors did the same.

Though some adult visitors seemed uncomfortable with the forced intimacy, most welcomed the moment.

When convo ended, the visitors watched student leaders orchestrate the orderly and mostly silent exit of over 750 adolescents, a feat of organization and discipline the leaders pull off every day. After witnessing the community spirit of convo, and the impressive display of student leadership, the curious outsiders got to see for themselves how the other core pillars worked. They walked from the gym through a grassy open field to the Leahy House dormitory. In the small room where the Velvet Rope kids meet, a handful of visitors encountered Dr. Lamourt. A bear of a man, with a name ideally suited to a Harry Potter villain, Ivan Lamourt is a pushover for kids, and the kids—who pop into his office, or his home—know it. He explained to the visitors that as soon as students are admitted to St. Benedict's, they go through a thorough emotional screening. "Most schools do an educational assessment," he said, but what good does it do if they aren't screened for depression, or anger, or any of a dozen other emotional imbalances that can severely disrupt a student's ability to learn? Once the assessments are complete, each student is graded according to need, ranging from those who seem to be holding things together, but should be watched, to the ones with serious enough traumas in their lives to require immediate one-on-one counseling, along with additional help in the classroom. For students who are between those extremes, the counseling center recommends Unknown Sons, Alateen, or one of the other group interventions.

"With that kind of counseling, a kid can just come in and unload," Lamourt explained. "What's the difference between that and going to see a tutor?"

A couple of things about St. Benedict's make those sessions more effective than they might be elsewhere. The school's group structure mixes kids from different grades and accustoms them to talking through issues with others who might be older, or younger, than they are. The school's economic and social demographics suggest that many of them deal with the same issues, either personally or within their own families, and when they share their histories in these groups, others recognize and identify with them.

To prove his point, the psychologist turned to Tareek, who was among a handful of students the counseling center had invited to meet with the visitors. "Do you want to tell everybody your story?" Hesitantly at first, Tareek opened up to the roomful of strangers, explaining in a hushed tone that he goes to the weekly Alateen meeting because both of his biological parents had addictions. "My mom, she was addicted to drugs, and my dad, he's an alcoholic," he stated matter of factly. Then he offered the briefest glimpse of his troubled past: "We had to survive on our own, me and my brother."

Across the room, fourteen-year-old Raúl told his story. "My mom is addicted to drugs," he said, his voice flat, his eyes darting nervously from Lamourt to the visitors. "And I go to the grief group because one of my friends passed away." Rey was there too, and he gave his version of what in just a few moments had become a distressingly common account. "My father's an addict, and I think it runs in the family line to my grandfather and even my great-grandfather." He said that attending the Alateen group meetings on Monday mornings had become an important part of his life at St. Benedict's. "You can feel you're the only one with this problem, but seeing that others are dealing with the same thing is helpful."

Tareek seconded that. "It's been helpful for me too. I'm learning that I'm a lot like my father, though I'm not as destructive as he is."

As he does in his group counseling sessions, Lamourt encouraged Tareek to open up more. "Do you want to bring up what we talked about in the boardroom yesterday?" he asked gently, referring to an additional emotional assessment that the center was conducting. It can strike outsiders as intrusive, but St. Benedict's students get accustomed to sharing their histories. Tareek calmly revealed to the room full of strangers what he'd told me weeks earlier, that he sometimes felt like he didn't belong anywhere. Then he added something I'd never heard him say: "I put on some paper that I didn't value my life."

I could tell that it was a lot for the visitors to take in. The eyes of one woman who was president of a school board in a nearby town teared up as she listened to Tareek. Lamourt tried to add perspective, telling them that despite the multitude of hurts Tareek has suffered in his young life, he's developed formidable emotional defenses. Knowing the extent of Tareek's trauma had led Lamourt to urge him to come in for individual counseling, as well as to attend the Alateen meetings. The visiting educators, especially several of the women, seemed dismayed by Tareek's disconsolate story, and their inability at that moment to comfort him.

The session moved on and one of the visitors asked how such a vigorous counseling program could ever be implemented in a public school, with all its privacy laws and budget constraints. It was one of several attempts they made to draw a distinction between what could be done at a private school like St. Benedict's and what their school boards would tolerate. Lamourt focused on the group counseling sessions, and emphasized the fact that students did not need their parents' consent to attend. He felt that if public schools tried to establish similar groups, they'd reach far more students, and reach them more effectively, than traditional counseling ever could. A doctorate in psychology isn't required to run the groups, he said. "Sometimes the kids do it." That's when Rey, who I'd watched run Alateen meetings, commented that students who participate in the groups learn empathy by listening to each other.

One of the visitors felt that everything the psychologist and the students had described is easier to undertake at a place like St. Benedict's because the school can expel the unruly students who make group sessions unmanageable.

"That's not true," Lamourt countered. He leaned in, as if getting ready to tell a secret. "We deal with the kids we have." This is another dividing line that separates St. Benedict's from other schools. Their goal is not to control students so they are less disruptive in class. There's an understanding, deeply rooted in the place, that though some kids come from stable, comfortable homes, many others carry with them a bundle of complications, what the staff refers to as "the ugly." The ugly is the inner reality that students live with, their past selves wrapped in all the anger, resentment, fear, loneliness, and despair that is their world, and that, like the dog crap they sometimes get on the bottom of their shoes, they track in with them when they come to school. At St. Benedict's, they don't ignore the ugly, or try to keep it out of the school. They prepare themselves to deal with it.

* * *

The visitors' next stop was the pool. They spread out on aluminum bleachers as Chris Firriolo, founder and president of Victory Road, explained the logic behind the water adversity challenge, known as the WAC, that they were about to witness. Many of St. Benedict's students do not have access to pools, and they lack the cultural and family connections to swimming that can help make them confident in the water. "Blacks are more than five times more likely to drown than whites," he stated. Father Ed had come to Firriolo looking for a way to build up every student's strength and courage, pumping into their character a skill set that can be applied to a range of life experiences. He also wanted to make sure that they knew enough to keep from adding to the already disturbing drowning statistics.

Firriolo was ready to demonstrate the results of that effort. He stood atop an eight-foot-high platform at the deep end of the pool, and began to call up students who were dressed in school clothes, carrying their backpacks. "Swimmer, step up to the tower," he announced. Many of the visitors had their phones out, ready to record. "Experiential opportunities," they heard the instructor say, "are lessons for life." A student then mounted the platform. "Swimmer, secure your mask." The student pulled on a blacked-out swim mask, and inched toward the edge, with Firriolo grabbing the back of her sweatshirt. "Swimmer ready." The student raised her left hand and placed her palm over the mask to hold it secure. After a second, she raised her right hand and gave a thumbs-up. "Swimmer three, two, one . . . step." As she moved forward, Firriolo made sure she cleared the edge of the platform as she plunged into the thirteen-foot-deep pool. Some visitors gasped. One lifted her shoulders, closed her eyes, and shuddered.

One after the other, students ascended the platform, donned a blacked-out mask, and stepped in, clothes, shoes, backpacks, and all. They had already completed five weeks of intensive training during the summer term of their second year. Firriolo would later tell me that the point of the challenge is to accustom students to switching from emotional focus to what he called mission focus. "When we're focused on our emotions, we're not going to be able to accomplish our goals. When we're able to check that and remain very emotionally neutral, and focus on the challenge in front of us, that's where we're going to have a higher rate of success in accomplishing our goals."

The most chilling part of the challenge was yet to come. Once they had surfaced, the students quickly removed their backpacks and shoes. Then—still wearing their blacked-out goggles—they attempted to take off their pants and trap air inside the legs so they could be used as a personal flotation device, a potential life saver in a real disaster. As one student was attempting to scoop air into his pants, an instructor in the water—a former Navy SEAL—swam up to him, jumped above his head, and pushed him down. As soon as the student resurfaced, the instructor dunked him a second, then a third time. To confuse and disorient him as if he had been in a boat that was sinking, the instructor splashed water in the student's face. It didn't work. Just as he'd been trained, the student proceeded calmly, tying knots in the legs of his pants so they held air and could float him to safety.

All second-year students receive this training, but only those who can swim and tread water sufficiently well have to go through the plunge, whether they want to or not. I learned that when Natalia, the girl from Irvington who'd been caught vaping, underwent her own water challenge a few months earlier, she'd kept a secret for the entire five weeks of the summer course. She had almost drowned at a water park when she was thirteen, and she dreaded having to go through the water challenge at St. Benedict's. But she had set her mind to completing it because she knew that just as it had been mandatory for her to walk the entire fifty-plus miles of the Appalachian Trail to get her school colors, she would have to complete the water challenge to maintain her membership in the St. Benedict's community. She started summer term in the group of kids with the least skills in the water, and the most fear. All of them received extra instruction in swimming and treading water. With help from Naval Academy volunteers, Natalia quickly progressed from the red group to the yellow group, and then green, the highest level, where ascending the platform was compulsory in order to complete the course.

"I knew I was probably going to fail the last part, the drowning part, but I kept trying," she told me. Firriolo was on the platform with her as she inched to the edge. He's seen some students who were absolutely terrified of jumping. "Tears come out of their eyes, shaking, shaking, deathly afraid, to a point where we have them and we're ready to 'three, two, one—step' and they're reaching back to grab on."

Firriolo waited for Natalia to give the thumbs-up sign indicating that she was ready. He said he knows that none of the executives he trains have to go through what St. Benedict's students confront, so if the kids need extra time, he gives it to them. But in the end, they must find the courage to jump. "The whole point is facing your fears, right?" he said. "Having the courage to rely on the training, right? When things go sideways, you're going to fall back to the level of your training. You know you can tread water. You know you can swim fifty meters, okay? You're going to get into that water, right?"

With her eyes covered by the mask, Natalia couldn't see a thing.

The pool was dead silent. All she knew was that the water was far below her, and she had no choice but to move ahead. It was just a step. Forward. One single step.

Before she could think about it, she was in the water. She managed to remove her backpack, shoes, and pants, but before she could inflate the legs of her pants, the instructor pushed her down. She came back up coughing and confused. "The only thing I told myself was that I wasn't going to take my blindfold off, because when you take it off, that means you quit, you're done." She kept trying, but the instructor saw how much she was struggling and he eventually took off her mask, ending the test. "I was the last person to go so it was really quiet and everybody was watching me," she recalled. The instructor tried to calm her down, but she was too upset to calm down. It wasn't because memories of the water park had resurfaced, she said, but because she had failed to complete the mission.

Some of the visitors who had come to St. Benedict's without any idea what to expect were left shaken by the demonstration. Most were impressed once they understood how well the students had been trained to deal with such extreme situations. Nonetheless, they were certain their own school boards would never approve such a program. Firriolo told me that he's incorporated multiple safety precautions into the exercises, and brought in additional staff so that there are redundant safeguards. Still, he said, it was only Father Ed's obsessive drive to ensure that his kids are strong and independent that made it possible for the program to be run at St. Benedict's. "There's no other school in this country that is doing what the students here at St. Benedict's Prep do," he told me. Of course, other prep schools offer swimming lessons, and teach emergency response. "But when it comes down to experiential training," he remarked, "and the difficulty that the students face during their four years, there's nowhere else like St. Benedict's."

* * *

When the educators broke for lunch, Cass tried to summarize what they'd seen and heard that day. "We're here to say that there's more than one way to educate kids." He bemoaned the over-reliance on performance indicators and test scores. (I never saw St. Benedict's display its own SAT and ACT scores anywhere.) The lack of attention to loneliness, depression, and abandonment have had a devastating impact on the ability of kids, especially city kids, to learn. St. Benedict's, he said, proves there are better ways to teach.

A panel of educators then presented ways that they have replicated St. Benedict's methods in their own schools. One panelist conceded that in her school in Milwaukee, they hadn't yet achieved the kind of trust needed to push kids into the deep end of a pool, but they do organize students into small groups and provide intensive orientation for freshmen before the regular school year begins. Mark Comesañas, the alumnus who spoke at the first convocation of the year, described how, when he worked in a Newark charter school, he adopted the practice of students silencing a room by simply raising a hand. And as head of the My Brother's Keeper group in Newark, he makes sure that young people get to interview every new staff hire.

The vision that Cass tried to convey at the symposium, of a school that tends to the heart as well as to the mind, is not a mirage. St. Benedict's may be unique, but much of what it does can be replicated in other places, as the panelists showed. The foundation stones of community, accountability, and emotional health, combined with an appreciation for the educational value of real life experience, have proven to be an antidote for the urban ills that vex so many other cities.

* * *

Most of the visitors were gone by the time St. Benedict's senior leadership team gathered in Room 11 that afternoon, in the main hallway of the old building, just off the Trophy Room and Father Ed's office.

Had the visitors been there, they would have witnessed an unrehearsed example of the impact the four pillars have on imperfect students who are constantly challenged by life.

When Dean Rodriguez walked into Room 11, he was steaming mad. Lucia and Rey's cell phone collection policy had been followed daily since July, yet it was clear that the system had broken down. Rodriguez, an acerbic Spaniard who is as comfortable with complex Spanish conjugations as he is with laying tile and doing home renovations, kept daily records of student discipline, noting absences, lates, and dress code violations. And he kept track of how many phones were collected each morning before convo.

When Kaleb's group turned in its bag that morning, it should have contained fifteen or more phones, but it held only one. And Rodriguez knew Kaleb's group wasn't alone in skirting the rules. Phone collection had grown lax as group leaders ignored omissions, or gave their friends a pass when they hadn't handed theirs in. "Father Ed has seen these numbers," Rodriguez lamented, "and he's already ripped my ear off."

The door to Room 11 swung open and Father Ed walked in wearing a face that looked like anything but the proud headmaster of the successful school the visitors had toured that day. "Who's responsible?" he asked the seniors. He was talking about the phones that were not being collected, but he could just as well have been addressing Rey and the others whose misdeeds in December had upset the school's balance. Since the winter term had started in January, much of what Rey had put in place at the start of the school year had come undone. Kids were skipping group meetings in the afternoon, and walking over garbage in the hallways. Students were getting progressively rowdier at convo. They were ignoring the dress code, and routinely trashing cafeteria tables and the school grounds. "You guys stink right now," the headmaster admonished the seniors, laying out the ways they were harming the school. "If you, as leaders, are lax, the younger ones think it's okay to cut corners too. If you cheat on a test, they'll cheat." Like personal and corporate reputations, St. Benedict's own standing took a long time to build. But he knew it could be lost in an instant. If you can't or won't act like leaders, Father Ed warned them, echoing his threat to the honor code committee weeks before, he vowed to bring up younger guys to replace them. "You're not going to run this thing off the rails," he growled. He turned and left the room, an awkward silence trailing behind him.

It was clear to everyone that Father Ed was upset about more than the phones. Rey must have sensed it too, because he stood up and asked for a chance to speak. A long line of black hoodies twisted toward him as though he were still senior group leader, even though they knew he wasn't. "I'm not sorry for what I did, because that's a personal thing. I'm sorry I put us in this situation where we look like we're a cluster fuck of a class and we don't know how to function. That's what I'm sorry about." He proceeded to take the blame for what was going wrong, understanding the destructive image that he and the other cheaters presented to the rest of the school. Because of their individual bad choices, the entire leadership hierarchy had lost credibility, and that undermined the moral standing of the whole senior class.

"I represented all of us, and I fucked it all up."

Noah sat a few feet away. Although he had spoken at the symposium earlier that day, Father Ed had never announced that he was in charge, and that hurt his ability to lead. Rey sensed that the uncertainty was making a bad situation worse, and he wanted to set the record straight.

"Whatever Noah's vision is, and how he wants to approach it, is how it's going to be approached." He was brimming with emotions—shame, anger, frustration—but he was also determined to do what's right. He tried to erase any doubt about who was in charge. "There's no going to me behind his back. None of that."

Watching quietly from the other side of the room where he'd been seated, Noah seemed to waver between his respect for his friend, and his stubborn doubts about his own ability to lead. Rey scanned the row of seniors, all wearing their black hoodies, all now living under the same shadow that had enveloped him since the end of last term. "I'm not here as a member of the leadership team. I'm here as a member of the senior class. And however I can help you guys get us back on track, I will." There were still almost five months left in the school year, enough time for them to try to repair their legacy, which lay in tatters, and to ensure that Father Ed doesn't at some point in the future add "'24" to the list of the worst classes he's ever had.

He asked if there was anything else he needed to clear up. Some of the seniors thought that there was.

"Do you plan to own up to everything you guys did that put us in a bad spot?" one asked. Was Rey prepared to say what he just said in front of the whole school the way the kids who had texted about the soccer team did, another wanted to know.

Dean Rodriguez stepped in to referee. He and Father Ed had repeatedly told Rey not to make any public statements about what had happened while the investigation into the cheating was ongoing. Nonetheless, Rey let the others know he was prepared to do whatever they felt was right. "I don't have a problem talking to anyone about it." Whenever anybody asked him about the exam, he told the whole story. He'd do the same to the entire senior class, even the whole school, if that would help repair the bonds that he had so obviously broken.

It then was Noah's turn to make clear that he was the senior group leader even without an official announcement of the switch. He acknowledged that discipline had slipped, and slipped badly. He pointed out that half of the leaders who were supposed to attend the meeting that afternoon hadn't bothered to come. He knew it would take a lot to right the ship, and he was ready to lead the way. "The only way we're going to get through this," he stated firmly, "is that it's got to be all of us."

CHAPTER 16

Order on the Court

COACH BADGER'S FRESHMAN basketball team was in the opening minutes of a January home game against rival St. Peter's Prep when things started turning sour fast. The Marauders from Jersey City had scored a pair of giveaway three-pointers with what seemed like an open invitation from the Gray Bees to add more, and Badger had holed himself up in the tranquil zone he establishes in front of his bench during most games. While he's there he's a study in self-control, wise in the ways of the game, a resolute mentor who rarely yells but always means business. That's a far cry from the Anthony Badger who wore number 11 for St. Benedict's in the mid-1970s and was, in his own words, one "tough, skilled hombre," a scrappy point guard who went chest to chest with anyone on the court, regardless of how much bigger or stronger they might be. "I was an absolute animal on the court. Not a nice guy. I'm a nice guy off the court, but on the court, it was war." Now, his only concession to intensity is his predatory crouch, bent forward at the waist like he might try to claw back one of his own players who'd just ignored everything he'd tried to pass along since their first meeting last summer.

A total of forty-four boys, including little Raúl, had shown up during the two days of tryouts Badger held just after the freshman overnight. Unlike the varsity Gray Bees' team that is stuffed with elite foreign players and transfers from top-ranked basketball programs, everyone on Badger's freshman team was a walk-on. "I coach the kids that come across my doorstep. Whoever I get, that's who I get." He quickly winnowed the roster down to the fourteen he guessed had the greatest speed, the most advanced skills, or what he considers the ballsy "street moxie" that transforms a mediocre ball handler into a hardwood terror. For the three months before the season officially started in November—when he'd invited me to one of his practices in Shanley Gym—he simply encouraged them to focus on getting into top physical shape, and regularly sent them motivational emails to fire up their passion for the game.

At one practice, I watched him address his athletes in a gentle but no-nonsense tone. "The first thing I want to say to you guys is we start practice at 3:30. If you get here after 3:30, we have an issue." He wore a white T-shirt printed with St. Benedict's Basketball and the familiar logo of Adidas—the school's official sponsor—gray pants, black athletic shoes, and a whistle on a lanyard around his neck. Of the fourteen boys who'd made the cut, only six had shown up on time and were sitting in the stands. They were a motley crew of assorted sizes and shapes, outfitted in mismatched gym clothes that a few were already outgrowing. But each wore pristine basketball shoes that looked like they might have cost half a monthly tuition payment.

For most of the next hour, Badger did not let them touch a basketball. They sprinted back and forth across the Shanley Gym floor in a workout he calls suicides. Some of them looked impossibly small and young, and none more so than Raúl, easily the slightest, thinnest youth on the team.

"You have to run all the way," Badger hollered, focusing his comment on Raúl and a few others who were doubling back several feet before reaching the turnaround marker. "If you don't, you're cheating the process, and you're cheating yourself." When they were sufficiently winded, he brought out basketballs and started them dribbling, passing, and blocking. "If you get tired, let me know," he told them. "But we're not going to stop." By the end of the practice, they all panted like racehorses. "It wasn't a bad effort," the coach conceded, "but we've got a lot of work to do on the little things." And when it comes to basketball, for Badger all the little things are big things. He ended the practice by calling everyone to the center of the court where they placed their hands on top of each other's, and shouted, "One. Two. Three. Benedict's!"

Over the next few weeks, he worked them hard as he attempted to transform them into something resembling a team. When they wheezed during sprints, he sarcastically asked them how old they were. When he had them do pushups, and Raúl's back was rubbery, his knees touching the hardwood, Badger shook his head in disbelief. At one practice, he chided a player he caught wearing an earring, something he'd specifically prohibited. When they started working on basic skills, he outlined his conviction that defense wins most games, and that's what he wanted them to focus on, even if they were far more interested in shooting and scoring.

* * *

Had they listened to him, they may not have been trailing St. Peter's 30–20 in that January home game. Coach Badger called a time out. The defensive instincts he tried to drill into them had obviously not made the impact he'd hoped for, and there were plenty of signs that St. Peter's would keep pulling ahead unless something changed. He put in Raúl, who showed off the jump shot that had earned him his spot on the team, but by the end of the third quarter, Benedict's lost all chance of catching up. The final score was 64–38, the team's worst drubbing of the season so far.

Coach joined me in the bleachers after his game ended and we watched the JV players warming up for theirs. Although he'd much rather win each game, this loss didn't bother him much. His goal as coach since he returned to the school in 2021 had been to prepare the young men for lives off the basketball court. "I tell my kids all the time that I'm here to help them become better people, better students, et cetera. And if they become better basketball players too, that's great." He was on the property a lot during the season, and I watched him interact with his players on and off the court. When he saw one of them in a hallway, he almost always stopped to chat, but it was rarely about basketball. How are you doing? he'd ask. How's your family? How are your grades? It surprises the kids as much as it initially surprised me, this basketball zealot, St. Benedict's Hall of Famer, who asks about school not sports. He's the kind of coach who holds eight a.m. Saturday practice, but shows up at seven for any kid who wants to put in an extra hour. And for every video clip on dribbling or hook shots that he sends his players, he sends one on building up personal traits like dependability and resilience.

He knows that few of his players are as pumped up about basketball as he was when he scored 1,200 points over his four years at St. Benedict's back in the era before the three-point shot. He realizes they don't have the same skills and court smarts he developed playing in the bumpy asphalt "parking lot" near his home on Brenner Street, or at the "Salt Mines" as the courts at Newark's Grover Cleveland Elementary School were known when he was a kid. His classmate and friend Kevin Washington told me that at St. Benedict's, Badger "was respected on the court, a student of the game who was always in the gym," as well as being a generally humble guy despite the star status his basketball prowess earned him. Badger played in a few varsity games as a freshman, became the regular point guard as a sophomore and continued there through his senior year, going up against guys who went on to play in the NBA, including Hollis Copeland, who became a small forward for the New York Knicks in the early 1980s.

Now as coach, he levels with his players, many of whom show up on King Boulevard with notions of playing varsity, even of eventually heading to the NBA. In the last eighteen years, he tells them, only a handful of freshmen have played on the varsity team. It is the same tough love message that he delivered the previous year to Jokari, who promptly ignored it, believing he'd be the exception. He wasn't. On that January night when the freshmen lost to St. Peter's, he was on the court warming up for the JV game, and still dreaming of making varsity. He'd spend most of this night on the bench, as he had for much of the season, as the JV team also succumbed to the visitors from Jersey City.

As a dejected Jokari and the others slumped off to the locker room, the most highly anticipated game of the night got underway. The varsity Gray Bees, ranked sixth, were taking on the undefeated St. Peter's Marauders. The bleachers that had been sparsely filled for the freshman game a few hours earlier were now packed. And many of the parents, alumni, and fans from both schools got their first look at something never before seen on King Boulevard. The newly organized St. Benedict's cheer team, in the blue and white uniforms the girls had designed, ran into the gym to perform. Less than four years after Sabrina and the others "broke in," here were a line of girls, most of them African Americans, in short skirts, navy sweaters, and white shoes, some with big white bows in their hair, all wearing the broadest smiles, stepping high and leading cheers as the boys varsity basketball team warmed up.

"I tried to dissuade them," said Father Ed, who had joined us in the bleachers. "I asked them why a bunch of girls would want to cheer for a bunch of guys instead of playing basketball themselves."

The answer was out there in the center of the line of girls. Natalia hadn't let the trouble she got into for vaping in the locker room derail her from her goal of starting a cheer team. She had been taking dance lessons since she was a child, and starting in her freshman year at St. Benedict's she had talked to friends about putting together a cheerleading team. At first she got plenty of pushback. Other girls had the same idea before, she was told repeatedly, but nothing ever came of it. Father Ed? Forget about it. His first words were, there's no money.

No place to practice. Most St. Benedict's girls wouldn't be interested in cheerleading. But he had misread the girls division. When Natalia and a friend held an interest meeting, about thirty girls showed up, and she knew they were on to something real. She was prepared to do everything from raising money for uniforms—that she'd design herself if necessary—to planning practices and choreographing routines. She only needed the headmaster's okay.

She expected Father Ed to put up a fight, but after his initial pushback he surprised her. He was willing to go along with the idea, so long as the girls took the lead. "He didn't think the boys had ever said they wanted cheerleaders, but we weren't doing it for the boys," Natalia told me, pride obvious in her tone. "We were doing it for us. That's something that we actually wanted, and the girls have been wanting, since before I came here."

Within a week of their first official meeting, they had raised all the money they needed for their uniforms. They bought skirts and shoes online. The advancement office provided sweaters. Natalia's sense of pride in her accomplishment could have been a cheer in itself. "We did it all ourselves," she beamed.

As the varsity team warmed up, the girls performed their routines to hearty applause from the bleachers. At one point, Father Ed left the stands and joined them in a cheer that got the crowd's attention.

The varsity basketball team handed St. Peter's its first loss of the season, a 46–42 squeaker.

* * *

Before spring baseball and track eclipsed the winter-time basketball season, one more big sporting event filled the gym, and it was another unusual demonstration of St. Benedict's robust embrace of community. It was the second annual game pitting St. Benedict's boys against a squad from the New Jersey State Police, an event that Rey had initiated the year before. For him, going up against the troopers was more than a game. Ever since the morning he awoke to find a SWAT team in his bedroom, he'd struggled with his relationship with police, as well as with his father. Both represented the worst parts of his life, dousing him with the unshakable feeling that drug dealers and guys with badges would always block him from getting out of the city, or getting the city out of him.

It took time, and many counseling sessions, for Rey to improve his relationship with his father. As he developed a clearer understanding of how living in the city without much education had trapped his dad, he stopped resenting the way he had hurt their family. That opened up space for him to re-examine how he felt about police. He and a few other students had worked to expand the Building Bridges program that Father Ed had started with the New Jersey State Police a few years earlier. Every month, troopers and students form teams that face off in physical adversity competitions. Rey upped the ante with the troopers, challenging them to a full court basketball game. The troopers won that first match.

A year later, on a Thursday in the middle of February, the troopers were back, and the Gray Bees were itching for a victory. (Lucia and the St. Benedict's girls would go up against female troopers in a Building Bridges volleyball game in April, and they would win.) Noah was at the podium to welcome the troopers. During the singing of "In the Cross," Tareek and Jokari came down from the bleachers to stand arm in arm with the troopers as they swayed to the Gospel hymn. When it ended, Noah handed Father Ed the mic. "In the monastery, when you do something twice in a row it becomes a custom," he said, addressing Col. Patrick J. Callahan, superintendent of the state police, who had come to the school that morning. "When you do it three times, it becomes a tradition," he warned Callahan. "You can't stop."

Noah then invited the troopers to suit up, while he and the other St. Benedict's players did the same. Until they got back, Father Ed riled up the crowd by taking hook shots from near center court. The seventy-eight-year-old priest managed to get a few in, but then he lost range. He moved closer and still missed, eliciting groans from the crowd with each try. But he didn't quit. His black robe whirling around him, he kept shooting. Ten. Twenty. Thirty shots, many of them outrageous air balls that earned him heckling from the stands. He kept shooting until finally, as the state police team jogged onto the court in their dark blue shorts and T-shirts, he made a buzzer beater. He raised his arms triumphantly, and the bleachers erupted.

With the troopers warming up on the court, St. Benedict's challenge was clear. A former Division 1 college basketball player was out there for the troopers. He was so tall and so fast running drills that the boys' only hope of winning was that the brace on his knee meant he was past his playing prime. None of St. Benedict's varsity basketball players had suited up. Instead, by agreement, seniors with court skills represented the school. Noah was one of them. After he had changed into shorts and a St. Benedict's white tee, he walked to the center of the gym and grabbed the mic. But instead of hogging the spotlight, he handed the mic to Rey, who had also suited up, to officially kick off the game. It was another example of the understated style of leadership he had projected in his few weeks of being unofficially in charge. Rey laid out his hope that the game would lead to greater understanding between police and teens. When the names of the troopers were announced, each one received polite applause. When it was St. Benedict's turn, Noah was given a hearty welcome, as were the others, including Rey, a sign that most of his classmates had already forgiven him.

After the tipoff, St. Benedict's youth, speed, and familiarity with the court gave them a slight advantage. They were not as tall as the tallest troopers, and they didn't rebound with the adults' raw power. But when they turned on the speed, they sprinted ahead of the older men. Rey drove the ball down court, weaving slyly past the troopers who guarded him. He bullied his way to a sweet spot beneath the backboard,

and it looked like he might try to toss the ball up and in before anyone could block him. But instead of taking the shot himself, he passed
the ball to Noah, who dropped it in neatly for St. Benedict's first two
points. At that moment, a student dressed as a gray bee, the school's
mascot, circled the court, taunting the troopers by shaking his cloth
stinger at them. The costume covered every inch of the student but his
shoes—which I could see were black suede loafers with a silver clasp
across the vamp. That's when I knew that Jokari had made it to the
court, not as a player but as a mascot.

Rey and Noah's teamwork had put St. Benedict's on the scoreboard.
It also seemed a gracious symbol of the way they had handled the transfer of power. What it hadn't done was pave the way to a victory. The
game ended with the troopers handing St. Benedict's a second straight
loss, 69–46. For the troopers, the game was all about image. Colonel
Callahan is no stranger to Newark, or the dark legacy the state police
still have in the city. His father, Mick, was one of the troopers sent to
Newark in 1967 to help quell the civil disturbances.

"I was thinking about it this morning as I was getting dressed," he
said after the game ended, decked out in his quasi-military French blue
jacket with gold-striped trousers and Sam Browne belt. Troopers like his
father had come to Newark to raise their firearms against young Black
men like those at St. Benedict's, on streets within shouting distance of
the abbey. More than half a century later, they had come face-to-face
again in the same part of the city. But this time they had confronted
each other on a basketball court instead of a dark and dangerous street.
Most of the kids in the gym knew little about the riots, and they'd had
limited experience with state troopers or city cops. But no one expected
it to stay that way.

"Look, we still have a long way to go," Callahan acknowledged when
I spoke to him. "But this is a program that shows how alike we are and
not the differences." At least when they are facing off over a basketball,
not a gun.

Father Ed had given Callahan a heads-up that Rey needed to be "pumped up a little bit," after all that had gone wrong for him. The colonel pulled Rey aside, put his arm over his shoulder, and talked to him privately. Rey was seventeen years old, soon to be eighteen, with his whole life ahead of him. Cheating on the exam had been a grave mistake, and there was no way to undo it. What mattered most, the colonel reminded him, was learning from his mistake, and getting back to being the leader he was before he took that test. He told Rey that organizing the Building Bridges basketball game, and seeing that it continued for a second year, showed he had talent that any college, or corporation, would value. You are the kind of person, he told Rey, who "has that vision to see what is not" and then can make it come to be.

CHAPTER 17

The Seeds You Sow

AFTER THE FRESHMEN on Coach Badger's basketball team ended up losing a few more games than they won all season, he sent each of his fourteen players a personal evaluation. In it, he mentioned neither wins nor losses. He didn't single out game highlights, nor did he remark on individual achievements or shortcomings. Instead, he emphasized their progress in the three areas of athletic and personal growth that he'd set out for them at their first meeting in August: physical, mental, and emotional conditioning, which they'd worked on every day on and off the court. And he ended the note with an inspirational quote like the ones he'd sent them all season. This final one was aimed not at the basketball court, but the long path of life: "Those at the top of the mountain didn't fall there."

As Coach Badger knows better than most, the tug-of-war between the school and the street is ceaseless, each class of freshmen carrying in their own unique challenges. It isn't always possible for the school to rinse the city from its kids, nor give them all the tools they need to bridge the gap from where they started to where they want to end up. The difficulties that students like Raúl, Tareek, and Rey confronted this year are just a preview of the adversity that awaits them. Regardless of their grades, their honors, or their titles when they graduate, there's no way to know if what they've learned here will be enough to get them over the obstacles they will encounter in the years ahead.

But in the time I spent at St. Benedict's, I found that it's the lives of alumni after they leave the safe harbor of the abbey grounds that truly reveals the power of what takes place here. The list of successful alumni of the restructured school is long, including well-known names like *Washington Post* columnist Jonathan Capehart '86, TV host Kevin O'Connor, '86, and actor and singer Cameron Bernard Jones, '06, as well as a Hall of Fame full of athletes, all of them solid proof of what the school does right. And there are legions of alumni who've gone on to solid, successful, and fulfilling lives, their individual triumphs after difficult beginnings the proof of their inner strength. But when it comes to resilience and courage, few graduates can attest to the power of St. Benedict's to shape a life, then mend it once it's been broken, with greater conviction than Coach Badger himself. There usually isn't enough time during basketball season for him to relate his enigmatic past to his players, nor explain to them that he had to climb, claw, and crawl his way to that mountaintop in the quotation he sent them. But he willingly offers up details of that other life to those who ask, and they reveal much about the enduring power of the virtues that St. Benedict's instills.

After Father Ed drove him and Kevin Washington the three hours to Susquehanna University in Pennsylvania in 1977, Anthony Badger dreamed of continuing to dominate the basketball court just as he had at St. Benedict's. But it soon was obvious that his hot-shot record at Benedict's didn't guarantee him playing time at Susquehanna, where his teammates had similarly stellar records and were bigger, stronger, and faster. He made the varsity team his first three years by switching from offensive shooter to defensive guard, but he didn't get to play as much as he wanted. By his senior year, his coach let him practice with the team every day, but never put him into a game the whole season, something he's vowed to never do to any kid on one of his teams.

He stayed in touch with Father Ed, and the headmaster promised that there would be a place for him at the school when he graduated. Badger earned a degree in sociology and in 1981 returned to
St. Benedict's where he worked as college admissions counselor, taught
a sociology class, and coached the freshman basketball team. He was
twenty-two and single, a kid from dirt-poor Scotia, South Carolina,
with a college degree, who was living on the edge of Newark's Ironbound
section, and enjoying the kind of life his parents could have only imagined when they left the South. But like so many young men with money
in their pockets and empty spaces in their hearts, the city held out many
temptations for him. At first it was marijuana, but because he never
moved at anything but full speed, he quickly escalated to cocaine, while
still functioning as educator and adviser at St. Benedict's. But it didn't
take long for the road he was on to lead him to heroin.

"I was here working but I was spiraling," he recounted one afternoon as we sat in one of his old classrooms, the sun dipping low enough
to cast deep shadows over the cramped desks. His candor reminded
me of the Alateen sessions I had observed at the school. No hint of
shame or embarrassment poked through his telling of the difficulties
of his past. He told me that Father Ed and the other monks had recognized that he was in trouble and offered to help. He lied to them
and said his problem was gambling, and he promised to get it under
control. When his habit worsened, and his self-control weakened, the
headmaster sent him to a psychologist who was a Benedict's alumnus.
Badger lied to him too, this time saying that the issue was depression,
but assuring the psychologist that he knew how to tame it. Eight years
after receiving his first paycheck at St. Benedict's, he walked away from
Newark Abbey and lurched into the dark corners of the city. "For two
years I basically lived underneath the earth," is the way he describes his
life then. He had one set of dirty clothes. One pair of worn-out shoes.
Feeding his addiction became his life, and he brushed off the entreaties
of others, including the monks, who wanted to help. "When people

want to help you, and you don't want to help yourself, there's nothing that can be done."

It didn't take long for him to run into trouble with local cops who, with their post-riot reputation of having little compassion for Black men, regularly hauled him to jail. When he was back on the street, he was beaten and robbed by other junkies, and when local dealers cut him off because he couldn't pay, he drifted across the Hudson River to New York City.

With nothing there to remind him of his past life, he was sucked into the dangerous urban underworld of drugs and crime. He lived each day with the same intensity that had allowed him to dominate the basketball court but now without any personal integrity: panhandling, grifting, begging for money and scraps. Two years and a few months of wandering the streets by day, defending himself in homeless shelters at night, led to the moment—and he has isolated it precisely—that he remembered he was a Benedict's man. It started on a fine spring morning that turned into a rolling catastrophe. When a man he didn't know approached him looking for drugs, Badger helped him score. The man turned out to be an undercover cop. He arrested Badger and hauled him off to central booking. A technicality led to the steering charge being dropped, and Badger was free to go. Time had mostly lost its meaning but this day was different. He had missed his morning dose of methadone, and he knew that if he didn't rush, he wouldn't get to the treatment center before it closed. He got there too late. That's when he realized that he'd been in such a hurry to get to the center, he had neglected to retrieve his identification card from the police. Without it, he couldn't get into the men's shelter where he'd been staying overnight.

Sick because he hadn't had his methadone, and worried about spending the night on the street, he wandered around the city. Withdrawal symptoms turned his stomach and clouded his mind until all he could think of was making the sick go away. He made his way to Stuyvesant Square Park on 16th Street and Second Avenue where he recognized some of the addicts who hung out there. He took it for granted that because he was just like them, they'd help him make it through the night. They told him to get lost. It was getting late, and he realized that for the first time in his journey through his addiction and homelessness, he was completely alone. And that set his mind racing. He'd heard stories of homeless men being harassed, attacked, even set on fire as they slept. He had no friends or family he could ask for help. The community he thought he belonged to had turned against him. He swallowed whatever pride he had left and followed two bedraggled homeless men to a dumpster and watched them rummage around for cardboard and pieces of foam to use for their beds. He did the same. When they found a spot on a nearby sidewalk beneath an overstory of scaffolding, Badger put down the trash he had recovered near them. Although the other men were physically close, they could have been on another continent. They were in their own world and cared little about him. Nor did he care about them. He was with them, but he was alone. He didn't belong.

It was still dark, maybe four a.m., when he started pacing the sidewalk, taking stock of the life that was looking increasingly like a waste of all his talents. Tired as hell, he was feeling miserable because he hadn't had his methadone. And he was scared. He was no stranger to the dangers of the street. During his years "underneath the earth" he'd overdosed three times, had a gun pointed to his head at least as often, had been beaten so badly by another addict that he'd landed in the hospital. All that had toughened him considerably. But this, this was different. He looked at the cardboard he'd pulled from the dumpster, and the shapeless lumps that were the men he'd followed as if they had the secret to his survival. Was he really like them? Was he really the stinking, disheveled, hollow-eyed addict that the guys in the park had chased away? What about the college graduate, prep school teacher, elite member of Newark's basketball royalty? It was a paradox like Theseus's ship. Had the person he is now replaced the person he'd been ten years before? Or did that man still exist despite the change?

As the interminable night wore on, his sickness worsened. He sank deeper into despair. He was tired of feeling sick, tired of feeling unmoored, tired of the whole drug scene and the wretched people in it. It was then, he told me, that without seeking it, what St. Benedict's had instilled in him resurfaced, faintly at first, but unmistakably. It wasn't the mathematics he learned in class, or the U.S. history. Not even basketball mattered. As important as all that had once been to him, it wasn't what a man who'd made the mistakes he made needed at a time like this. "It was all the foundational stuff they put in place" that counted now, he said, the beliefs that had been embedded so deeply in him he'd forgotten they were there. He once had the discipline it took to show up, on time, in uniform. Every day. All year. He had people who cared about him, who gave him a varsity letter jacket that he couldn't have paid for himself. Who drove him all the way to Susquehanna University. They were the people who helped him and expected nothing in return. They were the ones who had taught him about empathy, about brotherhood, about fighting for what truly matters. And never, ever, giving up. Despite all the years that had passed, he knew he surely was more like them than he was like the guys wrapped in rags who were snoring next to him on the sidewalk.

By the time the sun rose that morning, he was standing at the front door of the methadone clinic, in line to get his daily fix. Inside the treatment center one of the counselors who knew him remarked on how squandered he looked. "You ever think about a residential program?" she asked him. She knew of one on the Lower East Side of Manhattan that would take him, and right there and then he made up his mind to do it. As he stabilized during his first days in recovery, he regained enough of his past self to get in touch with his mother and let her know where he was. She must have passed along his whereabouts to the monks at St. Benedict's because not long after a letter from one of them arrived at the rehab center. The monk told Badger that he mustn't let his struggles define him because "there is life on the other side of addiction."

In a little more than a year after entering the program he was completely off drugs and ready to rebuild his life. He cycled through a series of jobs, none of them highly skilled but all requiring the discipline he learned at St. Benedict's. He eventually landed a position as a mental health aide at a treatment center in Lower Manhattan, and for the next twenty years worked for a succession of drug treatment and social work programs in New York City. "Everything I was doing to get better was done with them in mind," he said, speaking of St. Benedict's. In 2003, when he was in his early forties, he met a smart and pretty bank compliance officer from Brooklyn named Debra Elaine, and after a brief romance, they married. A decade later, the Archdiocese of New York (he refers to it as "the Arch") hired him as a caseworker and later appointed him manager of New York area youth programs, including CYO basketball, the same kind of league he played in at Shanley Gym before he enrolled at St. Benedict's.

When COVID hit, the "Arch" restructured many of its programs, including some that Badger managed. His financial adviser told him that he and Debra had saved enough to simply retire, which he gladly did. (She kept working.) Being retired freed him to return to St. Benedict's and volunteer to coach the freshman basketball team, what he calls the best non-job he's ever had.

"This place planted the foundation of my life," he told me that afternoon at the school. It was a statement of firm conviction, the testimony of a man who'd lived in darkness and survived. The reasons he strayed so far during those turbulent years are many, and even he finds it hard to explain why it started, or exactly why it ended when it did. But he believes that his time at St. Benedict's—the confidence the monks instilled in a poor Black kid, the lessons about perseverance and stability that their very presence in Newark conveyed, their dedication to helping others and to tending to matters of the heart as well as the mind—helped pull him back. He willingly concedes that without the lessons of Newark Abbey, his own story might not have brought him where he is now—financially secure with time enough to visit his mother in her nursing home every week and spend countless hours back on the hardwoods at Shanley, helping kids to get as much out of the game, and out of St. Benedict's, as he did.

He's been around the school long enough that he's coached generations of the same family, and some of the kids who played for him decades ago still call him coach. Leon McBurrows—who ran away during the freshman overnight—played on a summer league team that Badger coached. They are neighbors now, living in the same suburb on Newark's outer ring. And like Badger, McBurrows swears that St. Benedict's changed his life.

He surely didn't appreciate the school in the months after he ran away from the freshman overnight, but he eventually came to embrace its way of life. After graduation, he enrolled at the University of Bridgeport, and while there he was arrested when he locked his keys in his own car and was seen trying to jimmy the door. The white policeman handcuffed him, pushed him into the back of his cruiser, and took him to the station. Being accused of stealing his own car angered him, but instead of lashing out he kept calm and was able to prove to the desk sergeant that the car was his own.

McBurrows told me that in all honesty, he had not been thinking about St. Benedict's that day in Bridgeport. But years later, when he looked back on the episode, he realized that the lesson of St. Benedict's and the wise words of the monks had guided him that day, whether he knew it then or not. The four years on King Boulevard had altered his Newark-bred DNA and like a long-lasting vaccine, stealthily provided immunity against a type of stupidity that could otherwise have ruined his life. Instead of acting out his rage, he considered his options and chose intellect over anger.

He graduated from Bridgeport, and began a career with New Jersey Bell, later Verizon, working his way up to an executive position in systems engineering and field operations, until a stroke in 2013 forced him to retire. A few years ago, he returned to King Boulevard with a special message for Father Ed. "I had to tell him I was sorry," he recalled. "It was important to me to apologize for the way I behaved in freshman year and how much I hated Benedict's."

It took a while, he said, but he realized that without St. Benedict's, the confused, biracial kid he was then might have been consumed by his drug-addled Newark neighborhood. "When I was growing up, most of us weren't expected to live past twenty-five years old. I'm going to be fifty-nine soon and most of my classmates are still here." He thinks that's a hell of an accomplishment for a bunch of white guys in a Black city.

"We never thought of them as white saviors or anything of the sort." He said it with a defensive tone, as if he found the idea absurd. "We respected them for exactly who they were, not what color they were. Their system worked. It worked for all of us."

* * *

St. Benedict's held fast in Newark for one hundred years before youths like Anthony Badger and Leon McBurrows came along, and a measure of the resurrected school's success since 1973 wouldn't have been possible without the support of those previous generations. Many pre-1973 alumni recognize the degree to which St. Benedict's shaped them by giving back to the school, and they have done so to a degree that would make most similar institutions jealous. Men like the late Charles Cawley, '58, who founded the MBNA Bank, attended a far different school from the one that exists today, yet they remained loyal to the mission, and provided millions to preserve the Benedictine presence in Newark. But no alumnus is more identified with the school's rebirth than the one Father Ed has his arm around in a small photograph in the Trophy Room, inches away from Ransford Gyan's soccer player of the year award. In the photo, Father Ed wears his priestly collar, a short-sleeve shirt, and a cautious smile. Next to him in a light blue dress shirt is Robert E. Brennan, '62. In the oversized trophy case that stretches across the room and rises almost to the ceiling, it is the only photograph on display. But it is far from the only way that Brennan is present at St. Benedict's.

He was one year ahead of Dennis Leahy in the mostly white days before the riots shattered Newark, and by a mixture of fate and luck they've remained friends since. An Irish kid from Newark whose father and four brothers all graduated from the prep school when St. Benedict's men were destined to rule the city, and lots more, he wasn't a particularly good student, but he possessed the same kind of street smarts that many St. Benedict's guys had. He could talk tough, and he knew how and when to bluff. He went into business, got comfortable on Wall Street, started his own company, First Jersey Securities, and made a ton of money. He starred in a series of TV commercials, seated in a sleek helicopter flying past the Twin Towers of Manhattan or over the Grand Coulee dam, beckoning, "Come Grow with Us."

Brennan made so much money so fast that when he was still a young man, he started giving it away in spectacular style. An initial $10,000 gift to St. Benedict's kicked off a sweet period for the monks, who watched as their radical idea of reopening the school with no money, no business plan, and no clear idea of how it all was going to work, took off. Brennan kept writing checks until his donations totaled more than $15 million. The money went toward building the new gym and pool complex that bears his parents' names. His money helped cover the cost of renovating the abbey church and monastery, with enough left over to remake the old school into something the monks never could have imagined—a premier prep school run for the benefit of poor city kids.

Brennan's flamboyant success on Wall Street caught the attention of financial authorities. In 1995, the Securities and Exchange Commission charged him with securities fraud and ordered him to pay creditors $75 million. Seton Hall University, where Brennan had earned his undergraduate degree, and where he had been a member of the board of regents for a dozen years, stripped his name off an athletic center on campus that he'd funded. But despite pressure from some alumni, St. Benedict's kept the Brennan name on its athletic complex.[1]

Some of the school's supporters were embarrassed that the monks had accepted tainted money, regardless of what it meant for the school's survival. Robert J. Braun, a classmate of both Father Ed and Bob Brennan, and the long-time education reporter at the Newark *Star-Ledger*, questioned the morality of accepting Brennan's money, and wished that the monks hadn't taken a dime. He publicly confronted Father Ed in his columns, and reported the headmaster's defense.

"It's not an easy issue for us, but Bob has been a spectacular friend, not just to us but to individual kids whose lives he has changed," Father Ed told Braun, who published the quotes in the newspaper in 1995. "Do we judge the morality of every person who sent us a donation?" he asked.

A few years later, those quotes resurfaced when Brennan was hauled into a federal court in Trenton, accused of hiding assets when he declared bankruptcy to avoid paying the $75 million of his court-ordered judgment. Father Ed testified as a character witness for Brennan, claiming that without his continued support, St. Benedict's "would have disappeared long ago."

The prosecution grilled him on the morality question, and brought up the statements he made in Braun's article. Father Ed dodged the attempt to corner him. He reiterated that he had never asked Brennan to explain in detail the legal issues he was involved with because he said it was too complicated for him, a simple priest, to understand.

"But what would stop you anytime from picking up the phone and calling Mr. Brennan, your friend, and asking him, 'Hey, Bob, why'd the court ask you to pay seventy-five million dollars?'" asked the prosecutor.

That's when Father Ed let his Newark roots show. He defended the decision to accept Brennan's money with the same brawny pragmatism that has marked his long tenure at St. Benedict's. "What would stop me? That's easy. Kids getting shot at, a kid whose parents are on the street, it's—there's—I can give you a whole list of things that would stop me."

Brennan was convicted of bankruptcy fraud and spent the next decade in federal prison. Since being released in 2010, he has split his time between New Jersey and Florida, where Father Ed visits whenever he is in the state to raise funds for St. Benedict's. Brennan has not attended the annual alumni communion breakfast at the school for several years, but invariably someone recalls the stunt he pulled at the breakfast in 1983. Then-abbot Melvin Valvano had been negotiating for months to purchase an old camp near the Appalachian Trail in Sussex County, New Jersey, to use as a retreat for city-bound monks and their students. The abbot was deeply disappointed to find out that someone had swooped in and bought the camp out from under him. When alumni gathered in the cafeteria for their communion breakfast that year, Brennan surprised everyone by presenting the abbot with the deed to the camp, which he had secretly purchased for them. Since then, that hundred-acre property has become an integral part of St. Benedict's backpacking project, which this year was a rite of passage for every freshman, whether or not they had any desire to end their first year at St. Benedict's lugging a heavy backpack up and down a rugged trail in a distant corner of New Jersey.

CHAPTER 18

Trial by Trail

FOR EVERY ST. Benedict's graduate of the last fifty years, coming back to the school is a challenge to the passage of time. They are likely to see Father Ed and the familiar core group of monks roaming the halls, moving more slowly or maybe limping, but however improbably after so much time, still there. Alumni can't help but be touched by this complex linkage to the past, and when someone at King Boulevard recognizes them by name decades after they graduated, they can feel like they too have passed through the years unchanged from the adolescents they were so long ago.

If, however, they happen to show up at the property in late April, their homecoming may trigger the same twin emotions of excitement and dread they experienced when they prepared to take on the challenge of hiking the Appalachian Trail when they were freshmen. Nobody knows that better than Cass. He completed the backpacking project as a fourteen-year-old in 1987, and he's helped run it since he got his college degree at Notre Dame and came back to St. Benedict's thirty years ago.

"You are joining a long tradition of people just like yourselves taking the challenge of going out into the wilderness," Cass told the entire class of freshmen as they assembled on St. Benedict's lower playing field on a Monday morning in late April 2024. There was a keen sense of summer already in the air and a sky so clear and blue that the glimpse of Newark rising over the field looked positively hopeful. The students who lined up in ragged rows before him came from as close as Newark and as far away as Mongolia. They represented many different faiths and spoke a dozen different languages at home. Some fit the physical profile of fourteen-year-old boys, and others were already man-sized tall and broad. They had gone through the challenges that St. Benedict's had thrown at them all year, and only days before had endured final exams for their winter courses. Now, after a spring break that lasted just a long weekend, they were embarking on the biggest challenge of all.

Cass outlined the task ahead—hiking more than fifty miles of the rugged Appalachian Trail from High Point State Park in the extreme northwestern corner of New Jersey down the rocky spine of the Appalachian mountain range as it plunges through the state before emerging at the awesome Delaware Water Gap, where the famous river has cut a monumental passage through the wooded peaks. They would carry on their backs everything they need for their week-long trip, regardless of the weather. In his three decades on the trail, Cass has experienced temperatures that have topped 100 degrees, and dipped below 20. He's hiked through fierce thunderstorms, tempests with hail the size of golf balls, terrifying lightning, and howling wind. He's confronted bears and rattlesnakes and spooky noises in the middle of the night. All that, and more, awaits them. The trail would exhaust them. They would be scared. They would miss their moms. And some would be sorely tempted to give up. But he assured them that whatever elements they encounter, whatever conditions they might run into, "we will face them. And we will face them together."

Most of these teens have never spent a long night in the intense dark of the woods, where sylvan quiescence magnifies the scampering of a squirrel so it can sound like an attacking bear to those who are scared to be there. They've never cooked for themselves, or navigated using trail markers that, if missed, can doom them to wander aimlessly for hours. They've never had to bandage a blister, treat an infection, or poop in the woods.

Individually, they won't learn enough to make it through a week on the trail, and do it safely. "But together, as a team, you will," Cass promised them. This is not only the basic rule of the trail, but also of the monastery and the school. It is an echo of Mark Comesañas's spiritual message about being of one accord. Students are constantly reminded that they belong to a community, and that what the community needs outweighs what any individual wants.

Teamwork. Togetherness. Leave no one behind. All that is part of the tradition that Cass passed along to this new generation of hikers. To make his point, he told them a tale of how, when he was a freshman who was just as bewildered as they are now, one of his teammates got to school late and the bus taking them to the mountains left without him. When his team set up their tent they realized that the guy who missed the bus had been assigned to bring their tent poles. They spent a miserable couple of nights trying to keep their tent from collapsing.

"You are accountable to one another," Cass told them. If that means showing up at the house of the guy with the tent poles to make sure he gets on the bus, then do it.

* * *

Before the freshmen set foot on the trail, they were put through a brief regimen of physical conditioning. Kaleb—whose pants legs rose steadily higher above his ankles since last July, who had put his heart into urging his classmates to turn to each other and shout "I Love You. You're worth it"—had metamorphosed into hard-ass Commander Kaleb, assigned to lead the thirty-nine boys of Maroon company through the most sustained challenge of their first year at St. Benedict's. Assisting him was Everett, the rower who lost both his colors and his membership on the rowing team after the championship soccer game. Given the second chance he pleaded for in his public apology, he had earned his way back into the community.

Outfitted in trail gear, his socks pulled up over his pants legs in the approved anti-tick outfit, Kaleb warned his company that the trail is "both a physical and mental challenge." They might think of themselves as tough city kids but this, he told them, is different. In his own freshman year hike, a teammate grew so tired and sore that he came close to tears. "Go on without me," he whimpered. "I'll find my own way home." But as team captain, Kaleb had assured him that no one would get left behind. While the exhausted hiker caught his breath, his teammates transferred some of the weight from his pack to theirs. He still struggled, but they stayed together step by step through the woods until everyone made it to trail's end at the Water Gap.

Basic trail training for the girls was conducted separately but conveyed the same readiness message. As a member of the track team, Sheridan had no trouble with the physical conditioning the girls were put through. She is a trim, five-foot-two, 109-pound runner and jumper. She easily completed the pushups, sit-ups, and planks that others struggled with. Sprint relays proved to be a test for some girls, but not for her. Even in hiking boots, she ran effortlessly. When the girls had to repeat the relay, this time in an awkward, head-down, insect crawl, one struggled so much that Sheridan had to jog out and coax her across the finish line.

With 187 teenage hikers hitting the same section of the Appalachian Trail, Cass had to spread them out to keep them from overwhelming the woods or the camps where they'd spend most nights. They left Newark in separate companies over three consecutive days. Sheridan and the girls of Burgundy company were among the first to leave. They departed early on Saturday morning after receiving a blessing and a few words from Father Ed, who was struggling. Just a few days earlier Aurora, a St. Bernard–pit bull mix the monks had recently rescued to keep it from being put down, had lived up to her reputation for being overly reactive toward other animals. Father Ed had taken her for a walk on the property one morning and she had dashed after a squirrel, pulling him headfirst down a set of concrete steps.

"Despite the horrible, almost catastrophic fall I took, I'm here," he told the girls, while suppressing the smirk that crept across his badly bruised cheek. He cautioned them not to make excuses for themselves when the trail gets tough, which he assured them it would. "Carry out whatever you carry in, and always watch your language because other hikers will know you are from St. Benedict's." And before giving them a short blessing, he reminded them of the number one rule of the trail: stay together.

The section of the Appalachian Trail that the students hike starts about a mile and a half below the High Point monument in an auxiliary parking lot where the buses are unloaded. Several Naval Academy volunteers, both men and women, accompanied the hikers, although they had instructions to leave all map reading and directions to Sheridan and the other girls who were picked to serve as navigators, even if their team takes a wrong turn.

Despite strict orders to leave home anything that was not essential, some girls were bent under backpacks so loaded down with blankets, pots, and who knows what else that they may have weighed more than the girls themselves. As they waited for the signal to start, a few of them took out bottles of soap and started blowing bubbles. Sheridan was eager to get going, her long braids encased in a scarlet bonnet that she let hang over her shoulder. She said that it felt unreal to actually be starting the hike they'd been anticipating since they'd entered St. Benedict's.

As Sheridan made final adjustments to her pack, she told me that she'd never gone camping or spent any time in the woods. She was nervous about it, but also determined to prove that she could do something as physically taxing, and outside her comfort zone, as hiking the trail. She said she also hoped to learn patience, which doesn't come naturally to her. The day before the hike started, she'd competed in a track meet, running a relay, jumping the hurdles, and even clearing a modest seven feet in the pole vault. She was used to going full speed, and expected others to do the same. But she'd been told many times already that on the trail the team can go no faster than its slowest member. She then put me on notice: I shouldn't expect to talk to her when she crosses the bridge at the end of the trail because she'll be crying.

The morning was ideal for backpacking—serene sun, a cozy breeze, and a well-marked section of trail that was mostly dry. Sheridan's team, the Bisons, took off in high spirits, setting a brisk pace. In no time they were singing, going through a play list that ranged widely from rap to pop before settling into a ragged rendition of "Wheels on the Bus." It made me think that despite their casual bravado, these fourteen-year-old girls were more anxious about being in the woods than they let on. By the time they stopped for lunch, Sheridan, a self-professed picky eater, leaned against her backpack, pulled out a bag of pretzels, and leisurely snacked on them until her captain gave the signal that their break was over and it was once again time to hit the trail. The girls weren't able to keep the same pace throughout the rest of the day. The Bisons' captain, who was even smaller and slighter than Sheridan, had to move from the back of the line, where the captain normally stays to make sure there were no stragglers, to the front, the position of the slowest hiker. Sheridan took her place in the rear. But even with the switch, the captain was so burned out by midafternoon that someone else had to carry her pack while she caught her breath.

The first few boys teams set out from the same High Point parking lot the following morning. Some of them also had ignored advice about limiting the weight in their packs. I counted at least four who were carrying battery-powered fans. One had a football. And I watched Michael, who with Finn and Raúl belonged to the eight-man Eagles team, stuff a full-sized rubber mallet into his backpack. On their first night on the trail, I stood by as he used that mallet to pound in the stakes for the monster tent he'd carried. He'd convinced the others that it made more sense to carry one big tent they could all fit into than several small ones. The tent belonged to his family and he assured his teammates that his mother had shown him the proper way to set it up. With him giving instructions, it took the Eagles nearly twenty minutes and a lot of arguing to get the huge tent in something resembling its intended shape. Michael blamed the delay on them being so tired after their first day on the trail; they'd surely do better next time. After all the teams picked at their dinner of ramen noodles, I pulled Michael aside to find out how he was doing. He conceded that putting up the tent had been more complicated than he expected, and he described the ramen as awful. This first day on the trail had drained this cocky freshman who earlier in the year had described himself as having a big ego. "The trail's already humbled me," he said. He also admitted that he was homesick. "I miss my mom a lot," he said. "I really want to see my mom."

Before Raúl turned in that first night, he told me that the physical conditioning he'd attained during basketball season, along with the practice hikes the Eagles had taken during the leadup to the trail, had prepared him well. He suspected that the same cousins who had warned him to beware of the freshman overnight had exaggerated how exhausting the hike would be in order to scare him. As long as he drank enough water to keep from getting dehydrated, he said he'd be all right. Still, there were four days to go and he didn't expect it to be easy. In fact, he didn't want it to be. He hoped to prove that, despite his size, he could face big challenges, just as he had when he tried to convince Coach Badger that he was good enough to dribble past players on opposing teams who towered over him.

It was getting dark, and Commander Kaleb shouted for Maroon company to quiet down and go to sleep. It had been a long day for all of them, starting out in the familiar streets of home, and ending in the deep woods they'd never seen before. Raúl hesitated to head back to Michael's big tent. He said he wanted to tell me something else. "Since the overnight, I've grown more as a man," he said, referring to his initial encounter with St. Benedict's expectations of him last summer. He sounded like he wanted me to think of him, and St. Benedict's, in a certain way. "That's what the school is about, you know, to prepare you for life." Then he said good night, and headed back to the Eagles' tent which, despite the encroaching darkness, was easy to find because it was by far the biggest tent of any in Maroon company.

* * *

On day two, both the girls and the boys camps awoke with their first of many aches, blisters, and complaints but with a budding sensation of accomplishment. Sheridan had slept in a tent with three other girls—her first-ever sleepover—and was surprised by how loudly some girls snored, and how uncomfortable the ground can be if you have to sleep on it. Word had spread that one girl on another team had been injured in a freak accident. A bear bag with food the girls had hung from a tree limb had snapped its fastener and fell just as she was passing underneath. Cass, who's trained in wilderness medicine, got her an ice pack, and determined she would be able to continue the hike. When they finally got underway, forty-five minutes later than planned, some girls thought their packs felt heavier than before and they complained that they were carrying too much water. Their captains assured them that they would need every drop.

The long line of hikers snaked noisily through the woods. Sheridan called out for one of gospel singer Kirk Franklin's tunes. As they sang, they ran into thru-hikers who said they were trekking the entire 2,190 miles of the Appalachian Trail from Georgia to Maine. Black and Latino kids in the woods are a rare sight, and at first the hikers weren't sure what to make of it. When I explained the trail project to them their eyes widened. They thought that bringing city kids into the woods was inspired, and they expressed their wholehearted support. A few said they thought every school in the country ought to have something like it.

Besides the miles they walk on the A.T. itself, St. Benedict's hikers also have to cover more than eleven erratic up-and-down miles as they make their way to and from the camps where, because their groups are so large, they are required to set up overnight. Those off-trail miles traverse steep old roads, long since abandoned, or rough trails bushwhacked up and down mountainsides without regard to how taxing they would be for hikers. They had to take one of those steep access roads to a 4-H camp where they overnighted. Rutted in spots, the road was difficult to walk in daylight, and treacherous for a number of teams that got there after sunset. Kaleb's Maroon company had made good time and was first to arrive at the camp. It was midafternoon, and Raúl and the other Eagles were giddy as they looked over an expanse of neatly trimmed grass facing a lovely lake, anticipating a restful evening under the stars.

Their joy was short-lived. Kaleb announced that as a way of proving their mettle, the whole of Maroon company would forgo that idyllic site and instead make camp where he and his team had set up two years earlier when he was a freshman. Exhausted hikers who had already dropped their packs grudgingly put them back on and followed Kaleb to an overgrown hillside, filled with bramble and tree fall, and with hardly a foot of level ground. Kaleb tried to fire them up by acknowledging that the site where he and Everett had camped as freshmen was challenging, to say the least, but in the spirit of brotherhood, and to prove just how tough they were, Maroon company would spend the night there, leaving the grassy area they first saw for the brothers in the White company, which hadn't yet arrived.

Tired, hungry, and confused, Kaleb's company verged on mutiny. They groused without mercy, wondering why their commander had passed up an ideal spot and instead chose an area that looked like a dump. Kaleb seemed genuinely surprised by their reaction, and even more so when Cavill Henriques, a St. Benedict's English teacher with years of trail experience and the title of field commander, told him he didn't blame the boys for complaining. Kaleb countered: If it was good enough for us as freshmen, it should be good enough for them. Henriques quietly reasoned with him. As commander, the decision about where to camp was certainly his to make. But if he insisted on forcing everyone to honor this nod to his own history and tradition, he risked alienating the entire company. Kaleb swallowed his pride and brought everyone back to the flat, open field, which they eventually shared with White company.

Despite Cass's inspiring words about teamwork and staying together, the boys were quickly discovering that hiking in teams of eight is far more difficult than hiking alone. The willingness to follow someone else's lead isn't instinctual for many of these kids, and some team leaders struggled from the outset to control uncooperative teammates who refused to defy the code of city streets and let another student tell them what to do. While Finn led the Eagles through mile after mile of hiking without much issue, Kaleb's cousin Derek, who has the towering physical presence of a leader, was unable to corral two unruly hikers, and that was hurting his entire team, the Owls. One of the trouble makers was a state champion sprinter who refused to slow down. The other just didn't want to be there. His boots went unlaced, he broke the belt on his backpack, and the faster the sprinter charged ahead, the more he lagged behind.

Derek repeatedly called back the sprinter when he wandered so far ahead he was almost out of sight. At the same time, his recalcitrant hiker frequently stopped short and absolutely refused to take another step. No matter what Derek said to them, neither would listen, which led him to eventually wonder where disrespect ended and outright defiance began. The constant disputes put the Owls in a sour mood and convinced Derek that he was falling short as a leader. Cass had cautioned all the captains during their training not to turn to the adults on the trail if their leadership was challenged because doing so undercut their authority. But had he talked to the midshipmen, they'd have told him that this critical aspect of leadership can be a test for them as well.

At the Naval Academy, they receive classroom theory about leadership, but it's out in the field, with unpredictable conditions of weather and the challenges of time, terrain, and team dynamics, that they actually learn what it takes to convince others to follow their lead.

As we hiked hour after hour, and I rushed from the girls expeditions to the boys, I didn't notice any of them taking more than a passing interest in what they were seeing, hearing, or feeling in the outdoors. Even when I spied elusive pink lady's slippers blooming along the trail, I couldn't get these fourteen- and fifteen-year-olds with their legs in perpetual motion to slow down to take a second look at the relatively rare wild orchids that must grow for years before they blossom. One of the first directives in *The Rule of St. Benedict* is to bring every effort to completion, and these kids were single-mindedly focused on reaching the end of the trail. We passed the gnawed-at trunks of huge trees that beavers had downed to create a pond, and no one noticed. A plague of gypsy moth caterpillars spurred no questions, and the sight of four-inch long millipedes on the rocks we crossed only elicited screeches and Sheridan's high-pitched "I don't do bugs" affirmation.

Still, there was time for more than racking up miles. For a good half hour one day, I listened to Kaleb debate another hiker about the relative merits of Popeyes versus Wendy's as a breakfast venue. I heard a lot of talk among the Bisons about dating and hair extensions. They were intent on accomplishing everything the boys did, and they spent many moments wondering where the boys teams were. By the third day, Sheridan was still gabbing away jovially at the end of the line of hikers, casually using the Bison flagpole as her walking stick, the banner as soiled and sweaty as she was.

They ended their third day on the trail at a YMCA camp, a favorite of the hikers because it was the only place they are allowed to have a campfire. A mama bear and her cubs gave them a fright when they ran across an open field, close to their tents. The girls organized games, and some of them got muddy, which led to another leadership test. The camp only had a few showers, which were strictly off-limits to the hikers. But one girl managed to sneak in and wash off. When the leaders found out, they decided that in the interest of equality, she should be forced to roll in the mud again. The other girls who would have loved to wash off several days of trail grime heartily approved.

Because the next day's hike was one of the shortest trail segments, the girls didn't set out until noon, with the temperature in the low 80s. Some of the Bisons were already hurting before they began the climb up the steep and partially caved-in road they had easily descended the day before. I watched two girls at the end of the column hold hands as they walked, encouraging each other to press on.

The grueling climb up the mountainside, in the midday heat, at the start of a fourth day on the trail, tested their wills and taxed their spirits. They rejoiced when they saw that Father Philip was waiting for them with containers of water at the next road crossing. After a short break and some of their last remaining snacks, they got back on the trail for another long hike that ended at a shady ravine where they could take off their packs. Alexander Melchor, a burly 2013 graduate who is dean of the girls division, encouraged them to eat, drink, and refill their bottles because there wouldn't be another chance to get water until after they ended the hike at the Water Gap the following day. The final challenge that afternoon would be a long, steep, exhausting ascent up Bear Mountain, as rocky and rough a section of the trail as they'd encountered since leaving High Point.

When all the girls had eaten their last snacks and topped off their water bottles, they assaulted Bear Mountain together, a tapped-out column of sagging bonnets and weary shoulders ascending slowly in the last minutes of daylight. The line of climbers slowed down whenever one girl slipped. And it stalled completely when one of them was clearly struggling to the point of exhaustion and couldn't go on. Other girls offered to take heavy items from her pack and carry them on their own backs. At the ridgeline, the trail leveled off, giving the slowest girls a chance to catch up. It was already getting dark by the time they reached the place where they'd spend the night. A nearly full moon, bright as an approaching high beam, crested the ridge. With no camp nearby, they had to set up their tents on rocky outcrops and rough patches of stony ground flanking both sides of the trail. They worked quickly and efficiently, having had the benefit of a week's practice. But they were still getting used to the sounds of the forest. When a strange noise frightened one of the girls, Melchor told everyone to grab a pot and follow him. With images of the mama bear and her cubs at the YMCA camp still fresh, they banged on their pots, hoping to scare off any wild thing lurking in the shadows. They found nothing.

It was deep-woods-dark by the time Melchor called the girls to gather around him. They crawled out of their tents already in their pajamas and sleep bonnets. "I'm proud of every single one of you for pushing yourselves to the limit," he said. By now, the girls were calling him Papa Bear, and they listened to him as they might have listened to their father. "This is one of those challenges that not everybody can do." All the girls in Burgundy company who started at the High Point parking lot were still on the trail. There had been no major mishaps, no serious injuries, no personality clashes severe enough for anyone to have been sent home, as had happened in previous years. Melchor told them that the remaining eight miles were mostly downhill, and could be completed, if they kept a steady pace, in about four hours. "It's really just packing up, getting ready to go, and we're gone."

Kaleb and Maroon company reached the same spot the following evening. The Eagles mastered the final climb up Bear Mountain with relative ease, but one of the Owls stumbled several times. Exhausted, he grunted that he just couldn't go on. Derek and the other Owls, including the ones who had defied him earlier, helped him up and spurred him to continue to the campsite, which was just a few minutes away, telling him that they'd all be home by the same time tomorrow.

They arrived at their campsite a few hours earlier than the girls had, and set up their tents with plenty of daylight left. By now, Michael and the Eagles had gelled into something like a coordinated team. After arguing about it for several nights, Michael had agreed to change the sequence of steps they followed in setting up the tent, and that speeded up the process considerably. It took them just five minutes that last night, lightning speed compared to almost twenty the first time they'd tried. Michael beamed.

Once their tents were up and their sleeping bags unpacked, Maroon company gathered at a nearby outcropping they had christened Pride Rock. Kaleb congratulated them for toughing it out and maintaining such good spirits while under stress. The two midshipmen who had hiked with them acknowledged how impressed they were by the boys' perseverance. And Field Commander Henriques, who had completed the hike ten times already, tried to put the trail experience into broader perspective. For some of you, he said, the biggest challenge has been simply walking. "How many of you got blisters?" At least half raised their hands. "How many ran out of water at some point?" A few more. And how many were miserable because of the people they were with? Nearly every hand shot up.

"One of the most difficult things about this project is not the hiking. It's working together. Trying to make this work as a team." How do you deal with people who are hugely different from you? Who have different abilities from you? Who think that things are funny that other people don't? It was the essence of leadership that he was asking about, and Derek, the Owls' uncertain captain, could have told him how he had overcome the challenges of guiding his unruly team. Despite the contrariness of the quick-footed hiker who constantly bounded far ahead, and the Owl with unlaced boots who dallied at the tail end of the group, Derek had continued talking to them as equals, and responding to them whenever they too needed help. As he had learned about leadership in St. Benedict's *Rule*, his example was more important than were any of his words. He had moved ahead without complaining, not even about the defiant ones, and pitched in when any member of the team faltered. He had reached an accord with the impatient one and the laggard, and that had helped the entire team conquer Bear Mountain and, Derek was certain, would carry them all the way to the Water Gap. Working cooperatively is difficult but necessary, Henriques told Maroon company. And though he didn't spell it out to the exhausted hikers, sprawled over Pride Rock as a glorious amber moon rose over the cliffs, it is also one of the most important and challenging aspects of life.

* * *

The girls were so eager to get going that last morning on the trail that they were up at five and hit the trail before six. Just as the commanders had forecast, the final day's hike was over in about four hours. Sheridan rolled an ankle on some rocks, but that didn't slow down her or her team. At trail's end, Cass greeted every girl with a hug and slipped a small, embroidered patch into their hands to signify their completion of the project (an artifact some would treasure for years but others would never want to see again). They then crossed over a small wooden bridge that marked their passage into the St. Benedict's community, entitling most of them to leave behind the gray shirts they wore throughout their freshman year and put on the black uniforms that would mark them as members of the community when they return for the new school year in a few weeks.

After Sheridan and the Bisons clopped over the bridge, they gathered in a circle to jointly celebrate their accomplishment. As soon as they clasped hands, Sheridan teared up, as she had predicted she would, and was too emotional to say anything. But the Bisons' tiny captain spoke up and said she was proud of each of them. She admitted that she had struggled to keep up, and she knew that others had too. "I know it was hard," she said. "We all had our problems. We had our tough times. We had times we didn't want to keep going. Times we wanted to quit.

But we pushed through, and we got it done. I am so proud of y'all. I love y'all." Then someone shouted, "Let's give it up for Sheridan. She got through them bugs."

As the Bisons emerged from the woods, Lucia and Kymberli were there to congratulate them for completing the trail, and symbolically welcome them into the St. Benedict's community.

By the time the Eagles and the rest of Maroon company crossed the bridge the following day, they and their packs were dripping wet. Thunderstorms had blown through just as they were waking up, and continued on and off for the final four hours on the trail. Cass greeted them at the bridge, gave them their patches, and encouraged each soggy team to express their feelings to each other. But unlike Sheridan's Bisons, the Eagles were in no mood to rehash the hike. And they certainly weren't going to shed any tears. When they crossed the wooden bridge they gathered in a tight circle, arms over weary shoulders. In his low-key way, Finn said that as captain, he was happy that everyone had made it to the end without getting hurt. He was relieved that they all had completed the challenge, and he was actually thankful that it had rained that last day because it gave them the right to brag that they had put up with everything that nature had thrown at them. Michael thanked the others for keeping things on a high note, even when they were down. Raúl said the hike hadn't been as exhausting as his cousins had told him it would be, but he was glad it was over and he didn't think he'd ever do it again.

The Bisons and Eagles had completed the trail without suffering any major setbacks, but when I checked with Cass, he was unusually frazzled. In the thirty years he'd been involved with the trail project, he said he'd never dealt with so many accidents and mishaps. The Bisons and the Eagles didn't know it, but nearly a dozen hikers on other teams had sprained their ankles, knees, or shoulders. A few more had stumbled and hit their heads, one serious enough that he'd been airlifted to a hospital (where doctors cleared him). One team got lost for several hours, and another had so many disciplinary problems that it had to be disbanded. And for the first time in his three decades on the trail, Cass sent one student—a girl—to the doctor's office with what he thought was an abscess but turned out to be a blistering spider bite.

In the week after they completed the trail, all the hikers were required to write an essay describing how hiking had changed them. Many wrote that they found out things about themselves they hadn't even been searching for, which is a virtue of hiking whether it's a month on the *Camino de Santiago*, or a stroll in a local park. Some, to my surprise, even soaked up a little appreciation for nature and the outdoors. Raul's essay neatly summed up what the whole effort meant for these city-hardened kids. "Walking through forests and climbing mountains isn't just about getting from A to B," he wrote. "It's about finding out who you really are." He felt that the trail proved he was "tougher, more patient, and more grateful" than he ever knew. In other words, like most alumni, he came back from the mountains saying, "If I could do the A.T., I can do anything."

CHAPTER 19

Playing the Apron

WHILE THE FRESHMEN hikers were still sixty miles away pitting their inner strength against tradition and the trail, the rest of St. Benedict's students were taking spring term electives. Teachers are encouraged to prepare challenging courses for the five-week term that is devoted to special projects. The result can be ambitious offerings like Art, Nature, and Protest; Social Justice and Science; or classes that are more comforting than contentious, like golf caddying, organic gardening, and the New York City experience. One of the most popular spring term classes is Culinary Arts, aka Real Men Cook, which mixes the history and sociology of food with basic kitchen survival skills. Noah had pined for the class for years. In his mind, knowing how to cook for himself would make him a stronger, more independent man, and that was his ultimate goal. But he had been repeatedly passed over because seniors, who get first choice, filled the roster. This year, as a senior, he finally got his chance. While he was happy shopping for the ingredients to prepare *Fusilli alla Napoletana*, styled on a dish he and his mother share at a favorite local restaurant, Rey was forcing himself to face one of the most traumatic days of his young life, and do it in front of the entire school.

By this time Rey had abandoned all hope of regaining his leadership post, but it bothered him that he still hadn't explained to the rest of the school what he'd done, or why. He had repeatedly offered to make a public apology, but Father Ed and Dean Rodriguez insisted that he refrain from saying anything more. The year was coming to an end with many things left unsaid, which wasn't his style. To keep his honor intact, and redeem his character, he had agreed to play a leading role in this year's Stage Rage production as his spring term elective.

Of all the unique things that St. Benedict's does, Stage Rage is one of the most arresting, and the most revealing. Guided by the counseling team, and with direction from the theater director, a dozen students reenact on stage some of the worst moments of their lives. Just as the hikers trained before hitting the trail, Rey and the others involved in this year's Stage Rage spent several weeks in a classroom exploring their own psyches before moving to the auditorium. There, they took cues from Drama Guild director Patricia Flynn, who helped them produce skits that re-created a personal trauma from their past. Because most students have never been on stage, and never opened up so publicly about themselves, Flynn gently guides them through the process, mixing rudimentary stage direction with the revelatory analysis that the school's team of psychologists separately helped them tackle. "Play the apron," she tells them when they set up too far back on the stage and need to move closer to the audience to maximize their impact. But that closeness and intensity is more than a stage direction. She constantly pushes them to reach deeper into themselves, chiding some when their initial efforts come across as too literal. "All of you have really profound stories to share," she told this year's performers. "We're not going to do it superficially and disrespect you in that way."

One senior in this year's group tried to unravel the feelings of worthlessness and despair that had led him to attempt suicide. Another described how betrayed he felt when his mother was arrested on drug charges after being stopped for a routine traffic violation. Last year, Dr. Lamourt had encouraged Tareek to take part in Stage Rage. Tareek somehow managed to get over his reluctance to be in the spotlight and gave a stunning recounting of his mother's shooting. In a voice that sometimes waivered, he told the rest of the school that before the shooting, he didn't think men could be so violent toward women, "and certainly not my mom." Looking directly at his classmates, he seemed to harbor some guilt for not having protected her. He ended his performance by telling the audience that since the shooting, he's been exercising and lifting weights so he can stay strong "to help if people need me."

This year, it was Tareek who needed help. After his strong fall term, when he delighted his guardians by earning honors and running strong during the regular track season, he slid back into his old habits and, as a result, his grades tanked. At one point he stopped going to counseling so he could focus on his schoolwork, but even then he wasn't able to concentrate on his studies. Turmoil surrounded him. He broke up with his girlfriend and started spending more time with his biological parents. He was sent to Father Ed's office several times because of increasingly serious disciplinary problems. He fell into such a funk that he missed the state track championships where he had been expected to do well. Dr. Lamourt called the Haygoods and suggested that it might be best if Tareek left St. Benedict's temporarily for a more structured psychological program off the property. Father Ed told them not to be concerned about him missing class during that time away; it was far more important to tend to Tareek's heart than to worry about his grades. If the intervention got him back on track, he could rejoin his class before the school year ended and make up lost work.

Tareek was stable enough to return to St. Benedict's a few weeks before the end of spring term, and Dr. Lamourt thought that participating in Stage Rage again this year would give him an outlet for dealing with his inner turmoil. This time, the psychologist suggested that Tareek write and perform his own rap song, expressing things that other students might also be experiencing. Tareek agreed, but after several days of trying, he managed to write only a few words. Flynn scrapped the idea of a song and instead gave him the role of stage narrator, where the script would be written for him.

The other students, including Rey, wrote their own skits. Flynn pushed him to dive deeper into his inner self, forgoing the notion of re-creating the scene of him cheating on the history exam and instead, reaching into the part of himself that was responsible for making such a disastrous decision, and ask, Why?

Flynn had scheduled a number of performances in front of different groups of students at St. Benedict's as well as at other area schools. A big part of the value of Stage Rage comes from publicly raising complex issues that resonate with the audience, encouraging individuals who've experienced similar traumas to seek help. But just before the premiere, she had to scrap that schedule because Father Maynard Nagengast, the oldest monk at Newark Abbey who'd taught generations of students, died. He was a few months shy of what would have been his ninetieth birthday. The school scrambled to make time for a funeral mass that all students would attend. Most Stage Rage performances had to be canceled. That left just a single production that would be put on in front of the entire school.

* * *

On the day of the performance, Sheridan and the rest of Burgundy company filed into the auditorium, only recently returned from the trail and still wearing their hiking shirts. Kaleb led the Maroon company hikers to several rows on the right side of the center aisle. Flynn scurried around, giving last-minute instructions, and Dr. Lamourt stood ready to provide support in case the performance triggered upsetting memories for anyone there.

When it was time to begin, ten teenagers dressed entirely in black walked onto the stage that was empty but for a row of mismatched chairs. Each student silently took a seat and stared forward. Each wore a full-face plastic mask that they had marked to symbolically reflect who they appeared to be on the outside, as well hide who they actually were. On his mask, Rey had painted teardrops below the eye openings. On one cheek he drew a red, yellow, and green traffic light. On his forehead he put the S symbol of Superman, and wrote, "You're not who you say you are!"

Flynn barked "Action!" and the boys stood up and removed their masks. "The stories you are about to hear are the real-life stories of the students on stage, so please show the respect that it deserves," announced the first in line. "We're sharing our stories not only because it helped us, but because it might help you. This is Stage Rage."

Rey opened the set. Following Flynn's directions, he "played the apron," standing just a few feet from the edge of the stage to get as close as possible to the audience. Several classmates formed a circle around him. Each one represented a conflicting emotion that had tormented him in his worst moments of self-reflection. The narrator stood off to stage right, but it wasn't Tareek. When he had consistently failed to show up for rehearsals, Flynn put another student in his place. The understudy narrator set the scene: "Sometimes the hardest person to tell the truth to is yourself."

Rey and the other students are neither playwrights nor actors, but their presentations were so raw and so intimate, that their emotions captured the attention of the audience. No hand needed to be raised to maintain silence.

On stage, the other students circled around Rey, dressing him down with reproaching stares as each one crossed in front of him.

"You showed them exactly who you are," one cried out in a mocking voice. It was the sound of city streets talking.

"Your image is shattered." That was the humbled voice of the senior group leader, the role he had so wholeheartedly assumed, then foolishly, irrationally, bargained away.

The skit continued like that, one streetwise accusation countered by a contrite reckoning from alternating sides of Rey's complex character.

"Let's go find something to make us feel better."

"You can't come back from this. It's all pointless."

"We're untouchable, Rey. We can do whatever we want."

"You're worthless, Rey."

"It's too painful. Let's go cause some hell."

"You're just like your father."

Rey stood silently as the other players continued revolving around him. After he'd been thoroughly whiplashed by their words, when the conflicting dimensions of his character were left exposed and raw, he shouted a pronouncement that echoed the spirit of brotherhood and community that is at the heart of St. Benedict's.

"I can't keep fighting this alone. I need help."

It now seemed clear that during the first half of the school year, when he was the very image of the senior group leader—confident, firm, decisive—Rey had been playacting. He had tried to discard his identity as a kid from North Newark who came from a troubled family, and assume an entirely new role as the ideal senior group leader. He was on the property twenty-four hours a day, nearly every day. He was seeing Lucia, the most prominent girl in the school. Every aspect of his life related to St. Benedict's, and none reflected his father's Newark. Or so he thought. As much as he had tried to banish that part of his past, that aspect of who he was, he had failed and it was still there, still whispering in his ear that he deserved to get an A in U.S. History, no matter what it cost.

On stage, now alone, Rey spoke directly to the hundreds of students seated in the auditorium before him. His monologue had all the cadences of a counseling session with Dr. Lamourt. "I struggle to express myself in an authentic way because I don't know who I really am." Forfeiting his role as senior group leader had erased his identity. "I have an idea of the person I want to be, but I constantly act in ways that don't represent that person." He comprehended the difference between right and wrong, but there was something deep inside his heart that seemed to always steer him toward the worst outcome. "It feels like I left a path of destruction behind me in my search for identity," he lamented. That was the real consequence of his action in that overheated classroom in December. By cheating he had not only hurt himself, but had damaged the whole school. He had owned up to it, taken the consequences, and changed how he saw his place in the world. Now he was getting back into the fight. Standing on stage in front of his classmates, describing the disappointment he so obviously felt at letting them down, he was converting his personal trauma into a touchstone lesson for many of the young men and women sitting in the plush seats in front of him.

Rey left the stage after his skit, but he came back as a bit player in several others, including one where he played the role of Dr. Lamourt. The other performances were powerful representations of suicide, abandonment, and hopelessness. Tareek watched it all from one of the auditorium seats.

When the last skit ended, the performers returned to the stage and put their masks back on. The narrator urged the audience to reflect on what they'd seen and heard. "If any of these stories touched you in any way, or you see your own self in these stories, please get help and talk to somebody you trust." Then, after stunned applause, the performers removed their masks and sat on the lip of the stage to take questions. Most were directed at Rey, and, once more, he didn't flinch.

"I think everybody in this room knows the setbacks I had this year. And that was a major shock to my identity. This place is home for me, and I felt like I betrayed it directly with what happened. And that senior group leader image—senior group leader and Rey were one, and I didn't know who I was. Having your whole identity stripped down, and everyone in the room looking at me differently, was heavy and I'm still dealing with it, and it's something I'll be dealing with for years."

It was difficult to listen to him tear himself apart like that.

"Sometimes people who struggle the most may have the perfect image on the outside," he said. "It's important for adults not to give up on kids." As the kids are told when they prepare to hit the trail, it's easy to be in charge when things are going according to plan—"sunny and 75," is the way those perfect days are described. But it's when things go awry, and it's cloudy and cold and the expected turns upside down the way it did for Rey, that leadership is tested and character comes under the closest scrutiny. At those times, there's no way to fake it.

Although Rey had to bury his hope of regaining his title, nobody at St. Benedict's gave up on Rey. From the Building Bridges basketball game through intramural competitions and even Stage Rage and many small interventions when he lent Noah, Lucia, and other students a helping hand, it was clear that he still possessed the stuff of a leader. And at the senior awards dinner a few nights after Stage Rage, when members of the faculty toasted each graduating senior, Dr. Lamourt gave a brutally honest testimonial that touched directly on Rey's stunning fall from grace and the dignified way he'd bounced back. "Reynaldo experienced a tremendous setback this year," Lamourt addressed the cafeteria full of seniors and their parents. "However, instead of hiding, he committed to not only work on himself but to continue to be of service to those around him. Rey is a great example to all of us that it's not only about having grit, but you must use it with purpose. Make no mistake—this young man has great purpose."

As I listened to Lamourt stand up for Rey that night, I thought back to what it felt like when someone stood up for me when I was Rey's age, and had made decisions that were as calamitous as his. At the time it happened to me, I was struck only by the wonder of someone backing me when he didn't have to. Years passed before I could truly appreciate the profound difference that single act of support had on me, and what I have done with my life.

I know that it was similar for Anthony Badger. And I expect that it will be that way for Rey as well.

At the senior awards dinner for the girls division, to the surprise of no one, Lucia had been grandly feted. She won St. Benedict's highest honor, the presidential award, and because she was the first girl to win it after four full years in the school, it symbolically marked the final step in the successful creation of the girls division. When they held the same ceremony at the boys dinner the following night, eight young men were nominated for the presidential award. Rey was not one of them.

Abbot Augustine rose to announce the winner. All the nominees were worthy, he said, but only one could win, and that one was Noah.

At Rey's table, his mother tried hard to keep from showing how her heart was breaking. After all they had sacrificed for him to be there, and after all he'd achieved, it came down to this night full of disappointment. His father sat stone-faced, angry that there hadn't been any recognition of all that Rey had done for St. Benedict's before and even after he'd lost his post. Sitting with them, Rey did a respectable job of disguising his feelings. He applauded enthusiastically, his face registering neither resentment nor anger. Later, I asked him what had been going through his mind at that moment, and he told me that he didn't begrudge Noah his accolades, nor did he lash himself for the senseless actions that had cost him so dearly. He simply sat there in the midst of all those parents and teachers, alongside all the guys he'd known for four years, reviewing all that Noah had done to clean up the mess he'd inherited. And he'd had to concede that given how Noah had leaned right into that unexpected squall he, more than anyone else, even more than Rey himself, rightly deserved to come out on top.

CHAPTER 20

A Great Gettin' Up

THE FINAL DAYS of this historic fiftieth year of the resurrected St. Benedict's looked more like a revival meeting than the wrap-up of a prep school term. The school had erected a huge open-sided white tent on the green between the library and the Leahy House dormitory, and it became the temporary hub of activity, starting with morning convocation. Knowing that with only two days left before the start of summer vacation Noah would need help sticking to schedule, Father Ed sat on the temporary stage and called for calm. "If we're here till midnight, it's all right with me," he threatened after he failed to get the students' attention. The discipline that had prevailed during the year proved elusive that morning, and the background murmur that persisted under the tent ticked off the impatient headmaster.

"Whatever you feel is so essential that you're sucking the air out of the tent and inconveniencing seven hundred others just isn't," he griped. They struggled through the readings and hymns. When it was time for the energizing affirmation that Kaleb had delivered with such irrepressible spirit so often during the year, he stepped aside, and a classmate recited the familiar words instead. Kaleb accompanied him on the drums. The transition was a clue that he was already thinking about what would happen next year if, as he hoped, he succeeded Noah as senior group leader and would no longer be able to lead the affirmation because he'd have so many other duties. Leadership decisions for next year would be announced the following day. For now, Kaleb drummed with optimistic strength, total conviction, and under the big tent his drums boomed like an entire marching band.

Father Ed took back the mic to make announcements about the upcoming year. The most startling one had to do with the water adversity challenge, which the freshmen who'd just come off the trail would have to undergo in a few weeks. He intended to impose the same requirement that applied to the trail project, where finishing the entire hike is the only option. Under the new standard that he had developed with the Victory Road leadership group, the least-competent swimmers would have to jump into the pool blindfolded and fully clothed just as the competent swimmers had been required to do this year. The headmaster's only concession was that they would be spared the dunking by the ex-Navy SEAL.

"Tough times demand that St. Benedict's get even tougher," Father Ed explained. He was intent on ensuring that the word "preparatory" in the school's name meant prepared for life and all its hazards, injustices, and inequities.

* * *

The last major event of the academic year was also one of the most important. As this year so forcefully demonstrated, the actions and decisions of student leaders go a long way toward determining how well the school operates. Student leaders in both divisions pick their successors before passing the choices by Father Ed, who usually, but not always, concurs. Given how close this year's midterm snafu came to unraveling the entire year, picking the next leaders had taken on added importance. Noah and his team had conducted the search process in deep secrecy, and the suspense had left Kaleb unusually jittery. He had been interviewed for a leadership position a few weeks earlier, and he took it as a good sign that he had been called to a meeting fifteen minutes before the start of the last convo of the year. He believed that he had passed his final test—his performance as Maroon company trail commander—and that along with his roles as Prof. Blood group leader, freshman counselor, Fr. Mark Payne Institute host, and as a key member of the drum line and the Latin jazz band, along with giving his all as enthusiastic leader of the morning affirmation at so many convocations, his chances of getting what he wanted had been blessed.

He sprinted by me just before convo began, and the exuberant smile I expected was tempered. There'd been a change of plans, he told me as he rushed by, but he wouldn't say anything more. I soon found out why. When the leadership announcements were made, he was named one of the four section leaders, ranking just below the new senior group leader, Jonathan, the Seeing Eye dog trainer. Kaleb would not run convo, but he would lead Gray section, the one Father Ed picked on throughout the year.

No one leveled with Kaleb about why he'd been passed over for the top position. The mix-up over selecting the Maroon company's campsite during the A.T. hike had probably raised questions about his judgment. And the Prof. Blood group's deficient performance collecting phones suggested he may simply have been too nice a guy to be in charge of everything. But his disappointment at not getting the top spot was short-lived. He was determined to put his all into leading the Gray section. His gratitude for the school was undiminished, and he remained convinced that St. Benedict's had already made an enormous difference in his life.

"It teaches me what the real world is going to look like," he told me, already mature enough to understand the vagaries of fortune. "It teaches me that you have to invest in what you want. It shows me that people really care, even if for me, sometimes they have to step on my back to get me to do what I ought to do."

After the remaining leadership positions were filled, and the roster for the girls division leaders was announced, Father Ed injected a dose of reality. "Lots of schools in this country won't get this many kids that look like you together." He looked out over young faces from all over the world, representing a panoply of religions and beliefs, young women as well as young men who come together for the same purpose, putting aside any conflicts they may have with each other to sit shoulder to shoulder, and sing. He told them that outsiders coming upon such a gathering might see it as a threat. But here they were on this special ground, their voices united in song, their spirits aligned despite their differences. He referenced the line in Mahalia Jackson's hymnal "Great Gettin' Up Morning," that mentions "they'll be comin' from every nation," with a face full of admiration for the assembly before him.

* * *

On the first day of June, a thoroughly sweet and spring-like Saturday afternoon, the twenty-two members of the first class of St. Benedict's girls division to complete four full years at the school donned their garnet-colored gowns, put on their high heels, and showed off their long elaborately painted fingernails. Father Ed watched with a jaundiced eye as the girls he'd seen grow into young women strutted exuberantly into the big tent. "Here I am going all over the country raising money for them, and they're spending hundreds getting their nails done." He was grandstanding again. He understood that for these girls and their families, the expense of a fancy manicure was not an extravagance but an expression of gratitude and pride.

Parents and family were forewarned that there would be two separate parts of the commencement. First would come the formal section when each girl received her diploma. Then there would be singing, chanting, and unchecked expressions of the kind of joy that cannot be rehearsed. "When the Holy Spirit moves into a tent, something special happens," the headmaster predicted.

Even now, in the last few moments of their tenure at St. Benedict's, the school took pains to remind the girls of the importance of community. Staff called them to the stage not in the alphabetical order of their last names, but according to the groups they had belonged to since being drafted as freshmen. Each received her diploma from Abbot Augustine, hugged "Papa Bear" Melchor, shook hands with Father Ed, and clanged the Coker Bell, which is named after an alumnus who was Father Ed's classmate and who survived six years in a prisoner of war camp in Vietnam.

Their diplomas in hand, the girls listened to Sabrina Reves briefly narrate the girls division's creation parable. Then they lined up with faculty, alumnae, and a handful of female New Jersey State Troopers and poured their hearts into singing the familiar convocation songs, just as they had so many mornings before. The singing was both innocent and powerful, the sweet sound of those young voices flowing out of the tent, over the walls, and onto the rough streets of Newark's old Central Ward. Then Kymberli grabbed a mic and one last time belted out the St. Benedict's affirmation that ends with "You Go And Conquer!"

Lucia had the final word. She thanked Father Ed for all he'd meant to her since she was a toddler. During her four years as a student at St. Benedict's, the girls division had started flag football, fencing, cheerleading, and other teams. As senior group leader, she had helped introduce the tough new policies on phones, the dress code, and attendance, which had restored some of the character that had been lost during remote learning. She said the girls were respected and recognized for their own talents and were no longer willing to be overshadowed by the boys division. Personally, she had held her own alongside both Rey and Noah, projecting dependable student leadership even when the concept looked weakest. With the girls division enrollment expected to hit two hundred soon, she grandly told the parents and friends in the audience that she felt she had accomplished her number one goal as senior group leader.

"I can proudly say that the girls division is here to stay," she declared. The crowd roared.

When the boys gathered under the tent the next day, a handful of gray-haired men—members of what would have been the class of 1974 but who never graduated because the school closed—had been invited back fifty years later to receive their honorary diplomas. Abbot Augustine Curley was one of them. Just like the students, each one of them crossed the stage, received his diploma, and rang the Coker Bell.

As stand-in group leader Noah, like Lucia, had the last word. With a tremor of timidity still stuck in his voice, he recounted the struggles his class had endured, starting with the COVID lockdown. "No matter what was thrown at us, we stayed the course." He had never imagined himself giving such a talk, or standing in such a position. Just a year before he had his mind set on nothing more than being leader of one of the small groups. Instead, here he was, the face and voice of the school, the newest presidential award winner telling this huge tent full of people what it takes to stay the course, an apt metaphor for someone headed to the U.S. Naval Academy. He avoided placing blame, or leveling shame: "The class of '24 is a bunch of guys who can get it done." With their arms over each other's shoulders, swaying side by side under a pure white tent beneath a burnished Newark sky, they ended the ceremony with a soulful phrase of promise and prophecy that echoed along King Boulevard.

"You're gonna be so proud of me," they sang, a community of Black, white, and Latino, Christian, Muslim, and Hindu, all with a single resounding voice multiplying the same heartfelt message. "I'm gonna do this thing. Just you wait and see."

CHAPTER 21

And Ever Shall Be

HE TRIES TO hide it, but even after so many years, the end of each school year unsettles Father Ed. It's tough for him to let go of the kids, especially those like Lucia, who he's known since before they could talk. Or the ones like Noah, who he's watched grow from frightened boy to confident man. He once talked to me candidly about this cycle of school years coming to an end, and the gloomy way he described them took me aback because it differed so greatly from the upbeat, optimistic man I'd come to know. He referred to those final days as "small deaths" that bring many things to a close. I had to keep in mind that this is a man who stayed behind after the last graduate walked out of the building at the end of the school year in 1972 and the doors closed behind him, maybe forever; a man who drove Anthony Badger to college, but then had to watch as he sank into his addiction; a man who proudly sent presidential award winner Rob Peace off to Yale, but then mourned when he was murdered by a drug dealer just a few miles from Newark Abbey. Father Ed's dark admission seemed out of character for someone who usually displays such self-confidence, but I understood it better when he put it into the same kind of context he uses for the girls in his faith class. "The Lord talked about that, right?" he told me. "Unless you die, you can't experience new life."

And a new life is what awaited all those trail-toughened, water-challenged, deep woods survivors, otherwise known as St. Benedict's graduates. After sweeping many awards and successfully capping off her year as senior group leader, Lucia had her choice of universities, but her final decision was dictated by the strength of her commitment to her family and her community. Home, with her parents, her eight brothers and sisters, and her church, was where she felt she needed to be, so she accepted a generous financial aid offer from the New Jersey Institute of Technology, a five-minute walk down King Boulevard from St. Benedict's. She already had a plan: study business and marketing, put her considerable leadership skills to work and, she told me, "figure out who I am" without St. Benedict's and everything there that had demanded her attention for so long, including Rey. They had split up for a number of reasons, not the least being that he had made up his mind to go to college far from Newark. She had to put her passion for volleyball on hold because she's just too petite for NJIT's Division 1 team, but she planned to return to St. Benedict's to help coach her old team, and her younger sister Lilianna, who was about to enter her freshman year.

Every one of the young women who graduated from St. Benedict's on that beautiful Saturday in June continued her education. After finishing with a 3.32 GPA and winning the Benedictine Spirit Award, Kymberli received enough financial help from Monmouth University in central New Jersey to make her decision to go there an easy one. Others headed to NYU, Lincoln, Temple, and a broad range of competitive universities.

The boys division scored a similarly impressive record, with nearly every one heading off to university. None went to the Ivy League as in years past, but they'd been accepted to Northwestern, Holy Cross, and other top schools, and a few had won full scholarships. Over the summer, Noah enjoyed himself at graduation parties for his buddies at St. Benedict's as well as at home in Madison, before heading to six demanding weeks of basic training at the U.S. Naval Academy Preparatory School, a one-year stop before entering Annapolis. He seemed to be well on the way to achieving his number one goal in life: never walking in his father's footsteps.

Rey too had once dreamed of entering the Naval Academy, but he dead-ended the idea even before his debacle with the history exam. Now, because he wanted to get as far away from Newark as possible, he chose St. John's in Collegeville, Minnesota, 1,300 miles from King Boulevard. The sprawling campus of over 3,000 acres about 70 miles north of the Twin Cities is all male and predominantly white, but when Rey found out that a number of students come from the Bahamas every year, he figured it would be easy to find his own crowd.

After his gut-wrenching last year at St. Benedict's, he spent an easygoing summer with the security team at MetLife Stadium, where he got to see Lionel Messi compete in the Copa America. As soon as he got to St. John's, he joined the rugby team and hooked up with the volunteer fire department, his avocation to serve still fired up inside him. We kept in touch and he told me that looking back, he could see that St. Benedict's had dealt with his regrettable decisions about as fairly as was possible. He was glad he'd had a chance to explain himself to the whole school at Stage Rage, and he was proud of the way he had demonstrated in the months after he lost his leadership position that he could still lead. And like Noah, he felt that he had made a good start on his goal of separating himself from his dad's shadow. He admitted that his terrific year-turned-terrible had taught him a lot about his father, and himself.

"I used to say that I'm nothing like him, but I realize now that I have some of his best traits," he told me, "and some of his worst too," knowledge that, however painful, was essential.

St. Benedict's near 100 percent graduation rate, and its equally impressive number of students heading off to college, show how different this downtown prep is. In the context of the city where it is located, the results are remarkable. For many years, Newark's high schools were known disparagingly as dropout factories.[1] Mark Comesañas's My Brother's Keeper organization recently looked into the ragged performance of the city's secondary schools. Five-year graduation rates stood at around 76 percent for Black students throughout the district, but with wide disparities among schools. Technology High School, which was Rey's choice before his mother insisted on St. Benedict's, reported a zero dropout rate, while at Shabazz High School, which has an attendance counselor and an anti-bullying specialist on staff, only 45 percent of students finish.

Susanne Mueller, who besides her work on the honor code committee heads St. Benedict's seven-person college counseling team, advises students to aim for the best college with the best programs that won't saddle them with more than $30,000 in total debt by the time they receive their degree. Around 60 percent of the school's graduates stay in New Jersey and take advantage of the College Promise program for state residents that covers up to the entire cost of tuition at community colleges and public universities for families with incomes below $100,000. But getting into college is just one hurdle they have to overcome. While around 60 percent will graduate with a degree in six years, Mueller said the main reason the others don't complete their degrees is usually money, which is why she focuses on keeping costs, and debt, as low as possible.

* * *

Tareek's prospects for going to his dream college—Howard University—or any college that would allow him to become a teacher like his guardian Charity so that he could, as he told me, help another young Tareek or Jokari, had nearly evaporated by the time the year ended. Father Ed had worked out a schedule for him to get credit in summer phase for the classes he missed during his psychological intervention. That way, he could catch up to the rest of his class and conceivably graduate with them in June and then go on to college. But given all he'd been through, that seemed increasingly unlikely. Ryan, his guardian, had raised the possibility of putting off college temporarily and doing something else. He urged Tareek to consider joining the Navy, given

St. Benedict's connections with that branch of the military. He has told both his boys that their goal in life should be "You finish high school, you do something—college, the military, trade school—that equips you to be able to come back to Newark and afford to be able to live here as a homeowner," essentially, earning a pass to the middle class.

The avalanche of troubles that Tareek and Jokari experienced over the year shook their sense of security and left them uncertain about even their future at St. Benedict's. Just before summer break, both put the Haygoods on notice that they wanted to transfer to a public high school. Jokari had lost his position as freshman counselor and then, despite his scouting experience, was passed over for a chance to be a leader for the Appalachian Trail project—two big disappointments that dampened his motivation to complete his schoolwork. He told the Haygoods he thought he would be happier at Science Tech, a selective Newark public high school that his girlfriend attended. His GPA was close to the right range for Science Tech, but his record was inconsistent, and basketball and Boy Scouts clearly remained higher priorities than science. For his part, Tareek still harbored his dream of attending Arts High School, but his cumulative GPA was anemic, and he didn't have a major art project to work on the way most students there have by their senior year.

Despite their occasional misgivings about St. Benedict's, the Haygoods remained certain that it was still the right place for the brothers. They admit there have been disappointments, but they continue to be impressed whenever they attend an event at the school and see a student at the microphone taking the lead. And there have been many singular moments that touched them. When Tareek was struggling with Spanish, they met with Dean Rodriguez, who tried to set them straight about the school's mission. Charity remembered him saying that grades are just one measure of success. St. Benedict's teaches character and integrity, pushing kids through difficult challenges, and helping them bounce back after failures. She said she left such meetings telling herself that this is why St. Benedict's is what it is, and why it works for them.

"When they go on the trail," she went on, "we look at each other and say, 'This is why St. Benedict's.'" When they watched them tread water and use their pants as a flotation device, they thought, "This is why St. Benedict's." And when one kid in the pool struggled and the instructor told him to doggy paddle, and he doggy paddled all the way to the other end of the pool without anyone jeering but with everyone cheering, they again thought, "This is why St. Benedict's."

The Haygoods told Tareek and Jokari that they'd support them wherever they decided to finish high school, but they insisted that the boys take full responsibility for completing their transfer applications on time and on their own, or be prepared to put on their black hoodies again.

* * *

With the death of Father Maynard, the monastic community also faced an uncertain future. Their number had dropped to fourteen, and most of them were well past what is considered retirement age outside the abbey walls. The rules of the American-Cassinese Congregation, to which they belong, dictate that if the number of monks in a monastery falls to six or below, it is up to the president of the congregation to determine whether it can continue as a self-sustaining abbey. But unlike some religious orders with shrinking numbers that have put themselves on a "path to completion" by refusing to accept new members, these downtown monks remain hopeful, their optimism bolstered in recent years by a few young men—Brother Robert from Mexico, Brother Bruno from Connecticut, and an alumnus, Brother Thomas Hall, '06, who came to them from nearby Summit, New Jersey—who've pledged their lives to Newark Abbey. They have faith that they will be able to enlist more men, even if they do not come, as many of the current members did, through the classrooms of St. Benedict's.

For decades now, the Catholic church in the United States has struggled to recruit young men for its many religious communities. Along with the upheaval in the wake of the Second Vatican Council's reforms in the 1960s, and the profound societal changes in American culture since then, revelations of sexual abuse of children by priests and other religious men and women have left the church battered and dishonored. Hardly a parish, cloister, or house of any religious order has gone untouched. After the state of New Jersey temporarily lifted the statute of limitations in 2019, Newark Abbey was named in two lawsuits alleging abuse that occurred more than forty years ago, involving monks long dead. One monk who taught religion, psychology, and German at the prep in the 1980s was accused of abusing two teenage boys who had attended St. Benedict's elementary and prep divisions in the late 1970s and early 1980s. The monk died in 2012. A third lawsuit named a Benedictine brother who was not a teacher but who worked as sexton in St. Mary's Church almost eighty years ago and was accused of abusing an eleven-year-old boy in 1950. Since being filed, the three lawsuits have not been litigated.

When I asked Abbot Augustine about the lawsuits, he acknowledged their existence but declined to discuss them. He did give me a boiler plate statement saying the unproven accusations "are deeply disturbing," and that the monks "take all such allegations seriously." It was one of the rare instances that I encountered anything but full disclosure, but under the circumstances it was not surprising, and I understood how painful it must be for a community of individuals who have sacrificed so much to be questioned about something that may have happened so long ago. The abbot was willing to discuss a recent incident from 2022 about which there was little doubt. One of St. Benedict's staff was caught in a predator vigilante sting luring someone he thought was fourteen years old into a sexual liaison in the city of Harrison, across the river from Newark.[2] No prep students were involved, and the alleged activity took place far from school grounds. Both the sting and the man's arrest at his home in Jersey City were taped and available on the internet. The abbot told me that the college counselor and dean of seniors, a St. Benedict's alumnus and Ivy League graduate, had been fired immediately. He later pleaded guilty to one count of attempted criminal sexual contact, and was sentenced to a year of probation.[3]

National polls on the impact of the sex scandals in the United States suggest that the endless reports of abuse have so angered and disillusioned American Catholics that more than a third of them have considered abandoning the faith.[4] But most Catholics also told the pollsters that they still had confidence in their own local clergy, who they knew well and respected highly. The monks at Newark Abbey, especially the core group around Father Ed who've persisted at their work for half a century, remain enduring symbols of commitment to the children of Newark. City officials treat them as irreplaceable urban fixtures, while most alumni I spoke with can't imagine St. Benedict's without them.

And no monk is more indispensable than the man they call Fred. The tough old headmaster loves to brag about his reserves of strength and endurance. Although he no longer hikes the Appalachian Trail, he is a regular at the school's CrossFit box, and he's been known to take many-mile walks through Newark and the surrounding towns, delighting in the way he can surprise current and former students who don't expect to run into him so far from the property. He gave the entire community a scare when Aurora the pit bull yanked him down the stairs, and he made sure everyone knew that when the doctors at the hospital asked him what medications he was on, they thought they'd misheard him when he told them none.

He was less willing to let others know, however, that the doctors had also discovered a suspicious lump on his hip that they then successfully treated without the headmaster missing any school time.

The most pressing question facing St. Benedict's now is also the most delicate: What happens when Father Ed can no longer continue as headmaster? After all that he's meant, and still means, to the school, it is the question that nobody really wants to contemplate. Alan Fournier, a wealthy investor who has become one of the school's most generous benefactors, spoke for countless supporters when he told me, "Father Ed is what makes St. Benedict's what it is." As part of his continuing work helping the school, Fournier told me he's been focusing on "how to set St. Benedict's up for the post-Father Ed world and how to maintain what's there for another fifty or a hundred years." One scenario under consideration now would split leadership of the school into a triad. Father Ed would serve as President and Chief Mission Officer of the school, focusing on an overall vision for St. Benedict's for as long as he is able. A head of school would be appointed to take over day-to-day operations, while an executive vice president would oversee the business side.

But for now, the school functions as it has since 1973, with open arms, a big heart, and Father Ed firmly in charge. In the middle of the short summer break, he sent an email message to all students and staff, bringing them up to date on his recovery from Aurora's wild dash, outlining the details with the kind of bravado that simply adds to his legend.

Brothers and Sisters,

I have been working out every day, seven days a week, for the last five weeks and am in even better physical condition now than I was before my tragic accident. You, on the other hand, have no doubt been eating Cheetos, Cheez-Its, double-stuffed Oreos, and who knows what else during this break. I urge you to stay away from the vending machines, bodegas, and candy aisles in the shopping centers, and do something to get your flabby, mushy bodies into some kind of shape. And stop going to bed at 4:00 in the morning after being on TikTok all night.

Just thought I'd get you up to date on the happenings of my life over these last several weeks. I am focused, fit, and fired up for the new school year. Looking forward to seeing you. Pray for me as I do for you.

Signed,

Focused, Fit & Fired Up Fred

CHAPTER 22

Back to the Beginning

THE FIRST CONVO of the 2024–2025 academic year wouldn't start for at least a half hour, but Kaleb already was so revved up he couldn't stand still for more than ten seconds. Although he wouldn't be where he had dreamed of being—at the podium orchestrating everything as senior group leader—he would soon take his place in front of the bleachers as Gray section leader, one of St. Benedict's top men. When attendance was taken, his old section, Maroon, would be first to report. The Blue section, with his trail colleague Everett taking over as one of the group leaders, would come next, followed by White, and finally Gray, which he hoped would give him time to calm his first-day jitters and keep a proper tally based on what his group leaders shouted out. As excited as he was, he told me he'd have to keep the running count of absences on his fingers so he wouldn't mess up when it was his turn, for the first time, to authoritatively report the Gray section's inventory of all who were present, as well as those who were missing.

He worried for nothing. "Gray section down six," he called out firmly, confidently, and with the faintest outline of a self-satisfied smile.

At the other end of the gym, Natalia's group had been moved to an unfamiliar spot in the bleachers, close to where Sheridan sat with the blue bag holding the cell phones of all the girls in the Betty Edelen group, into which she'd been drafted. Sheridan had taken her first step up the leadership ladder, and now was one of the freshman counselors. Her uniform grays were gone, replaced by the official St. Benedict's black polo that she was wearing for the first time.

Oscar had been discharged from the Velvet Rope, and was back for a fifth year and one more chance to switch out of his grays. Raúl, still wearing gray, sat on the floor looking forlorn. He'd been denied his membership, and his black, because of piss-poor grades and a lousy attitude about any outside-the-classroom activity except basketball. He told me he was determined to get his black. He just didn't know when.

A hand went up. Voices quieted down. A lanky student with two-toned hair settled in behind the podium. "Good morning. Welcome to convo for July 29th. Let's begin with prayer."

And with that another year began at St. Benedict's. In style and substance, this convo was similar to all those that had come before. But the tone was more subdued than it had been when Lucia and Rey set the previous year alight. The large cast of alumni who had been invited to mark the fiftieth year of the redefined school was missing, except for one graduate who sat on a folding chair near Dr. Lansang's keyboard, wearing a St. Benedict's polo shirt and a pair of tan shorts. Tryouts for freshman basketball weren't scheduled to start for two weeks, but Coach Badger was already there, hoping to get a preview of the latest freshman class. He was scouting for boys who were taller than the rest, who moved with cool confidence, and who showed signs of being street tough. What he'd seen so far this morning hadn't impressed him. So many of these freshmen were puny, not ready for pushups, suicides, or defense drills. But it's like that at the start of most years. Tryouts would weed out the hotshots from those kids with real talent, and spotlight the ones who will allow themselves to be coached.

Out on the floor with the freshmen, carrying themselves like leaders, I saw Finn, the Eagles' team captain, and his medic Michael, both wearing their black polos and both part of the new corps of counselors guiding the freshmen who are as timid now as Finn and Michael were a year ago. Finn had finished the year with highest honors and a 3.93 GPA. Wrestling at 150 pounds, he'd won all nineteen of his matches. Michael had struggled to get his GPA to a decent 2.9 and, wrestling for the varsity team at 132 pounds, he only won two matches. But he'd grown bigger, stronger, and, he hoped, smarter, since then, and he expected to do better. I was surprised to see how a year at St. Benedict's had transformed both of them. The school seemed to have instilled self-confidence, empathy, and a desire to pass along what they've learned.

I noted a change in Michael that was especially telling. I remembered how, on the first night on the trail, he told me how much he missed his mom, sounding like a homesick boy. Now, here he was standing in front of me, taller, broader, his dreads replaced by a traditional haircut, explaining that his first year at St. Benedict's had been challenging, but not hard. Hard, he told me, looking me in the eye with a newfound maturity, was what he heard one of the former Navy SEALs describe as seeing your best friend killed in action. Despite the melodrama, I realized how much tougher these kids had become, and how much a year on King Boulevard—with all its challenges, adversity, and expectation—had prepared them for the uncertainties ahead.

And in their remaining years at St. Benedict's, they'd face other ordeals that would make them even more prepared for life outside the property. Father Ed had made good on his end-of-the-year promise to make every second-year student jump into the deep end of the pool. And there would be even tougher challenges ahead. Along with staff, he was drawing up an array of adversity tasks, including a simulated plane crash and water rescue staged in the pool, as well as an ultimate capstone challenge for seniors that would seal St. Benedict's reputation as the toughest prep school in America.

* * *

As I scanned the bleachers that morning, I was surprised to see Tareek and Jokari seated close to each other halfway up Kaleb's Gray section. Tareek's hair was now braided into tight rows and spirals; Jokari had kept the high-top fade with twists he had last year. Both had on their familiar black suedes with silver buckles. It wasn't easy to read either one, or why they were still there after being so determined to get out.

I found out that Tareek had not gotten far with his plan to trans- fer to Arts High. Instead, he'd taken a summer job at the Newark CityPlex 12 that was co-owned by basketball legend and Newark native Shaquille O'Neal, who in recent years had invested in residential and commercial projects that were helping the city bounce back. At the theater, Tareek did everything from cleaning up to making popcorn, and thought it was cool. After talking with one of the theater's guards, he got the idea of moving up to a security job that paid substantially more than he was making. When he found out he'd first have to take a qualifying test, he got the application, ordered the material he needed to study for the test, and hit the books—all on his own. It was a real sign, his guardian, Charity, told me, that St. Benedict's has had a positive im- pact on him despite his difficulties. He'd forgotten about transferring and was set to make up the course work he'd missed last year. They all hoped he'd break his record of flaming out after a strong start so that he could graduate with the rest of his class in June.

Two rows away, Jokari sat with his elbows on his knees, wearing a face that Father Ed has described at other Monday convos as being too washed out to play a dead man in an old Western. He had continued his quest to transfer to Science Tech, but the principal there had been lukewarm about his prospects. She wanted him to answer advanced math questions on a standardized test later in the summer. If he scored as high as her already enrolled students, she'd consider admitting him in September. But without any experience taking such specialized tests, the outcome was uncertain. So, for the moment, Jokari was stuck be- tween two worlds, and he didn't look happy.

Still, he had come to convo, on time and in uniform. And when Dr. Lansang tried animating the sleepy students, it was Jokari who first started clapping to the words "Today, I realized, I'm living in a miracle." He told me he planned to start his Eagle Scout Project soon, providing emergency medical kits for Newark public schools (he later changed it to something that had more meaning for him—a luggage drive for homeless kids). Although his aborted term as freshman counselor hadn't led to the assistant group leader position he'd hoped for, he still had ideas about improving the school, and, of course, playing basketball. There's no way to know for sure what will happen, but just as I planned to watch Tareek graduate, I expected to see Jokari march into a big tent with his group in a future St. Benedict's commencement.

It was a new year, with new goals and a new leadership team, one that was taking a much more laid-back approach than Lucia and Rey had a year before. For the first hour of this convo, neither Jonathan nor Benay, the new senior group leader of the girls division, had come to the podium. Finally, just moments before convo ended, they took the mic and welcomed several new teachers. Jonathan also introduced Bingo, the German Shepherd puppy he was training for the Seeing Eye organization, and that he said would be his constant companion throughout the year.

Focused, Fit & Fired Up Fred was subdued. No tales of past high jinks, no painful puns or humble bragging. His message was clear and straightforward: Don't assume this year will be like the last. He repeated what he had told me long before, that the school has to re-create itself every year, which now took on deeper meaning in light of what I knew he felt about school endings being like little deaths. Rey and Noah, Lucia and Kymberli, were gone. Ransford Gyan was playing soccer at Clemson. Aurora the pit bull had been sent back. But new life was beginning, and Fred was there, same as ever, ready to guide it.

* * *

After convo ended, I met up with Coach Badger. I'd once asked him what it had been like to walk the mile and a half between school and his former home on Brenner Street when he was a student in that first generation of the new St. Benedict's, and he invited me to walk with him any time I wanted to find out for myself. We had settled on this day to retrace his past. He hadn't walked that route in decades and had no idea how the stretch of Springfield Avenue that the newspapers had called "a mile and a half battleground" had changed since he'd last crossed through there.

We traced the fence that surrounds the abbey grounds as we walked down William Street to the intersection with Springfield Avenue. That section of the battleground has been utterly transformed into a modern urban thoroughfare, with no signs of the street's troubled past. Orderly rows of new townhouses line one side of the avenue, the massive new Metropolitan Baptist Church dominates the other. Farther up, the hundreds of small stores and luncheonettes of the 1960s had been replaced by chains like Popeyes, Sonic, and Dollar Tree that seem to spring up like weeds in every city. Badger walked briskly and steadily for a few blocks, then stopped at the two basketball courts adjacent to the city's Hank Aaron baseball field and looked them over approvingly.

We passed through a city that is 20 percent less densely populated than it was when Badger took this daily walk to St. Benedict's, with the population now hovering around 305,000. It also is less Black than it was then, and more Hispanic. Around 47 percent of the current population is identified as Black, while 37 percent is Latino, and 9 percent white. Like other cities, the face of business in Newark has changed drastically since the 1970s. Downtown now has skyscrapers, expensive condominiums, the fabulous Performing Arts Center, and a block away from City Hall, the Prudential arena where the New Jersey Devils and Bruce Springsteen play. St. Benedict's students have watched a new project, the forty-two-story Halo apartment tower, assume the title of tallest residential building in Newark's modest skyline, just a block away from their lower playing field. Broad Street has a new Whole Foods supermarket, which has proven to be a precursor in many urban neighborhoods to a real estate renaissance. And the old Ballantine Brewery, shut since St. Benedict's closed in 1972, has been renovated and remade into nearly three hundred modern apartments, a poignant symbol of Newark's rebirth in light of what losing the plant in 1972 meant for the city. But Newark is still far from booming. Pockets of poverty, abandoned buildings, and vacant land proliferate in many parts of the city. We walked past many fallow building lots on Springfield Avenue where houses and businesses have been torn down but no one has yet had the courage or the resources to rebuild.

As we continued our walk, we almost missed the small, sad triangle of grass at the intersection of Springfield and 15th Avenue, a few blocks away from the street where police stopped John Smith in 1967. Those few yards of city soil go by the official name of Rebellion Park, but it takes imagination to consider it a park. Besides the browning grass, and one spindly tree, there is a single block of granite shaped like a tombstone where we read the names of the twenty-six people who lost their lives in the days after Smith's arrest. On one line was William Furr, known to everyone as Billy, who was shot and killed by a Newark policeman as he ran away from a liquor store hugging a case of beer. He was twenty-four. Eloise Spellman's name was there too. The mother of eleven children was killed as she closed the window of her Hayes Homes apartment. And there was the name of Detective Frederick Toto, shot and killed by a sniper just a few blocks from the monument. Above them all a melancholy declaration carved into the stone read "We will forever remember the names of those whose lives were lost." On this day, Coach Badger thought it had been a long time since anyone had remembered that Rebellion Park was there. The planter in front of the stone marker was filled with dying, straw-colored grass. An empty Bud Light can was tucked beneath a wobbly sidewalk bench. Sorely disappointed in his city, Badger sighed. "They could have done more than this."

Much had changed along the avenue, but scattered here and there were bits of the old Newark that Badger remembered. It was just a little after nine in the morning and the Silver Key liquor store was already busy. He was surprised to see that Engine 6 firehouse was still open, and what used to be a bank up the street from it was still a working bank. We continued up the incline of Springfield Avenue, passing the CityPlex 12 where Tareek worked. "Holy mother of God!" Coach exclaimed when we got to West Kinney. What used to be the mammoth Hayes Homes housing project had been torn down and replaced by neat rows of townhouses, including a line of them facing the old Fourth Precinct, where the riots began. It is now Newark's Office of Violence Prevention and Trauma Recovery, which has helped substantially reduce the city's crime rate. Around the corner is the red brick building that once housed St. Stanislaus School and Lyceum. In yet another inspired transformation, it is now St. Benedict's elementary school.

As we neared Brenner Street where Coach Badger grew up, we looked for familiar landmarks but found none. Marty's Meats? Gone. John's Bargain store? Gone. What the Badgers had called the hot dog store, where Coach's mom sometimes took him and his brothers for a treat? Gone. Just before we reached South 10th Street—the end of that long-ago headline-designated combat zone—we walked by an abandoned three-story house where someone had draped an old bed sheet over the railing on the front stoop. As we got closer, we noticed a pair of dirty feet sticking out of a tumble of blankets. We didn't know if it was a man or a woman who was sleeping there, but their evident misfortune led Badger to recall the fear and self-loathing he felt when he had no alternative but to sleep on the street. "I've been there." He sighed. It had been the worst night of his life, and yet, he said, surprising me, he wouldn't trade any of his experiences—not even the bad ones like that—because without them, without all he learned about the world and himself on the street, what he learned about empathy from the monks, what he learned about resilience from the city where he was reared, he wouldn't be the man he has become. He's never forgotten what it was like to be strung out without a place to sleep, and when drug rehab centers invite him to speak about his experience, he lays out his entire life story so that his example might give others hope.

In the few steps left in our journey we passed the bumpy stretch of asphalt, with its makeshift backstop, and a hoop without a net, where Badger pursued basketball excellence. A block away from "the parking lot," his old three-story apartment building on Brenner Street was gone, replaced by a single townhouse. In place of the lampshade factory down the street stood a new apartment complex. The brownstone gatehouse to Woodland Cemetery was barely standing, littered with garbage and a weirdly out of place pair of women's high heel shoes standing upright amid the trash. The nearby abandoned house where he and other addicts had camped for weeks when he was at his "apex of stupidity" looked renovated and occupied.

I wondered how many of the people sleeping in doorways and abandoned buildings like the one we passed could have been helped had someone told them their lives had infinite value and their futures were without limit. I still didn't understand how, even with the boundless energy he possessed, Coach Badger had found the strength to escape the indignity of the street after diving so deeply into the drug scene. But as we walked through the tumbledown cemetery, along the paved paths now grown over with weeds, I kept thinking about what he'd said in summing up his life—how he wouldn't change anything, not even the ugliest, most dangerous parts—and I could hear Father Ed telling the kids over and over "your history is not a mistake," you are who you are because of your past self. You are going to make bad decisions; you're going to take wrong turns. There's going to be ugly in your life. But he always reminds them that it all becomes part of who you are, and as long as you recognize it, as Anthony Badger did, and years later so did Rey, you will have what you need to get back in the fight. And that is what matters most.

"We used to have the run of the whole place when we were kids," Badger mused as we walked through the overgrown lanes of the sadly neglected cemetery. Trash trees and weedy bushes have taken over large sections, covering some of the old headstones. "It's got me thinking about New York," he mumbled, looking out over the wild corners of the grave-yard. When he was homeless he, and the unfortunates around him, would have been attracted to such hidden spots. "They'd find any little space where they could be private for a while," he reminisced, the sadness in his voice matched by the wonder of how distant those times and that life now seemed.

Farther away from the surrounding streets, the cemetery seemed better maintained, or maybe just less abused. The asphalt pathway was broken up in spots, but still passable. Most of the tombstones were erect, and readable. The German names and the ancient dates had meant nothing to Badger and his friends until they learned about Newark's long and complex history. That's when the real meaning dawned on them, and it was both simple and profound: "There was more to this area than us," he had realized. More to time than just the present. More to a city than the names of the people who live there, and the monuments they leave behind.

We walked back to King Boulevard and briefly stopped in Shanley Gym, where the class of 2028 was still going through their week-long freshman orientation. The old gym looked small compared to Bob Brennan's top-tier gym across the street, but its basketball backboards still had their magic square painted on them, the square that Badger would once again encourage the hotshots on his freshman team to aim for when they try to score.

We stood at the bottom of a staircase near the gym as he described some of the ways he tries to inspire his players, focusing not on winning at all costs, although he likes winning more than losing, but on what they need to know to lead successful lives. Just then a Black youth in wire rim glasses and a gray polo shirt—obviously a transfer—hesitated before excusing himself and asking where he should drop off a form he had filled out to join the wrestling team. "It's my first day here," he offered apologetically.

Coach Badger told him to bring the form to the athletic director's office. "Do you know where that is?" he asked.

The confused student shook his head.

"On the balcony in the gym?" Badger hinted. "Right above where you just had convo?"

The youth looked confused, unsure how to get to where he needed to be.

Coach Badger had a good half century on him. He had just re-traced his own daily journey to the school several miles up and down Springfield Avenue, and along the way relived some of the worst moments of his life. As he looked at one of the newest prospective members of the St. Benedict's community, he had no idea how much ugly the young man had carried with him into the school that day, or how his history might weigh on him and the choices he'd make during his time there. And the young man hadn't a clue of the journey Badger had taken to get where he is, or how being there with him, and everyone else at St. Benedict's, would shape his own life.

"I'll take you," Coach offered.

I watched them climb the stairs, the uncertain young man following a step behind the tireless coach. It came to me then that the lessons of a place like St. Benedict's are as varied as they are endless. The school changes constantly, one class succeeding another, one year pushing into the next. But neither the school, nor the community that is Newark, ever changes completely. The remarkable stability of the monks, the passionate fealty of the staff, the steadfast loyalty of the alumni, the raw energy and potential of the students, and the undiminished hopes and dreams of this indomitable city have been woven into a tapestry of times past, present, and to come that defies the odds and bucks the trends, constituting an enduring force of good in a place that's seen its share of evil, and a lasting lesson in tolerance, empathy, and resilience for us all.

ACKNOWLEDGMENTS

ONE OF THE most familiar dictates in *The Rule of St. Benedict* calls for the monks to welcome with humility anyone who knocks on their door. I am indebted to Abbot Augustine J. Curley for opening the doors of Newark Abbey to me when I came knocking. As an archivist and historian, he understood my mission in writing this book and allowed me to range freely among the abbey's records, including the unflattering minutes of the chapter meetings from the crucial period leading up to the school's closure. The other monks I spoke with followed his example. They patiently answered questions, provided the materials I requested, and generally followed *The Rule* and made me feel welcome without attempting to inflate what they had accomplished at St. Benedict's. Father Albert Holtz was exceedingly gracious in permitting me to quote from his personal journal, which enabled me to re-create some of the emotional turmoil inside the monastery before and after the school closed, a powerful reminder that these men of faith are, after all, men with fears, convictions, and sensibilities like the rest of us. Father Philip Waters, Father Luke Edelen, Father Patrick Winbush, Father Maximilian Buonocore, and Father Mark Dilone all generously offered their time and insights. I've never met a tougher or more fearless bunch of guys. The young monks were particularly open with me, and

I appreciate the insights that Brother Thomas, Brother Robert, and Brother Bruno passed along.

And of course, there was Father Ed, one of the most extraordinarily decent, dedicated, and faithful men I've ever met. I've heard him described as Christlike, which seemed a stretch when I heard him cussing out the Gray section, but then was all too believable when I witnessed the ferocity with which he defended a troubled kid for the second or third time. A classmate once said of him that he was "about as good and decent as anyone could be and still be breathing," and I understand what he meant. It took a while to convince him to permit an outsider like me to study his school so intently, but once he agreed, he patiently shared his wisdom, his good humor, and his faith, even as he continually wondered why I was taking so damn long to write the book.

Inside the well-worn walls of the school, lay faculty and staff provided helpful guidance whenever I asked. Although she wears several hats and perpetually seems overcaffeinated, Michelle Tuorto found time to guide me through the prep school's academic curriculum and help me better understand the unique challenges she and her staff face in St. Benedict's classrooms. Deans David Rodriguez and Alexander Melchor provided a steady stream of insights that helped me immensely. Both also turned out to be upstanding hiking companions on the Appalachian Trail. Teachers Char-lotte Searcy, Susanne Mueller, Robert Cygan, and Brian Marricco all pitched in whenever I asked for help, as did a legion of others. I picked up many insights into the emotional state of the students through countless meetings with the counselors at St. Benedict's. Dr. Sinclair Davis welcomed me into his Unknown Sons group and helped me interpret the intense dynamics of those meetings. Charlesy Sheib and Simena Carey backstopped me on many psychological issues that arose. And I am particularly indebted to Dr. Ivan Lamourt, both as head of the extraordinary counseling center and as an alumnus and key player in St. Benedict's rise, for always being available to me, and of course, to all the kids who rely on him.

Dr. Glenn Cassidy was an enormous help in many things, providing history, perspective, and—during the trail challenge—a workable way of hiking with both the girls and the boys teams. Jesse Alexander, Jared Boone, Analisa Branco, Noreen Connolly, Frank DiPiano, Jim Duffy, Pat Flynn, Mario Gallo, Bobby Hastie, Daniel Kane, Grace Lenahan, Dexter Lopina, Sylvers Owusu, John Rowe, Mike Scanlan, and others on staff were unfailingly polite and ever helpful. I am grateful to Cavill Henriques for saving my hide on the trail, and to Dr. Dennis Lansang for helping me understand hydrates as well as Jersey Club music. I owe a special thanks to Sabrina Reves for reliving the girls' "break-in," and to Chris Firriolo and his staff at Victory Road for helping me understand what it means to focus on the mission. Paul Thornton, Mike Fazio, and Susan Kronberg were my first contacts at St. Benedict's, and they remained helpful and available throughout the time I worked on this book.

The extraordinary students at St. Benedict's, those named and the ones I gave protective cover, showed great courage in allowing me so completely into their lives. I appreciate their candor and their willingness to let down their natural teenage suspicion. I am especially indebted to Lucia and Noah, to Kaleb, Natalia, Raúl, Tareek, Jokari, Oscar, Everett, Sheridan, Finn, Kymberli, and Michael, and I wish all of them the absolute best as they carve their own way into the world. And then there's Rey, whose complex character dazzled and perplexed me, and ultimately helped me understand that although our history may shape us, it doesn't have to be our destiny.

Mark Comesañas, Leon McBurrows, Ralph Kevin Harris, Kevin Washington, and other alumni who gave their time to me and to the school show just what kind of mark St. Benedict's leaves on the young. And I remain astonished by the courage and good will of Coach Anthony Badger, and the way he bravely shares his past self, along with the man he has become, with everyone and everything connected to St. Benedict's. He is the ideal coach every athlete wants.

I value the time Alan Fournier spent explaining his vision for the school he didn't attend, and never even knew about until he saw it featured on television. I will always remember his telling me that a single morning at convo convinced him to spend a good portion of his time, and a substantial part of his fortune, making sure the school lasts for another century. Charity and Ryan Haygood helped me see the school and the city of Newark through the eyes of parents deeply indebted to both, and I came away with great admiration for them and their devotion to the city's children. Despite all the hardships Tareek and Jokari suffered in their early lives, they hit the jackpot when they walked into the Haygoods' home.

As I have done so often in the past, I once again turned to the extraordinary staff at the Newark Public Library's New Jersey reference room for help, and received invaluable assistance from Greg Guderian and many others. They truly are a treasure. Junius Williams, Richard Roper, and Mayor Ras Baraka all helped this white man better understand what the city of Newark is, and what it can be. My work was made easier by the excellent research and clear narrative in Thomas A. McCabe's *Miracle on High Street*, as well as Jeff Hobbs's gripping account in *The Short and Tragic Life of Robert Peace*. And once again my thanks to Father Albert Holz. It was in his *Downtown Monks* that I first encountered that felicitous and so apt description of Newark's men in black.

My eternal thanks go to my long-time agent, Stuart Krichevsky, who fought as long and as hard as I did to have this book published several decades after we first tried. The unbeatable Hannah Phillips recognized the noble nature of Newark Abbey and St. Benedict's and labored heroically to make sure their story got into print in a way that would captivate readers. Her keen eye and sharp sense of style improved every page, and Andrew Yackira, Allie Johnston, John Simko, and Michelle Meredith carefully curated my all-too-numerous corrections and emendations. The creative staff at William Morrow/HarperCollins—especially Brian Moore, who, despite my confusing and sometimes contradictory directions, designed a cover that is as striking as it is persuasive—made me look better in so many ways. Megan Wilson, Samantha Marks, and Odette Fleming at HarperCollins, along with Cindy Tavlin and Katherine Noyes at ECG Group, helped spread the word about St. Benedict's and Newark far and oh, so wide. Several of the early readers I turned to for guidance helped me immensely. My colleague Tim Padgett looked at my draft through the eyes of a seasoned journalist and converted Catholic. Another journalist I've known for decades, Al Frank, who also is a former seminarian, a current Catholic deacon, and an old Newark hand, backstopped all my references to religion, tradition, and church law. And Stephen Bloom, an author and avowed Catholic skeptic whose work I admire, examined every line, and questioned many of them. They all guided me when I went too far astray, and pushed me where I hadn't gone far enough.

As always, my great appreciation goes to my family, starting with my parents who allowed me to select St. Joseph's Boys High School, where I first entered the orbit of Brother David Van Hollebeke, FSC, a Christian Brother in the order of St. John de la Salle, who remains a mentor and friend. My crew of tough Jersey guys kept track of my progress and prodded me to finish this book while only occasionally grumbling about having to listen to yet another Newark story. My children Aahren, Laura Felice, and Andrés, and their families, put up with shortened vacations and interrupted visits throughout the time I was almost as present at "the property" as I was at home. And finally, my eternal gratitude and appreciation for Miriam, who has listened without complaint as I read to her every word of this and other books I've written. We met when she was at St. Joseph's Girls High School, and I sat across the hallway at St. Joe's Boys High School, two small-city kids with big-city dreams who were brought together from different parts of the globe by history, politics, and a quirk of fate, one of those moments that Father Ed describes as the extraordinary happening in the ordinary, and she has been showing me the best way to live, and to love, ever since.

NOTES

Chapter 1: Of One Accord

1. St. Benedict of Nursia, *The Rule of Saint Benedict: A Contemporary Paraphrase*, ed. Jonathan Wilson-Hartgrove (Paraclete Press, 2012).
2. Reading and rereading *The Rule of Benedict: Insights for the Ages*, (Crossroad, 1992) by Sister Joan Chittister, O.S.B., was an immense help in understanding how a 1500-year-old book could possibly be relevant today. Much of what I saw and heard at St. Benedict's reflected the clear-sighted interpretation of *The Rule* that is laid out in these pages.
3. Noguera, Pedro A., *The Trouble with Black Boys: And Other Reflections on Race, Equity, and the Future of Public Education* (Jossey-Bass; John Wiley distributor, 2008): pp. xxi–xxiii.

Chapter 2: A Showcase for Others

1. Cusick, James, "Mile and a Half Battleground," *Newark Evening News*, July 14, 1967, p. 1.
2. Biggest U.S. Cities, "Newark Population History 1840–2023," https://www.biggestuscities.com/city/newark-new-jersey, accessed January 2025.
3. Shipler, David K., "The White Niggers of Newark," *Harper's*, August 1972, pp. 78–83.

4. City of Newark, Office of the Mayor, *Model Cities Application*, April 25, 1967, accessed at the Newark Public Library, David Malaforte collection, Box #5.

5. *Development Prospects for St. Benedict's Preparatory School and St. Mary Priory 1966–67—1981–82*, Taylor, Lieberfeld and Heldman, Inc., New York, 1966.

6. Douglas Robinson, "King Warns Cities of Summer Violence," *The New York Times*, April 17, 1967, https://www.nytimes.com/1967/04/17 /archives/king-warns-cities-of-summer-riots-civil-rights-leader-terms -new.html.

7. "Newark Councilmen Spurn King's 'Powder Keg' Tag," *Newark Star-Ledger*, April 19, 1967, p. 14.

Chapter 3: Open Rebellion

1. Wineka, Mark, "July 12, 1967: When a Reluctant Salisburian Collided with History," *Salisbury Post*, July 13, 2017, https://www.salisbury post.com/2017/07/13/july-12–1967-reluctant-salisburian-collided -history/.

2. Governor's Select Commission on Civil Disorder, State of New Jersey, "Report for Action," February 1968, https://governors.rutgers.edu /governor-richard-hughes-and-the-newark-report/.

3. Cusick, James, "Trouble Centered on Man Few Knew," *Newark Evening News*, July 13, 1967, p. 4.

4. "Report for Action," p. 108.

5. Baraka, Amiri, *The Autobiography of Leroi Jones* (Lawrence Hill Books, 1997), p. 368.

6. "Seven More Slain in Riot," *Newark Evening News*, July 15, 1967, p. 1. Also Eagleton Institute of Politics, Center on the American Governor, https://governors.rutgers.edu/governor-richard-j-hughes-biography/.

Chapter 4: A Community Divided

1. Curley, Augustine J., O.S.B., "Monks in the City: A Unique New Experience," Archbishop Gerety lecture, Nov. 15, 2006, Seton Hall University, South Orange, N.J. Also at https://www.shu.edu/documents/monks-in-the-city.pdf.
2. McCabe, Thomas A., *Miracle on High Street* (Fordham University Press, 2011).
3. *Newark Abbey Chapter Minutes*, Feb. 24, 1971.
4. Porambo, Ron, *No Cause for Indictment: An Autopsy of Newark* (Holt, Rinehart and Winston, 1971), p. 61. Also at https://law.justia.com/cases/federal/appellate-courts/F2/451/49/71469/.
5. Tuttle, Brad R., *How Newark Became Newark* (Rivergate Books, 2011), p. 191.
6. Hayes, Giles, O.S.B., *Unto Another Generation* (Newark Abbey Press, 2006), p. 73.

Chapter 5: The Essence of Freedom

1. Holtz, Albert, O.S.B., *Downtown Monks: A Benedictine Journey in the City* (Morehouse Publishing, 2012).
2. Cook, Joan, "A New St. Benedict's Is Due," *The New York Times*, April 1, 1973, p. 90.
3. Holtz, Albert, O.S.B., Personal Journal, March 14, 1973, p. 105.
4. Braun, Robert J., "New St. Benedict's Bows with 90 Boys as Students," *Newark Star-Ledger*, July 3, 1973, p. 4.

Chapter 11: Brotherhood

1. Panico, Rebecca, "Man Found Guilty of Shooting, Paralyzing Friend He Found with His Ex," nj.com, Nov. 8, 2019, https://www.nj.com

/essex/2019/11/man-found-guilty-of-shooting-paralyzing-friend-he-found
-with-his-ex.html. See also https://www.njcourts.gov/system/files/court
-opinions/2023/a2522–19.pdf.

Chapter 17: The Seeds You Sow

1. Brennan, Robert E., *Brennan: The Record Stands* (self-published, 2023).

Chapter 21: And Ever Shall Be

1. Russakoff, Dale, *The Prize: Who's in Charge of America's Schools?* (Mariner
   Books, 2016), p. 31.
2. "Newark Prep School Guidance Counselor Accused of Inappropriate Contact
   Facing Multiple Charges," YouTube, Oct. 7, 2022, https://www.youtube
   .com/watch?v=m_ypqgZRRjI. Also https://patch.com/new-jersey/newarknj
   /newark-prep-school-dean-accused-attempted-luring.
3. Personal communication from the Hudson County Prosecutor's office,
   Oct. 15, 2024.
4. Jones, Jeffrey M., "Many U.S. Catholics Question Their Membership Amid
   Scandal," Gallup, March 19, 2019, https://news.gallup.com/poll/247571
   /catholics-question-membership-amid-scandal.aspx.